COLLINS

WORLD ATLAS

W9-CTA-670

CONTENTS

Collins World Atlas
first published 1986 by William Collins Sons & Co. Ltd.
Reprinted 1987, 1988, 1989, 1990

New Edition 1991
Maps © Collins and Collins-Longman Atlases
Statistics © Bartholomew

Collins is an imprint of Bartholomew,
a division of HarperCollins *Publishers*

12 Duncan Street
Edinburgh
EH9 1TA

Printed in Scotland by HarperCollins Manufacturing,
Glasgow

The contents of this edition of the Collins World Atlas
are believed to be correct at the time of printing.
Nevertheless, the publishers can accept no
responsibility for errors, or for omissions, or for
changes in detail given.

ISBN 0 00 447826 6

HarperCollins*Publishers*

Earth's Dimensions

Superficial area	510 066 000 km²
Land surface	148 326 000 km²
Water surface	361 740 000 km²
Equatorial circumference	40 075 km
Meridional circumference	40 007 km
Volume	1 083 230x10⁶ km³
Mass	5.976x10²¹ tonnes

A : ANDORRA
ALB : ALBANIA
AUS : AUSTRIA
B : BELGIUM
BANGLA : BANGLADESH
BA : BARBADOS
BULG : BULGARIA
CAMB : CAMBODIA
CZECH : CZECHOSLOVAKIA
E.Q.G. : EQUATORIAL GUINEA
GER : GERMANY
G.B. : GUINEA BISSAU
GR : GRENADA
GUAT : GUATEMALA
HUNG : HUNGARY
L : LUXEMBOURG
LEB : LEBANON
LI : LIECHTENSTEIN
M : MONACO
MA : MALTA
NETH : NETHERLANDS
S : SWITZERLAND
S.K. : ST. KITTS-NEVIS
S.M. : SAN MARINO
S.T. : SÃO TOME & PRINCIPE
S.V. : ST. VINCENT AND THE GRENADINES
T : TURKEY (in Europe)
U.A.E. : UNITED ARAB EMIRATES
V.C. : VATICAN CITY
YUGO : YUGOSLAVIA

© Collins

River Lengths

An Nīl (Nile) ; Africa	6695 km
Amazonas (Amazon) ; South America	6516 km
Chang Jiang (Yangtze) ; Asia	6380 km
Mississippi - Missouri; North America	6020 km
Ob-Irtysh; Asia	5570 km
Huang He (Hwang Ho) ; Asia	5464 km
Zaïre; Africa	4667 km
Mekong; Asia	4425 km
Amur; Asia	4416 km
Lena; Asia	4400 km
Mackenzie; North America	4250 km
Yenisey; Asia	4090 km
Niger; Africa	4030 km
Murray - Darling; Oceania	3750 km
Volga; Europe	3688 km

Lake and Inland Sea Areas

Some areas are subject to seasonal variations.

Caspian Sea; U.S.S.R. / Iran	371 795 km²	Lake Tanganyika; East Africa	32 893 km²
Lake Superior; U.S.A. / Canada	83 270 km²	Great Bear Lake; Canada	31 792 km²
Lake Victoria; East Africa	69 485 km²	Ozero Baykal (Lake Baikal) ; U.S.S.R.	30 510 km²
Lake Huron; U.S.A. / Canada	60 700 km²	Great Slave Lake; Canada	28 930 km²
Lake Michigan; U.S.A.	58 016 km²	Lake Erie; U.S.A. / Canada	25 667 km²
Aralskoye More (Aral Sea) ; U.S.S.R.	36 500 km²	Lake Winnipeg; Canada	24 514 km²

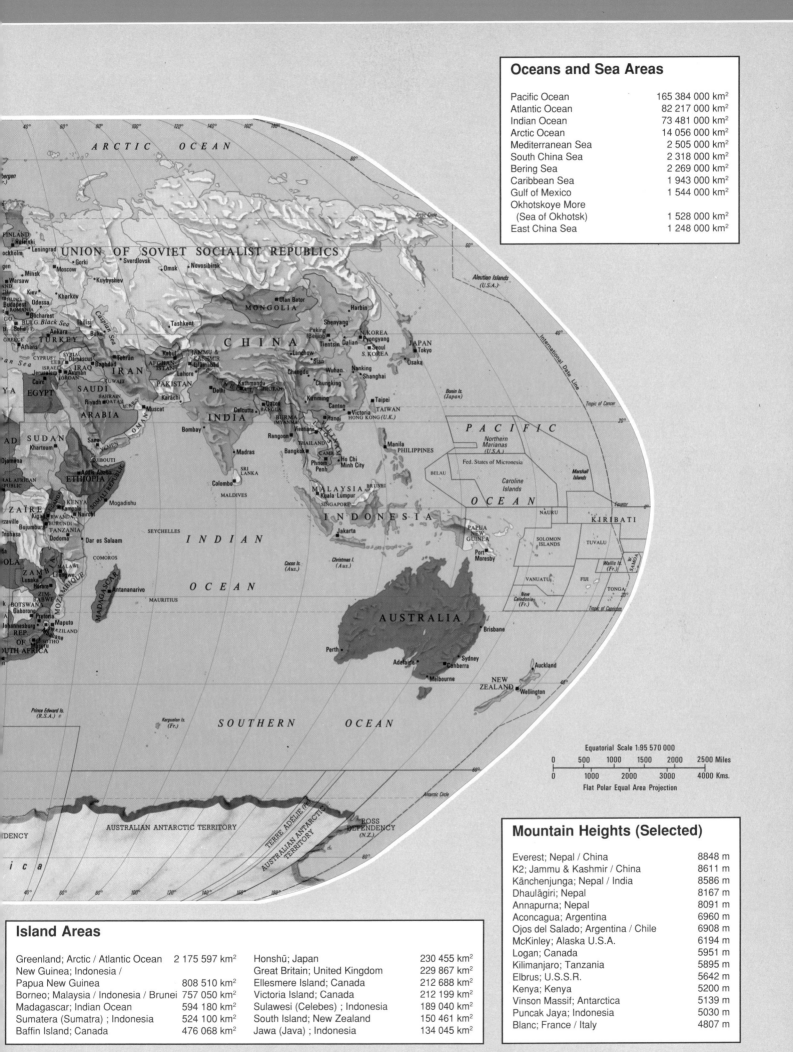

Oceans and Sea Areas

Pacific Ocean	165 384 000 km²
Atlantic Ocean	82 217 000 km²
Indian Ocean	73 481 000 km²
Arctic Ocean	14 056 000 km²
Mediterranean Sea	2 505 000 km²
South China Sea	2 318 000 km²
Bering Sea	2 269 000 km²
Caribbean Sea	1 943 000 km²
Gulf of Mexico	1 544 000 km²
Okhotskoye More (Sea of Okhotsk)	1 528 000 km²
East China Sea	1 248 000 km²

Mountain Heights (Selected)

Everest; Nepal / China	8848 m
K2; Jammu & Kashmir / China	8611 m
Kānchenjunga; Nepal / India	8586 m
Dhaulāgiri; Nepal	8167 m
Annapurna; Nepal	8091 m
Aconcagua; Argentina	6960 m
Ojos del Salado; Argentina / Chile	6908 m
McKinley; Alaska U.S.A.	6194 m
Logan; Canada	5951 m
Kilimanjaro; Tanzania	5895 m
Elbrus; U.S.S.R.	5642 m
Kenya; Kenya	5200 m
Vinson Massif; Antarctica	5139 m
Puncak Jaya; Indonesia	5030 m
Blanc; France / Italy	4807 m

Island Areas

Greenland; Arctic / Atlantic Ocean	2 175 597 km²	Honshū; Japan	230 455 km²
New Guinea; Indonesia / Papua New Guinea	808 510 km²	Great Britain; United Kingdom	229 867 km²
Borneo; Malaysia / Indonesia / Brunei	757 050 km²	Ellesmere Island; Canada	212 688 km²
Madagascar; Indian Ocean	594 180 km²	Victoria Island; Canada	212 199 km²
Sumatera (Sumatra) ; Indonesia	524 100 km²	Sulawesi (Celebes) ; Indonesia	189 040 km²
Baffin Island; Canada	476 068 km²	South Island; New Zealand	150 461 km²
		Jawa (Java) ; Indonesia	134 045 km²

Equatorial Scale 1:95 570 000

Flat Polar Equal Area Projection

3

ASIA

COUNTRY	POPULATION	AREA sq. km.	CAPITAL
AFGHANISTAN	15 814 000	647 497	Kābol
BAHRAIN	489 000	622	Al Manāmah
BANGLADESH	106 507 000	143 998	Dhaka
BHUTAN	1 483 000	47 000	Thimbu
BRUNEI	249 000	5 765	Bandar Seri Begawan
BURMA	38 541 000	676 552	Rangoon
CAMBODIA	8 055 000	181 035	Phnom Penh
CHINA	1 114 311 000	9 596 961	Beijing (Peking)
CYPRUS	694 000	9 251	Levkosía (Nicosia)
HONG KONG	5 681 000	1 045	
INDIA	811 817 000	3 287 590	New Delhi
INDONESIA	179 136 000	1 904 569	Jakarta
IRAN	55 208 000	1 648 000	Tehrān
IRAQ	16 278 000	434 924	Baghdād
ISRAEL	4 566 000	20 770	Yerushalayim (Jerusalem)
JAPAN	123 116 000	372 313	Tōkyō
JORDAN	4 102 000	97 740	'Ammān
KUWAIT	2 048 000	17 818	Al Kuwayt (Kuwait)
LAOS	3 972 000	236 800	Vientiane (Viangchan)
LEBANON	2 897 000	10 400	Bayrūt (Beirut)
MALAYSIA	16 942 000	329 749	Kuala Lumpur
MALDIVES	206 000	298	Malé
MONGOLIA	2 043 000	1 565 000	Ulaanbaatar (Ulan Bator)
NEPAL	18 442 000	140 797	Kātmāndu
NORTH KOREA	22 418 000	120 538	Pyŏngyang
OMAN	1 422 000	212 457	Masqaṭ (Muscat)
PAKISTAN	108 678 000	803 943	Islāmābād
PHILIPPINES	60 097 000	300 000	Manila
QATAR	422 000	11 000	Ad Dawḥah (Doha)
SAUDI ARABIA	14 435 000	2 149 690	Ar Riyāḍ (Riyadh)
SINGAPORE	2 704 000	602	Singapore
SOUTH KOREA	42 380 000	98 484	Sŏul (Seoul)
SRI LANKA	16 806 000	65 610	Colombo
SYRIA	11 719 000	185 180	Dimashq (Damascus)
TAIWAN	19 900 000	35 961	Taipei
THAILAND	54 448 000	514 000	Bangkok (Krung Thep)
TURKEY	56 741 000	780 576	Ankara
UNITED ARAB EMIRATES	1 546 000	83 600	
VIETNAM	64 412 000	329 556	Hanoi
YEMEN	11 619 439	527 968	Şan'ā

AFRICA

COUNTRY	POPULATION	AREA sq. km.	CAPITAL
ALGERIA	24 597 000	2 381 741	Alger (Algiers)
ANGOLA	9 747 000	1 246 700	Luanda
BENIN	4 591 000	112 622	Porto-Novo
BOTSWANA	1 256 000	600 372	Gaborone
BURKINA	8 798 000	274 200	Ouagadougou
BURUNDI	5 302 000	27 834	Bujumbura
CAMEROON	11 540 000	475 442	Yaoundé
CAPE VERDE	368 000	4 033	Praia
CENTRAL AFRICAN REPUBLIC	2 740 000	622 984	Bangui
CHAD	5 538 000	1 284 000	N'Djamena
COMOROS	484 000	2 171	Moroni
CONGO	1 940 000	342 000	Brazzaville
DJIBOUTI	456 000	22 000	Djibouti
EGYPT	53 080 000	1 001 449	Al Qāhirah (Cairo)
EQUATORIAL GUINEA	341 000	28 051	Malabo
ETHIOPIA	50 774 000	1 221 900	Ādīs Ābeba (Addis Ababa)
GABON	1 206 000	267 667	Libreville
GAMBIA	835 000	11 295	Banjul
GHANA	14 566 000	238 537	Accra
GUINEA	5 071 000	245 857	Conakry
GUINEA BISSAU	943 000	36 125	Bissau
IVORY COAST	12 097 000	322 463	Yamoussoukro
KENYA	24 872 000	582 646	Nairobi
LESOTHO	1 700 000	30 355	Maseru
LIBERIA	2 508 000	111 369	Monrovia
LIBYA	4 385 000	1 759 540	Tarābulus (Tripoli)
MADAGASCAR	9 985 000	587 041	Antananarivo
MALAŴI	8 022 000	118 484	Lilongwe
MALI	7 960 000	1 240 000	Bamako
MAURITANIA	1 969 000	1 030 700	Nouakchott
MAURITIUS	1 068 000	2 045	Port-Louis
MOROCCO	24 521 000	446 550	Rabat
MOZAMBIQUE	15 326 000	801 590	Maputo
NAMIBIA	1 817 000	824 292	Windhoek
NIGER	7 250 000	1 267 000	Niamey
NIGERIA	104 957 000	923 768	Abuja
RWANDA	6 989 000	26 338	Kigali
SÃO TOMÉ AND PRINCIPE	116 000	964	São Tomé
SENEGAL	7 113 000	196 192	Dakar
SEYCHELLES	67 000	280	Victoria
SIERRA LEONE	3 516 000	71 740	Freetown
SOMALI REPUBLIC	7 339 000	637 657	Muqdisho
SOUTH AFRICA, REPUBLIC OF	34 492 000	1 221 037	Cape Town (Kaapstad)/ Pretoria
SUDAN	24 484 000	2 505 813	Al Kharṭūm (Khartoum)
SWAZILAND	681 000	17 363	Mbabane
TANZANIA	24 802 000	945 087	Dodoma
TOGO	3 296 000	56 785	Lomé
TUNISIA	7 465 000	163 610	Tunis
UGANDA	17 804 000	236 036	Kampala
ZAÏRE	34 491 000	2 345 409	Kinshasa
ZAMBIA	7 804 000	752 614	Lusaka
ZIMBABWE	9 122 000	390 580	Harare

CITY	COUNTRY	POPULATION
CIUDAD DE MÉXICO (MEXICO CITY)	Mexico	19 396 000
NEW YORK	United States	17 931 000
TŌKYŌ	Japan	15 911 000
CAIRO	Egypt	13 000 000
SÃO PAULO	Brazil	13 000 000
SHANGHAI	China	12 500 000
LOS ANGELES	United States	10 232 000

CITY	COUNTRY	POPULATION
BUENOS AIRES	Argentina	9 970 000
SŎUL (SEOUL)	South Korea	9 646 000
RIO DE JANEIRO	Brazil	9 500 000
BEIJING (PEKING)	China	9 470 000
CALCUTTA	India	9 160 000
LONDON	United Kingdom	9 055 000
MOSKVA (MOSCOW)	U.S.S.R.	8 967 000
PARIS	France	8 706 000

NORTH AMERICA

COUNTRY	POPULATION	AREA sq. km.	CAPITAL
ANTIGUA AND BARBUDA	85 000	442	St John's
BAHAMAS	249 000	13 935	Nassau
BARBADOS	256 000	431	Bridgetown
BELIZE	180 000	22 965	Belmopan
CANADA	26 248 000	9 976 139	Ottawa
COSTA RICA	2 922 000	50 700	San José
CUBA	10 594 000	114 524	La Habana (Havana)
DOMINICA	81 000	751	Roseau
DOMINICAN REPUBLIC	7 018 000	48 734	Santo Dominigo
EL SALVADOR	5 207 000	21 041	San Salvador
GREENLAND	56 000	2 175 600	Godthåb/Nuuk
GRENADA	97 000	344	St George's
GUATEMALA	8 935 000	108 889	Guatemala
HAITI	5 609 000	27 750	Port-au-Prince
HONDURAS	4 951 000	112 088	Tegucigalpa
JAMAICA	2 392 000	10 991	Kingston
MEXICO	84 275 000	1 972 547	Ciudad de México (Mexico City)
NICARAGUA	3 384 000	130 000	Managua
PANAMA	2 370 000	77 082	Panamá
PUERTO RICO	3 293 000	8 897	San Juan
ST KITTS-NEVIS	49 000	266	Basseterre
ST LUCIA	148 000	616	Castries
ST VINCENT AND THE GRENADINES	113 000	389	Kingstown
UNITED STATES OF AMERICA	249 928 000	9 372 614	Washington

SOUTH AMERICA

COUNTRY	POPULATION	AREA sq. km.	CAPITAL
ARGENTINA	31 929 000	2 766 889	Buenos Aires
BOLIVIA	7 193 000	1 098 581	La Paz/Sucre
BRAZIL	147 404 000	8 511 965	Brasília
CHILE	12 961 000	756 945	Santiago
COLOMBIA	30 241 000	1 138 914	Bogotá
ECUADOR	10 490 000	283 561	Quito
GUIANA	90 000	91 000	Cayenne
GUYANA	1 023 000	214 969	Georgetown
PARAGUAY	4 157 000	406 752	Asunción
PERU	21 792 000	1 285 216	Lima
SURINAM	397 000	163 265	Paramaribo
TRINIDAD AND TOBAGO	1 212 000	5 130	Port of Spain
URUGUAY	3 077 000	176 215	Montevideo
VENEZUELA	19 246 000	912 050	Caracas

EUROPE

COUNTRY	POPULATION	AREA sq. km.	CAPITAL
ALBANIA	3 202 000	28 748	Tiranë
ANDORRA	50 000	453	Andorra
AUSTRIA	7 618 000	83 849	Wien (Vienna)
BELGIUM	9 883 000	30 513	Bruxelles/ Brussel (Brussels)
BULGARIA	8 981 000	110 912	Sofiya (Sofia)
CZECHOSLOVAKIA	15 651 000	127 869	Praha (Prague)
DENMARK	5 132 000	43 069	København (Copenhagen)
FINLAND	4 962 000	337 032	Helsinki
FRANCE	56 160 000	547 026	Paris
GERMANY	78 620 000	356 755	Berlin/Bonn
GREECE	9 983 000	131 944	Athinai (Athens)
HUNGARY	10 563 000	93 030	Budapest
ICELAND	250 000	103 000	Reykjavik
IRELAND, REPUBLIC OF	3 515 000	70 283	Dublin
ITALY	57 557 000	301 225	Roma (Rome)
LIECHTENSTEIN	28 000	157	Vaduz
LUXEMBOURG	378 000	2 586	Luxembourg
MALTA	350 000	316	Valletta
MONACO	28 000	2	Monaco
NETHERLANDS	14 891 000	40 844	Amsterdam
NORWAY	4 227 000	324 219	Oslo
POLAND	37 931 000	312 677	Warszawa (Warsaw)
PORTUGAL	10 467 000	92 082	Lisboa (Lisbon)
ROMANIA	23 152 000	237 500	Bucureşti (Bucharest)
SAN MARINO	23 000	61	San Marino
SPAIN	39 248 000	504 782	Madrid
SWEDEN	8 541 000	449 964	Stockholm
SWITZERLAND	6 647 000	41 288	Bern (Berne)
U.S.S.R.	286 717 000	22 402 200	Moskva (Moscow)
UNITED KINGDOM	57 205 000	244 046	London
YUGOSLAVIA	23 764 000	255 804	Beograd (Belgrade)

OCEANIA

COUNTRY	POPULATION	AREA sq. km.	CAPITAL
AUSTRALIA	16 807 000	7 686 848	Canberra
FIJI	727 000	18 274	Suva
KIRIBATI	64 000	886	Tarawa
NAURU	8 000	21	Nauru
NEW ZEALAND	3 389 000	268 676	Wellington
PAPUA NEW GUINEA	3 593 000	461 691	Port Moresby
SOLOMON ISLANDS	299 000	28 446	Honiara
TONGA	95 000	699	Nuku'alofa
TUVALU	7 000	24	Funafuti
VANUATU	143 000	14 763	Vila
WESTERN SAMOA	168 000	2 842	Apia

Map coverage extends to every part of the world in a balanced scheme that avoids any individual country or regional bias. Map areas are chosen to reflect the social, economic, cultural or historical importance of a particular region. Each double spread or single page map has been planned deliberately to cover an entire physical or political unit. Generous map overlaps are included to maintain continuity. Each of the continents is treated systematically in a subsection of its own. As an aid to the reader in locating the required area, a postage stamp key map is incorporated into the title margin of each map page.

Map projections have been chosen to reflect the different requirements of particular areas. No map can be absolutely true on account of the impossibility of representing a spheroid accurately on a flat surface without some distortion in either area, distance, direction or shape. In a general world atlas it is the equal area property that is most important to retain for comparative map studies and feature size evaluation and this principle has been followed wherever possible in this map section.

Map scales, as expressions of the relationship which the distance between any two points of the map bears to the corresponding distance on the ground, are in the context of this atlas grouped into three distinct categories.

Large scales, of between 1:1 000 000 (1 centimetre to 10 kilometres or 1 inch to 16 miles) and 1:2 500 000 (1 centimetre to 25 kilometres or 1 inch to 40 miles), are used to cover particularly dense populated areas of Western Europe and Japan.

Medium scales, of between 1:2 500 000 and 1:7 500 000 are used for maps of important parts of Europe, North America, Australasia, etc.

Small scales, of less than 1:7 500 000 (e.g. 1:10 000 000, 1:15 000 000, 1:25 000 000 etc.), are selected for maps of the complete world, oceans and many larger countries.

The actual scale at which a particular area is mapped

therefore reflects its shape, size and density of detail, and as a basic principle the more detail required to be shown of an area, the greater its scale. However, throughout this atlas, map scales have been limited in number, as far as possible, in order to facilitate comparison between maps.

Map measurements give preference to the metric system which is now used in nearly every country throughout the world. All spot heights and ocean depths are shown in meters and the relief and submarine layer delineation is based on metric contour levels. However, all linear scalebar and height reference column figures are given in metric and imperial equivalents to facilitate conversion of measurements for the non-metric reader.

Map symbols used are fully explained in the legend below. Careful study and frequent reference to this legend will aid in the reader's ability to extract maximum information.

Topography is shown by the combined means of precise spot heights, contouring, layer tinting and three-dimensional hill shading.

Hydrographic features such as coastlines, rivers, lakes, swamps and canals are clearly differentiated.

Communications are particularly well represented with the contemporary importance of airports and road networks duly emphasized.

International boundaries and national capitals are fully documented and internal administrative divisions are shown with the maximum detail that the scale will allow. Boundary delineation reflects the 'de facto' rather than the 'de jure' political interpretation and where relevant an undefined or disputed boundary is distinguished. However there is no intended implication that the publishers necessarily endorse or accept the status of any political entity recorded on the maps.

Settlements are shown by a series of graded town stamps, from major cities down to tiny villages.

Other features, such as notable ancient monuments, oases, national parks, oil and gas fields, are selectively included on particular maps that merit their identification.

Lettering styles used in the maps have been chosen with great care to ensure maximum legibility and clear distinction of named feature categories. The size and weight of the various typefaces reflect the relative importance of the features. Town names are graded to correspond with the appropriate town stamp.

Map place names have been selected in accordance with maintaining legibility at a given scale and at the same time striking an appropriate balance between natural and man-made features worthy of note. Name forms have been standardized according to the widely accepted principle, now well established in international reference atlases, of including place names and geographical terms in the local language of the country in question. In the case of non-Roman scripts (e.g. Arabic), transliteration and transcription have either been based on the rules recommended by the Permanent Committee on Geographical Names and the United States Board on Geographic Names, or as in the case of the adopted Pinyin transcription of Chinese names, a system officially proposed by the country concerned. The diacritical signs used in each language or transliteration have been retained on all the maps and throughout the index. However the English language reader's requirements have also been recognised in that the names of all countries, oceans, major seas and land features as well as familiar alternative name versions of important towns are presented in English.

Map sources used in the compilation of this atlas were many and varied, but always of the latest available information. At each stage of their preparation the maps were submitted to a thorough process of research and continual revision to ensure that on publication all data would be as accurate as practicable. A well-documented data bank was created to ensure consistency and validity of all information represented on the maps.

SYMBOLS

Relief

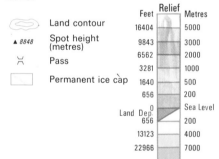

		Feet	Relief	Metres
Land contour		16404		5000
▲ 8848 Spot height (metres)		9843		3000
Pass		6562		2000
Permanent ice cap		3281		1000
		1640		500
		656		200
		0		Sea Level
	Land Dep.	656		200
		13123		4000
		22966		7000

Hydrography

- Submarine contour
- ▼ 11034 Ocean depth (metres)
- (217) Lake level (metres)
- Reef
- River
- Intermittent river
- Falls
- Dam
- Gorge
- Canal
- Lake/Reservoir
- Intermittent lake
- Marsh/Swamp

© Collins

Administration

———	International boundary
– – –	Undefined/Disputed international boundary
–·–·–	Internal division : First order
·······–	Internal division : Second order
▣ ◉ ⊙ ▢ ◌ ⊡	National capitals

Settlement

Each settlement is given a town stamp according to its relative importance and scale category.

1:1M-1:2½M	1:2½M-1:7½M	1:7½M or smaller
Major City	Major City	Major City
City	City	City
Large Town	Large Town	Large Town
Town	Town	Town
Small Town	Small Town	—
Village	—	—

Urban area (1:1M-1:2½M only)

The size of type used for each settlement is graded to correspond with the appropriate town stamp.

Communications

—— Tunnel – –	Main railway
⊕	Main airport
– – – –	Track

Road representation varies with the scale category.

═══ Principal road	} 1:1M-1:2½M
─── Other main road	
─── Principal road	} 1:2½M-1:7½M
─── Other main road	
─── Principal road	1:7½M or smaller

Other features

∴	Ancient monument
⌣	Oasis
⬡	National Park
▲	Oil field
△	Gas field
–·–·–	Oil/Gas pipeline

Lettering

Various styles of lettering are used-each one representing a different type of feature.

ALPS	Physical feature	KENYA	Country name
Red Sea	Hydrographic feature	IOWA	Internal division
Paris	Settlement name	*(Fr.)*	Territorial administration

BRITISH ISLES

ATLANTIC OCEAN

NORWAY

DENMARK

NORTH SEA

SCOTLAND

UNITED KINGDOM

ENGLAND

WALES

REPUBLIC OF IRELAND

NORTHERN IRELAND

IRISH SEA

NETHERLANDS

GERMANY

BELGIUM

LUXEMBOURG

FRANCE

Celtic Sea

English Channel

Relief

Feet		Metres
16 404		5000
9843		3000
6562		2000
3281		1000
1640		500
656		200
0		Sea Level
Land Dep.		
656		200
13123		4000
22966		7000

Scale 1:6 500 000

0   50   100   150 Miles

0   50   100   150   200   250 Kms.

Conic Projection

© Collins ◇ Longman Atlases Cbii

7

ENGLAND AND WALES

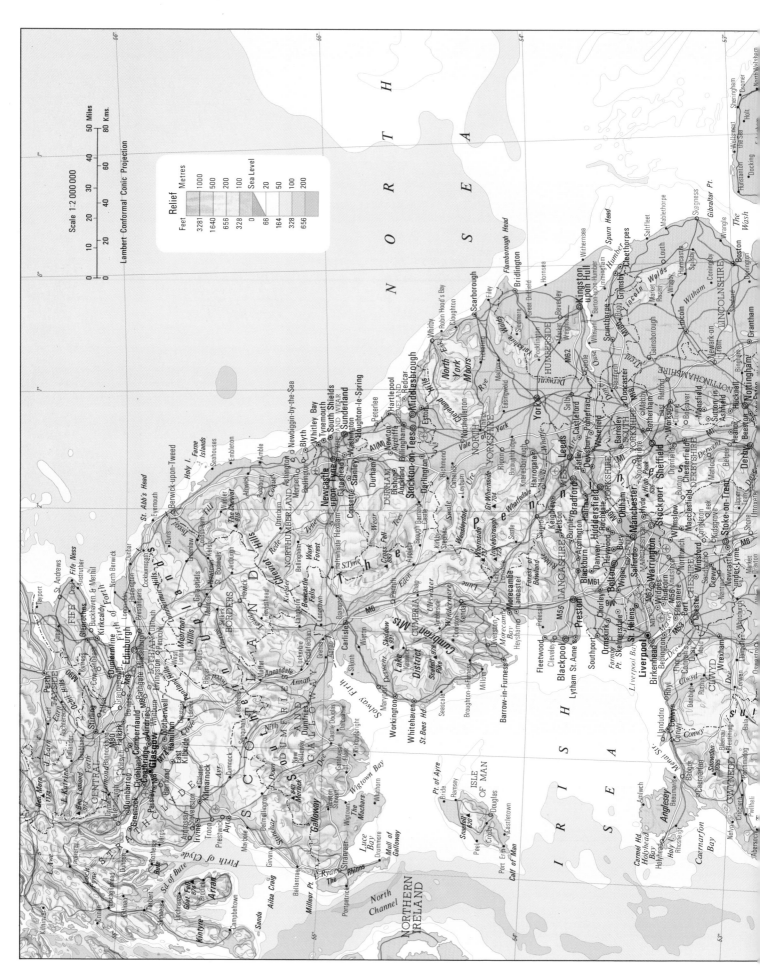

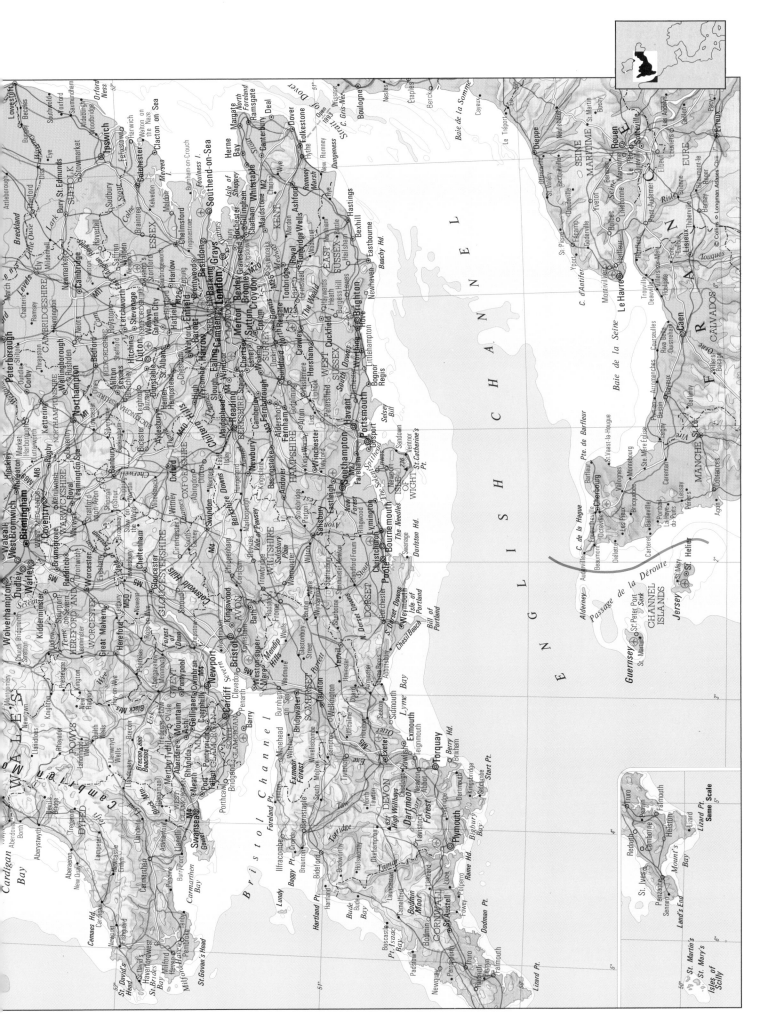

Relief

Feet		Metres
3281		1000
1640		500
656		200
328		100
0		Sea Level
66		20
164		50
328		100
656		200

Scale 1:2 000 000

0 10 20 30 40 Miles

0 20 40 60 Kms.

Lambert Conformal Conic Projection

© Collins ◇ Longman Atlases Cbiii

SCOTLAND

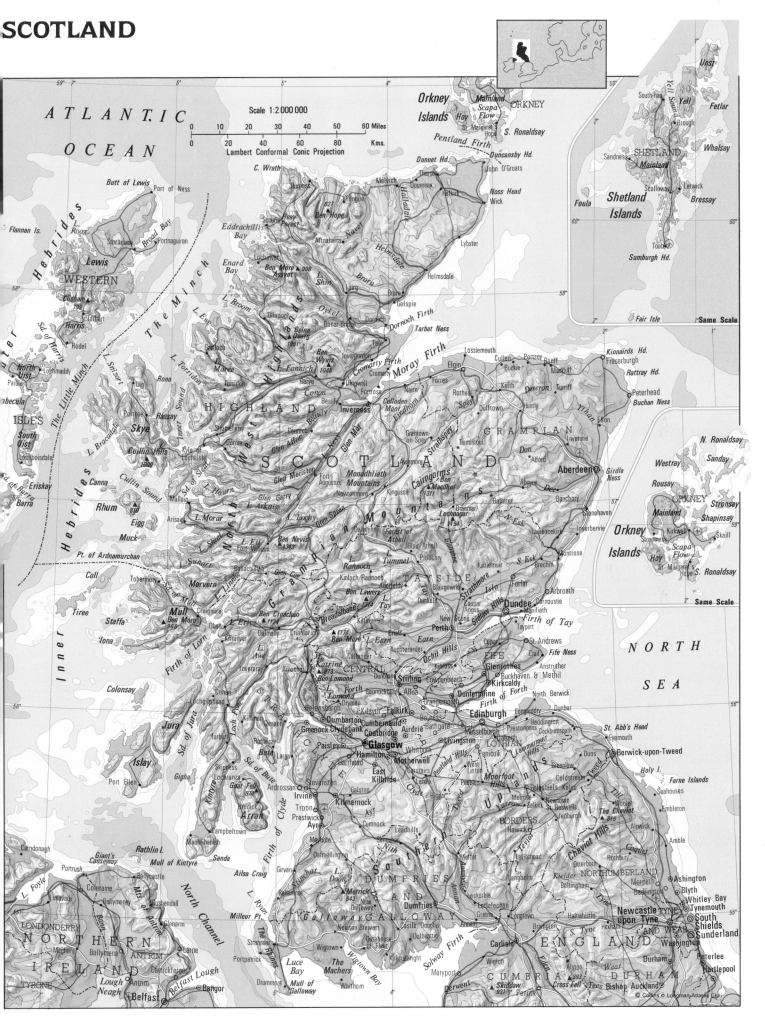

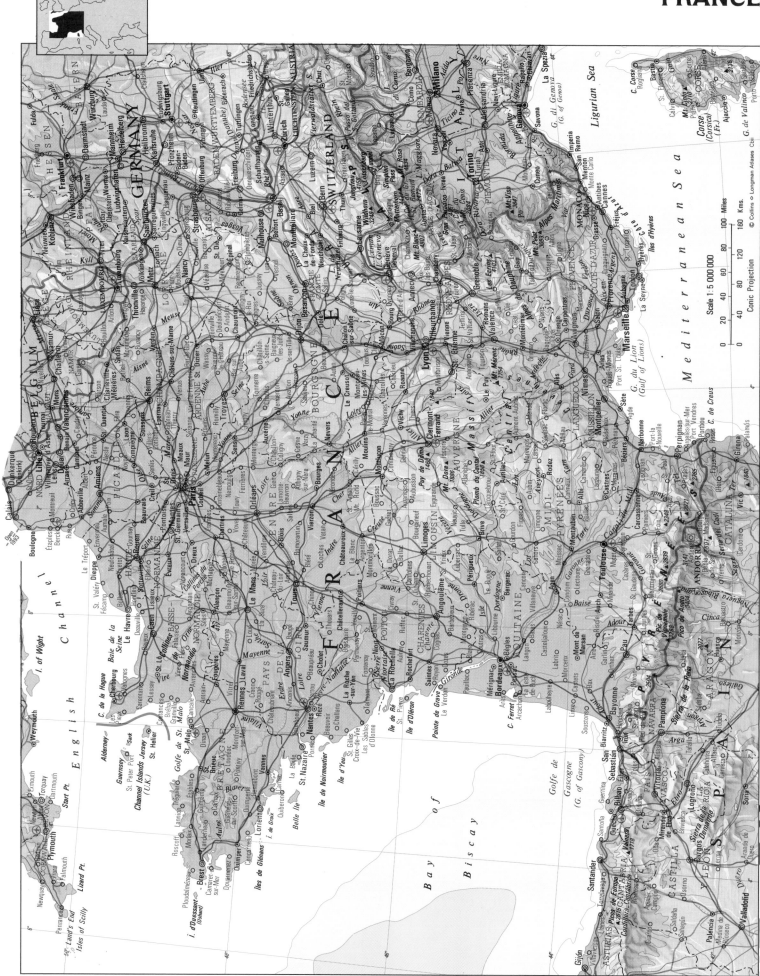

Scale 1:5 000 000

Conic Projection

© Collins © Longman Atlases Cbi

SPAIN AND PORTUGAL

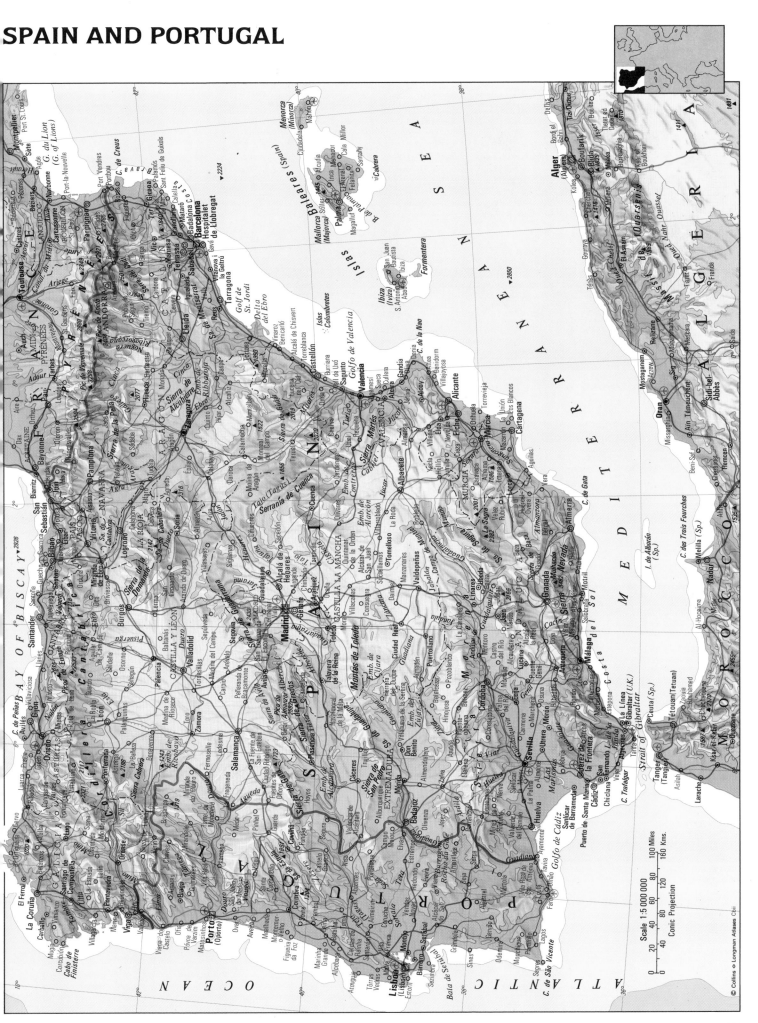

ITALY AND THE BALKANS

Scale 1:5 250 000

| 0 | 50 | 100 | 150 | 200 Miles |
| 0 | 50 | 100 | 150 | 200 | 250 | 300 Kms. |

Conic Projection

© Collins ⬦ Longman Atlases Cbii

CENTRAL EUROPE

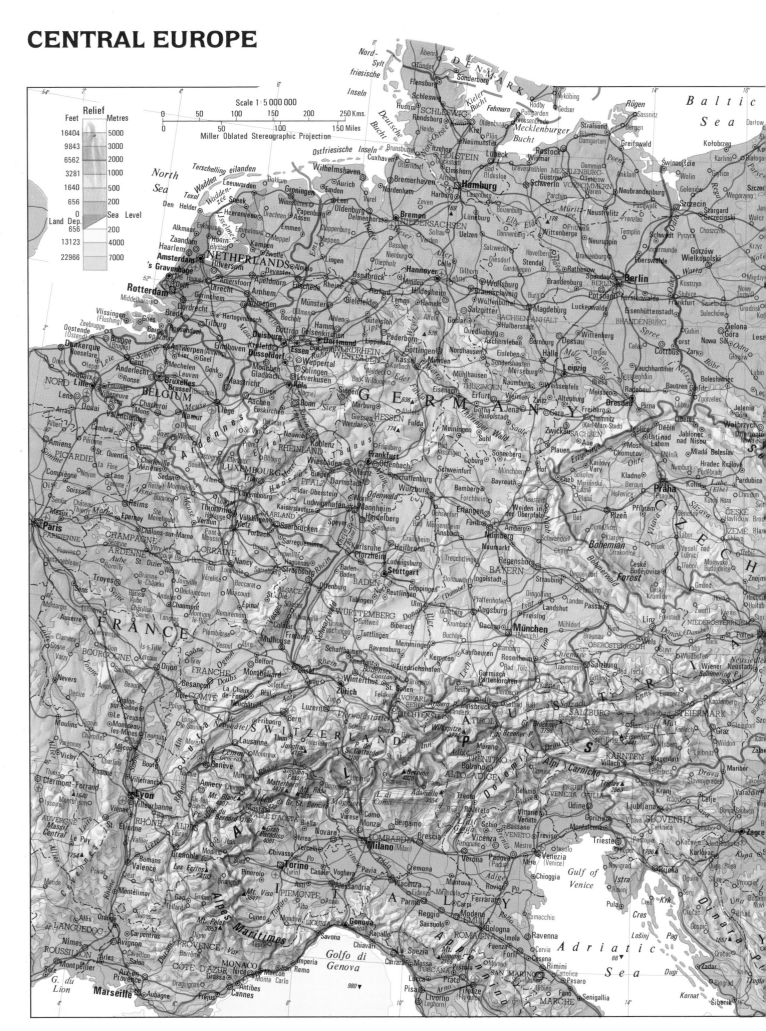

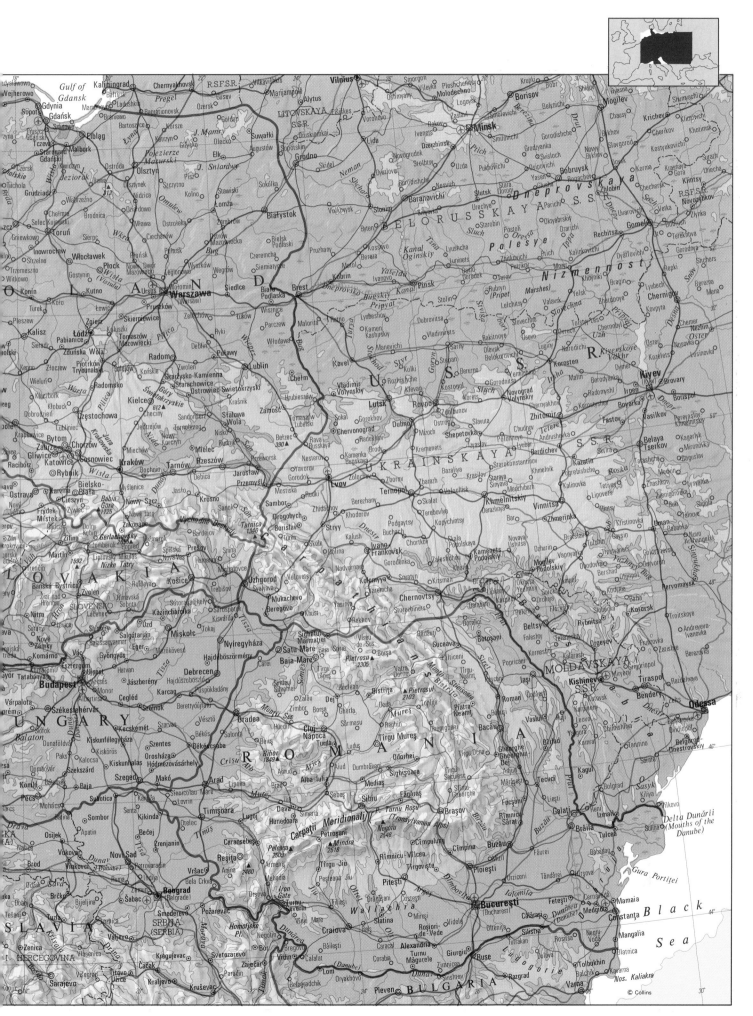

17

SCANDINAVIA AND BALTIC LANDS

ICELAND
on the same scale

© Collins

FAROE IS.
(Denmark)
on the same scale

Relief
| Feet | Metres | | | | Sea Level | | |
Scale 1 : 5 000 000
Conic Projection

ATLANTIC OCEAN

U.S.S.R. IN EUROPE

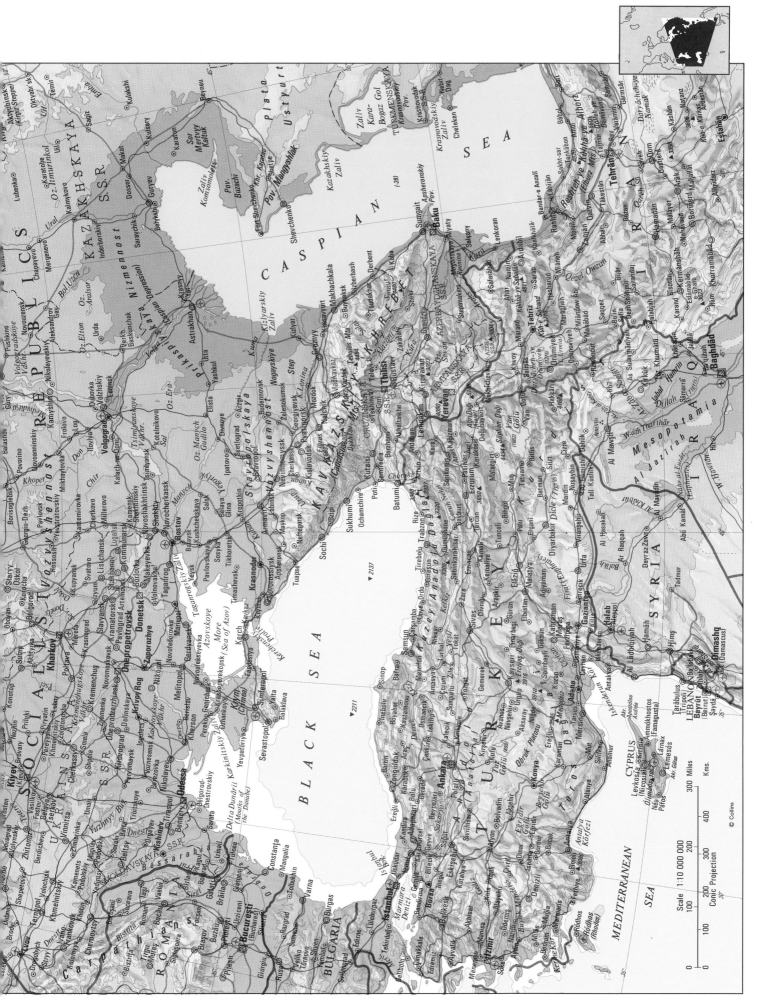

U.S.S.R.

MIDDLE EAST AND SOUTH ASIA

Scale 1 : 20 000 000

| 0 | 100 | 200 | 300 | 400 | 500 Miles |

| 0 | 200 | 400 | 600 | 800 Kms. |

Bonne Projection

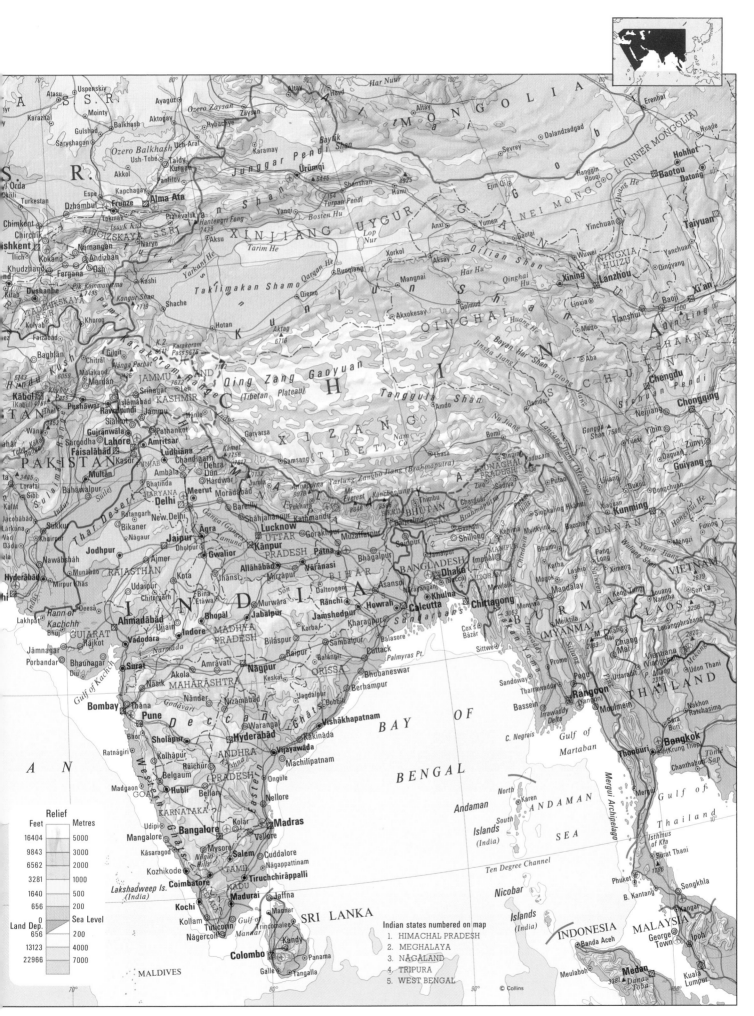

Indian states numbered on map
1. HIMACHAL PRADESH
2. MEGHALAYA
3. NAGALAND
4. TRIPURA
5. WEST BENGAL

Relief

Feet		Metres
16404		5000
9843		3000
6562		2000
3281		1000
1640		500
656		200
0	Sea Level	
Land Dep.		200
656		4000
13123		7000
22966		

© Collins

FAR EAST AND SOUTHEAST ASIA

Relief

Feet	Metres
16404	5000
9843	3000
6562	2000
3281	1000
1640	500
656	200
	Sea Level
0	Land Dep. 656
656	200
13123	4000
22966	7000

Scale 1:20 000 000

Bonne Projection

500 Miles
800 Kms.

Chinese state numbered on map

1. TIANJIN

JAPAN

NEW ZEALAND

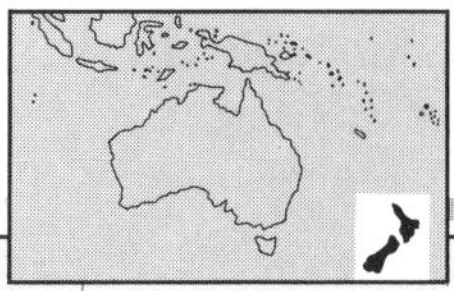

Relief

Feet	Metres
16 404	5000
9843	3000
6562	2000
3281	1000
1640	500
656	200
0	Sea Level

Land Dep.

656	200
13 123	4000
22 966	7000

NORTH ISLAND

SOUTH ISLAND

TASMAN SEA

PACIFIC OCEAN

North Cape
Ninety Mile Beach
Doubtless Bay
Mangonui
Kaitaia
Bay of Islands
C. Brett
Hewera
Paihia
Kaikohe
Hikurangi
NORTHLAND
Whangarei
Dargaville
Waipu
Bream Bay
Gt. Barrier I.
Warkworth
Hauraki Gulf
Helensville
Kaipara Harbour
Coromandel
Coromandel Peninsula
Takapuna
Auckland
Manukau
AUCKLAND
Manukau Harbour
Waiuku
Pukekohe
Thames
Mayor I.
Waikato
Waihi
Bay of Plenty
Morrinsville
Matakana I.
Huntly
Tauranga
Hamilton
Te Kaha
Te Araroa
East Cape
Cambridge
Matamata
Hicks Bay
Kawhia
Hikurangi 1754
Tikitiki
WAIKATO
Tokoroa
Rotorua
BAY OF PLENTY
Whakatane
Opotiki
Waipiro
Te Kuiti
Kawerau
Matawai
Tolaga Bay
North Taranaki Bight
Glennydale
Lake Taupo
GISBORNE
Gisborne
Taumarunui
Waikaremoana
New Plymouth
Inglewood
Ngauruhoe 2291
Turangi
Mt. Egmont 1518
Stratford
Ruapehu 2797
HAWKES BAY
Opunake
Normanby
Waiouru
Wairoa
Hawera
Patea
MANAWATU
Taihape
Napier
Hastings
Wanganui
WANGANUI
Waipawa
Waipukurau
Marton
Dannevirke
Palmerston North
Woodville
Foxton
Levin
Otaki
Masterton
Kapiti I.
Paraparaumu
Carterton
WELLINGTON
Porirua
Upper Hutt
Wellington
Lower Hutt
C. Palliser

Cape Farewell
Collingwood
Golden Bay
Takaka
D'Urville I.
Tasman Mts
Tasman Bay
Karamea Bight
Motueka
Nelson
Picton
Karamea
Richmond
Havelock
Cook Strait
Granity
Wairau
Westport
Butler
NELSON MARLBOROUGH
Blenheim
Cape Foulwind
Murchison
Seddon
Inangahua
Cape Campbell
Reefton
Mt. Travers 2338
Kaikoura Ra.
Clarence
Grey
Hanmer Springs
Greymouth
Lewis Pass
Waiau
Kaikoura
Kumara
Brunner
Hokitika
Cheviot
Ross
Otira
Arthur's Pass
Waipara
Whataroa
Pegasus Bay
Hanmer
Fox Glacier
Rangiora
Springfield
Kaiapoi
SOUTHERN ALPS
Darfield
Christchurch
Cascade Pt.
Mt. Cook 3764
Rakaia
Lincoln
Akaroa
Okuru
Tekapo
Ashburton
Leeston
Banks Peninsula
Pukaki
Fairlie
Canterbury Bight
Mt. Aspiring 3027
L. Wanaka
Twizel
Geraldine
Hawea
Wanaka
Omarama
Timaru
Milford Sound
Homer Tunnel
Arrowtown
Dunstan Mts
Kurow
Waimate
Queenstown
Cromwell
Naseby
Pukeuri
L. Wakatipu
Clyde
Ranfurly
Oamaru
Te Anau
Alexandra
L. Te Anau
Kingston
Lumsden
Eyre Mts
OTAGO
Palmerston
Roxburgh
Waikouaiti
L. Manapouri
Mossburn
Port Chalmers
Resolution I.
SOUTHLAND
Otago Peninsula
Ohai
Winton
Clarence
Dunedin
Puysegur Pt.
Nightcaps
Gore
Milton
Tuatapere
Wyndham
Clinton
Balclutha
Riverton
Edendale
Invercargill
Foveaux Strait
Bluff
Ruapuke I.
Stewart I.
Halfmoon Bay 980
Southwest Cape

Scale 1:6 000 000

0 — 50 — 100 — 150 Miles
0 — 50 — 100 — 150 — 200 Kms.

Conic Projection

© Collins ◇ Longman Atlases Cbii

PACIFIC OCEAN

SAMOA ISLANDS
Scale 1:7 500 000

Falealupo Aopo Fagamalo
Salailua 1857 Puapua
Matautu Lano Salelologa
Savai'i Upolu
WESTERN Matautu Apia Tiavea
SAMOA Sala'ilua Samoa
14° (U.S.A.) Manua Is.
Ofu Olosega
Tau
Pago Pago
Tutuila C. Matatula
Steps Pt.
172° 170°

FIJI
180°
Undu C. 15°
Gt. Sea Reef Vanua Levu
Lambasa Mbutha
Mbua Taveuni Yathata
Koro
Lautoka Viti Ngau Koro
Nandi Levu Sea
Singatoka Suva Lau
Group
Kandavu Passage
Kandavu
Scale 1:15 000 000
180° 20°

RAROTONGA
(N.Z.)
159°45'
Avatiu Avarua
Pokoinu 438
Aroarangi Te 653 Matavera
Manga Ngatangiia
21°15' 21°15'
Muri
Titikaveka
Scale 1:500 000
159°45'

NIUE
(N.Z.)
169°50'
Hikutavake Mutalau
19° Makefu Tuapa Lakepa 19°
Alofi Motutapu Liku
Bay Alofi
Avatele 66
Avatele
Avatele Bay
Tepa Pt. Vaiea Hakupu
Scale 1:1 000 000
169°50'

GUAM
(U.S.A.)
145°
Ritidian
Pt.
Pati Pt.
Philippine Mt Santa Rosa
Sea 262 Catalina Pt.
Agana Yigo
13°30' 13°30'
Orote Yona
Pen. Talofofo
Merizo Malojos
Inarajan
Scale 1:2 000 000
145°

VANUATU AND
NEW CALEDONIA
166°
Banks Is.
C. Cumberland C. Quiros
Espíritu 1880 Maewo
Santo I. Oba
16° Luganville Pentecost I. 16°
Malekula Ambrim
Epi Shepherd
Coral Islands
Sea VANUATU Emae Tongoa
170°
Vila Efate
Récifs
d'Entrecasteaux
Grand Eromanga
Récif Tana
de Lenakel
Cook Aneityum
20° 20°
166° 170°
Koumac
Voh 1628
Kone Houailou
Nouvelle Île Maré
Calédonie Yaté
(New Caledonia) Île des
(Fr.) Pins
Nouméa
© Collins
Scale 1:15 000 000

HAWAIIAN ISLANDS
(U.S.A.)

Haena • *Kauai*
Mana Kapaa
Niihau Lihue
Wahiawō *Oahu* Kailua
Honolulu *Molokai*
Maunaloa Honokahua
Lanai Wailuku *Maui*
Lanai City Hana
Kahoolawe Alenuihaha Channel
Upolu Pt. Honokaa
Waimea *Hilo*
Hawaii
Mauna Loa
Papa Pahala
Naalehu

Scale 1:10 000 000

KIRITIMATI (CHRISTMAS I.)
(Kiribati)

North West Pt. Main Camp
London
Paris North East Pt.
Bay of
Wrecks
South West Pt.
South East Pt.

Scale 1:2 500 000

TONGA
Scale 1:7 500 000
Vava'u 'Uta
Group Vava'u
Late

Kao
Tofua Ha'apai
Group
Fonuafo'ou
Nomuka
Group
Nuku'alofa Tongatapu
Group
Tongatapu Eua

MARQUESAS
ISLANDS
(France)

Hatutu
Eiao

Nuku Ua
Hiva Tai-o-haé Huka
Ua Pu
Hiva
Îles Marquises Oa Atuona
(Marquesas Is.)

Scale 1:10 000 000
Fatu
Hiva

EASTER ISLAND
(Chile)

Cabo Norte
Terevaka Bahia la
601 Pérouse
Isla de Pascua Cabo O'Higgins
(Easter I.) Cabo Roggeveen
Hanga
Roa Pta. Cuidado
Rano Kao
410 Cabo Sur

Scale 1:1 000 000

SOCIETY ISLANDS
(France)

Motu Iti *Îles sous*
Bora Bora *le Vent*
Tahaa
Huahine
Uturoa
Raiatea
Tetiaroa
Moorea *Papeete*
Papetoai
Îles du *Tahiti*
Maiao *Vent* Tautira Presqu'île
de Taiarapu
Îles de la Société
(Society Islands)

Scale 1:7 500 000

TAHITI
(France)

Papeete Papenoo
Pt. Arei
Tatai
Orohena
Punaauia 2277
Faaone
Isthme de
Taravao
Maraa Taunoa Tautira
Atimaono Vairao Pt.
Faaraa
Toanoano

Scale 1:2 500 000

Scale 1:60 000 000
0 200 400 600 800 1000 Miles
0 400 800 1200 1600 Kms.
Modified Zenithal Equidistant Projection

WESTERN AUSTRALIA

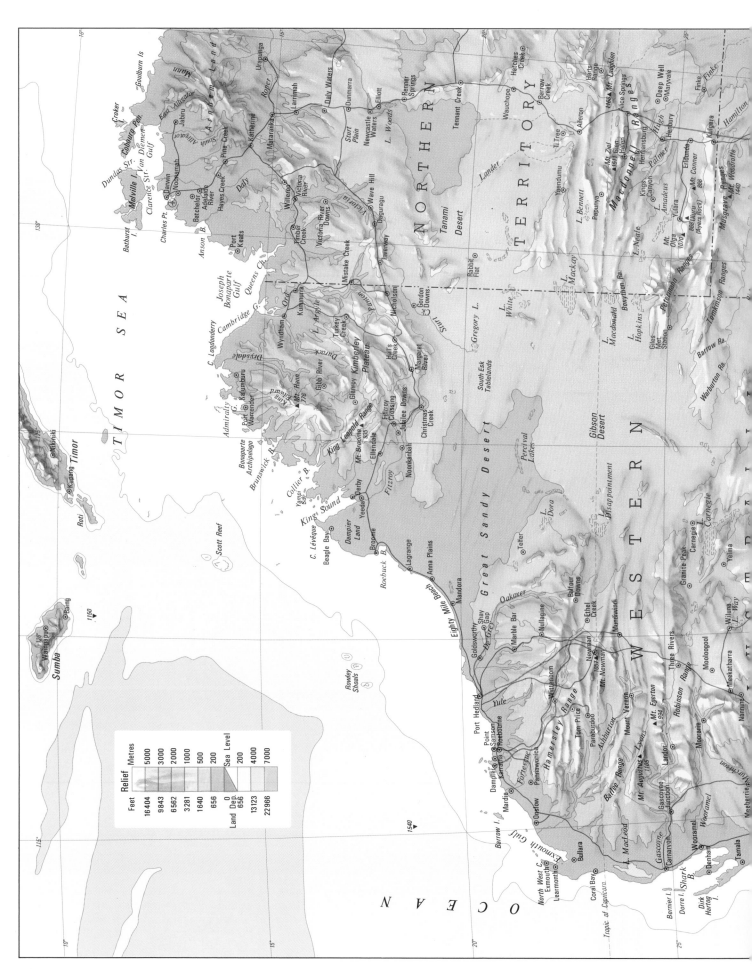

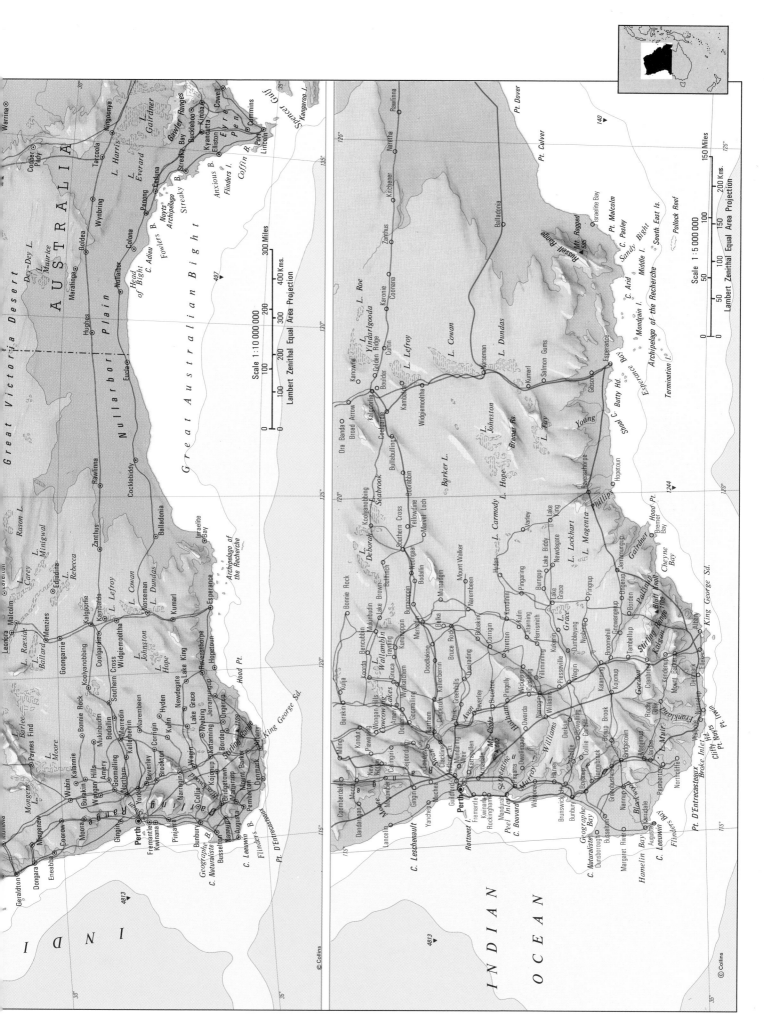

INDIA

AUSTRALIA

Great Victoria Desert

Nullarbor Plain

Great Australian Bight

Spencer Gulf

Kangaroo I.

INDIAN OCEAN

Scale 1:10 000 000

300 Miles

400 Kms.

497 ▽

Lambert Zenithal Equal Area Projection

Scale 1:5 000 000

150 Miles

200 Kms.

Lambert Zenithal Equal Area Projection

Perth

Fremantle

Kalgoorlie

Esperance

Geraldton

Kwinana

Stirling Range

King George Sd.

Albany

© Collins

© Collins

EASTERN AUSTRALIA

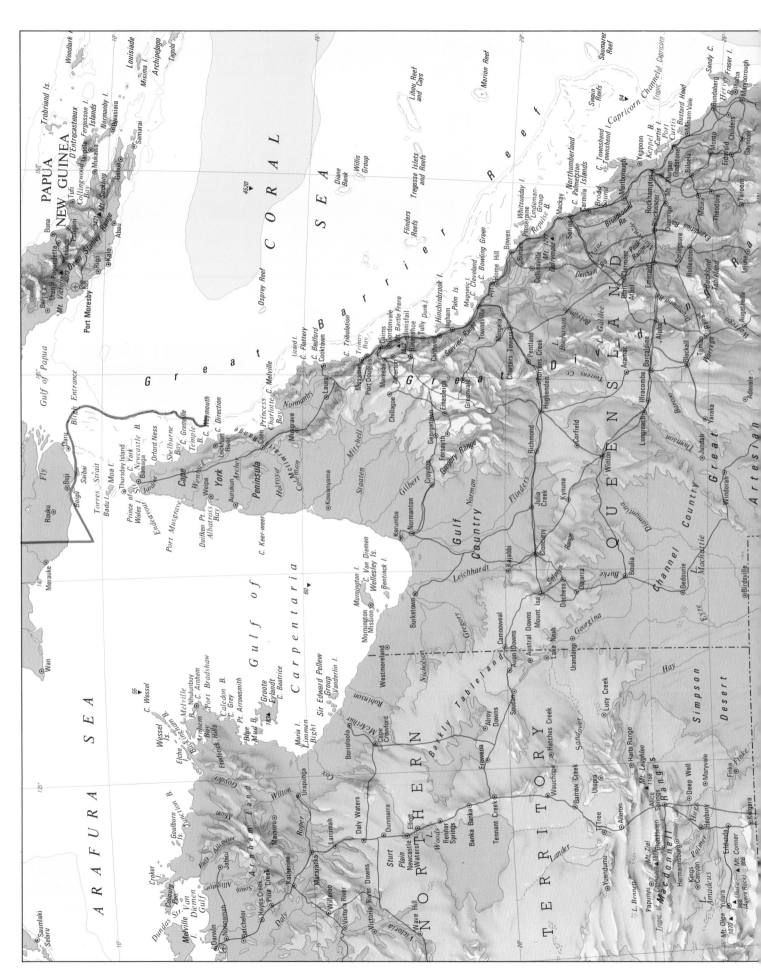

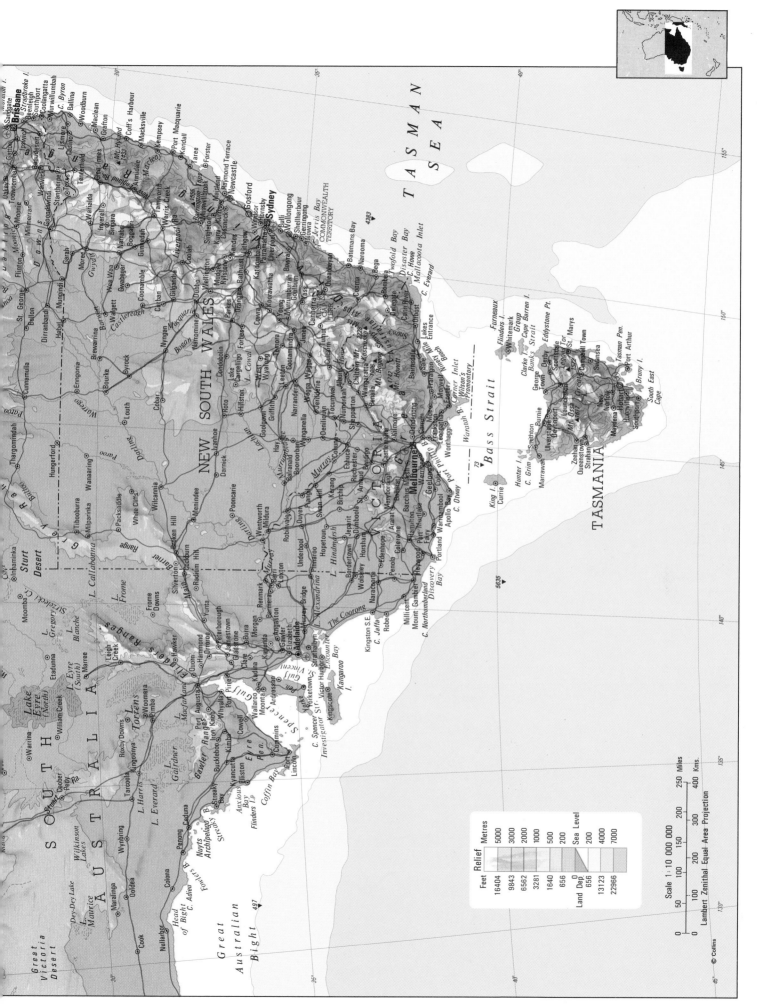

SOUTHEAST AUSTRALIA

CANADA AND ALASKA

Relief

Feet		Metres
16 404		5000
9843		3000
6562		2000
3281		1000
1640		500
656		200
0		Sea Level
Land Dep.		
656		200
13 123		4000
22 966		7000

Scale 1 : 17 000 000

0	100	200	300	400	500	Miles

0	100	200	300	400	500	600	700	800	Kms.

Bonne Projection

UNITED STATES

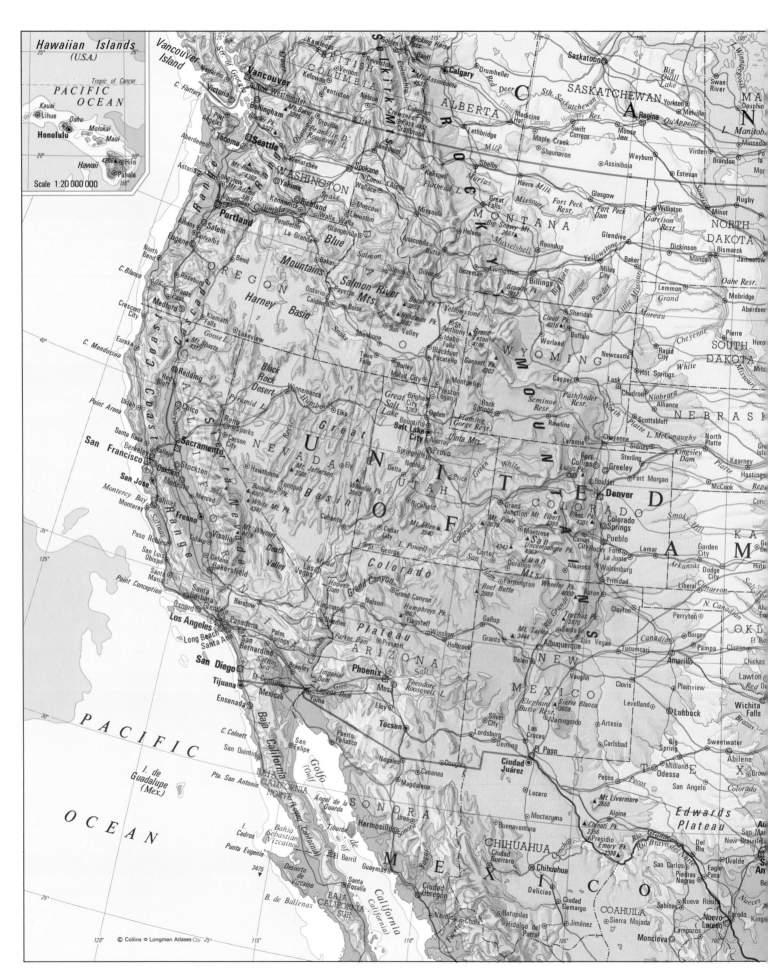

Scale 1:12 000 000

Relief		
Feet		Metres
16 404		5000
9843		3000
6562		2000
3281		1000
1640		500
656		200
0	Sea Level	
Land Dep.		200
656		4000
13 123		7000
22 966		

Bonne Projection

CENTRAL AMERICA AND THE CARIBBEAN

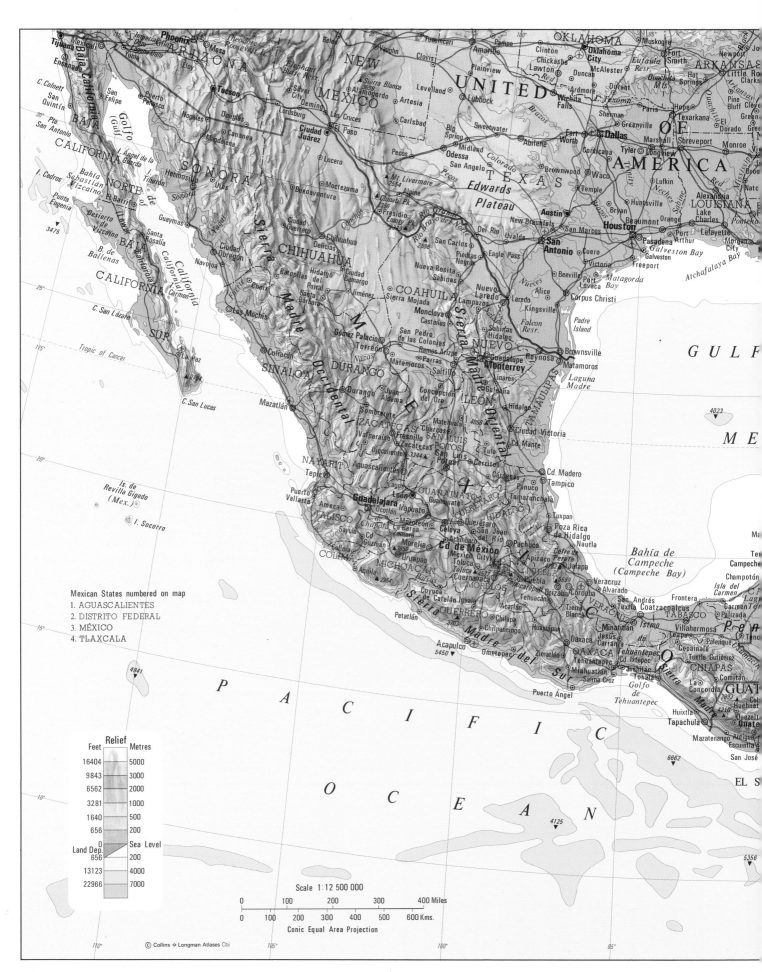

Mexican States numbered on map
1. AGUASCALIENTES
2. DISTRITO FEDERAL
3. MÉXICO
4. TLAXCALA

Relief		
Feet		Metres
16404		5000
9843		3000
6562		2000
3281		1000
1640		500
656		200
0		Sea Level
Land Dep.		
656		200
13123		4000
22966		7000

Scale 1:12 500 000

0   100   200   300   400 Miles
0   100   200   300   400   500   600 Kms.
Conic Equal Area Projection

© Collins ◇ Longman Atlases Cbi

TENNESSEE
Columbia
Asheville
NORTH
Chattanooga Cleveland
Spartanburg
New Bern
Fayetteville
Charlotte
C. Lookout
Rickwick
Huntsville
Gadsden
SOUTH
CAROLINA
Greenville
Anderson
Wilmington
corinth
Tennessee
CAROLINA
Rome
Athens
Florence
C. Fear
Atlanta
Anniston
Augusta
Orangeburg
Birmingham
Bessemer
Griffin
Columbus
Macon
Dublin
ALABAMA
GEORGIA
Savannah
Montgomery
Greenville
Andalusia
Dothan
Waycross
Brunswick
Pensacola
Tallahassee
Thomasville
Madison
Okefenokee Swamp
Panama City
Lake City
Jacksonville
St. Augustine
Apalachee Bay
Gainesville
Ocala
Daytona Beach
Sanford
Orlando
Cape Canaveral
Clearwater
Lakeland
St. Petersburg
Tampa
Fort Pierce
Bradenton
Sarasota
West Palm Beach
Fort Myers
Lake Okeechobee
Fort Lauderdale

ATLANTIC

OCEAN

GULF

OF

CO

Mississippi Delta

Key West
Florida Keys
Miami
C. Sable
C. Romano

Straits of Florida

La Habana (Havana)
Matanzas
Cárdenas
Archo. de Sabana
Pinar del Río
Marianao
Güines
Santa Clara
Sagua
Caibarién
Guane
Golfo de Batabanó
Cienfuegos
Sancti Spíritus
Ciego de Ávila
CUBA
Camagüey
Nueva Gerona
Archo. de los Canarreos
Trinidad
Victoria de las Tunas
Bayamo
Holguín
Banes
Isla de Pinos
Jardines de la Reina
Manzanillo
Sa. Maestra
S. Luis
Turquino
Santiago de Cuba
Guantánamo

BAHAMAS

Freeport
Grand Bahama I.
Great Abaco I.

New Providence
Nicolls Town
Nassau
Andros Town
The Bight
Andros
Rolleville
Gt. Exuma

Eleuthera I.
Rock Sound
Cat I.
San Salvador
Rum Cay
Long I.
Samana Cay
Crooked I.
Plana Cays
Acklin's I.
Mayaguana I.
Caicos Is.
Great Inagua
Matthew Town
Little Inagua
Turks and Caicos Is. (U.K.)
Turks Is.

Tropic of Cancer

La Blanquilla
Dragon's Mouth
Bonaire
La Orchila
Los Roques
La Tortuga
Isla de Margarita
Porlamar
Pampatar
Carúpano
Cumaná
Pen. de Araya
Barcelona
Maturín
Delta del Orinoco

Same Scale

Little Cayman
Cayman Brac
Grand Cayman
Georgetown
Cayman Is. (U.K.)

Windward Passage

Greater

Montego Bay
Black River
May Pen
Kingston
JAMAICA
St. Ann's Bay
Port Antonio

Île de la Tortue
Port-de-Paix
Cap-Haïtien
Môle St.-Nicolas
G. de la Gonâve
Gonaïves
Jérémie
Île de la Gonâve
Les Cayes
Port-au-Prince
HAITI

Puerto Plata
Valverde
Santiago
La Vega
San Juan
S. Cristóbal
Santo Domingo
Azua
Barahona

San Francisco de Macorís
Samaná
DOMINICAN REP.
La Romana
S. Pedro
Saona
Mona

San Juan
Bayamón
Arecibo
Mayagüez
Ponce
Caguas
PUERTO RICO (U.S.A.)

Hispaniola
Antilles

CARIBBEAN SEA

BELIZE
Belize
Dangriga
Punta Gorda

Gulf of Honduras
Is. de la Bahía
Pto. Cortés
Balfate
La Ceiba
Trujillo
C. Camarón
Tela
Yoro
S. Pedro Sula
HONDURAS
Juticalpa
Comayagua
Tegucigalpa
Danlí
Ocotal
NICARAGUA
Chinandega
León
Managua
Granada
Jinotepe
Rivas
Lago de Managua
L. de Nicaragua
San Carlos
S. Juan del Norte
C. Sta. Elena
Liberia
Pen. de Nicoya
Puntarenas
COSTA RICA
San José
Cartago
Limón
C. Blanco
Puerto Quepos
Golfo de Nicoya
Pta. S. Pedro
Pen. de Osa
Pto. Cortés
Pto. Armuelles
Pta. Burica
Isla de Coiba
David
Santiago
Pen. de Azuero
Chiriquí

Mosquitia
C. Gracias á Dios
Pto. Cabezas
Costa de Mosquitos
Prinzapolca
Río Grande
Rama
Bluefields
I. de Providencia (Col.)
I. de San Andrés (Col.)

Laguna de Caratasca

Laguna de Chiriquí
Golfo de los Mosquitos
Colón
San Miguelito
Gatun Lake
Balboa
PANAMÁ
Panamá
Penonomé
Archo. de las Perlas
Golfo de Panamá
El Real

Golfo del Darién
G. de Urabá

COLOMBIA

Netherlands Antilles
ARUBA
Curaçao (Neth.)
Bonaire
Willemstad
Pta. Gallinas
Pen. de la Guajira
Golfo de Venezuela
Pen. de Paraguana
Punto Fijo
La Vela
Coro
San Felipe
Tucacas
Puerto Cabello
Maracay
Valencia
Barquisimeto
Carora
Trujillo
Valera
Mérida
Guanare
VENEZUELA
Santa Marta
Ríohacha
Uribia
Maracaibo
Cabimas
Ciudad Ojeda
Sa. Nevada de Sta. Marta
Barranquilla
Ciénaga
Sabanalarga
Cartagena
Turbaco
Calamar
Magangué
Montería
Sincelejo
Cúcuta
San Cristóbal
Bucaramanga
Pamplona
Barrancabermeja
Arauca

Puerto Rico Trench
San Juan
Bayamón
Arecibo
Mayagüez
Ponce
Caguas
Carolina
PUERTO RICO (U.S.A.)
Vieques
St. Thomas
Virgin Is. (U.S.A.)
St. Croix
Anegada
Virgin Gorda
Tortola
Virgin Is. (U.K.)
St. Martin (Fr.-Neth.)
Sint Maarten (Neth.)
Saba (Neth.)
Sint Eustatius (Neth.)
ST. KITTS
NEVIS
Anguilla (U.K.)
St. Barthélemy (Fr.)
BARBUDA
ANTIGUA
St. John's
Montserrat (U.K.)
Pointe-à-Pitre
Marie-Galante
Guadeloupe (Fr.)
Basse-Terre
DOMINICA
Roseau
Martinique (Fr.)
Fort-de-France
ST. LUCIA
Castries
St. Kingstown
VINCENT AND THE GRENADINES
Bridgetown
BARBADOS
St. George's
GRENADA
TOBAGO
Port of Spain
San Fernando
TRINIDAD
Serpent's Mouth

Leeward Islands

Lesser Antilles

Windward Islands

Lesser Antilles

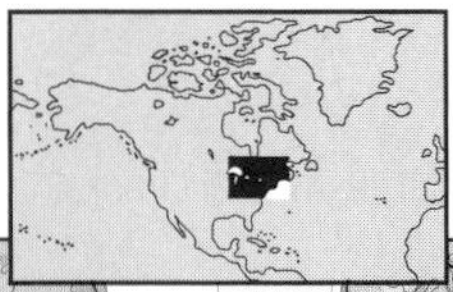

Relief

Feet	Metres
16404	5000
9843	3000
6562	2000
3281	1000
1640	500
656	200
0	Sea Level
	Land Dep.
656	200
13123	4000
22966	7000

Scale 1:7 500 000

Conic Equidistant Projection

© Collins

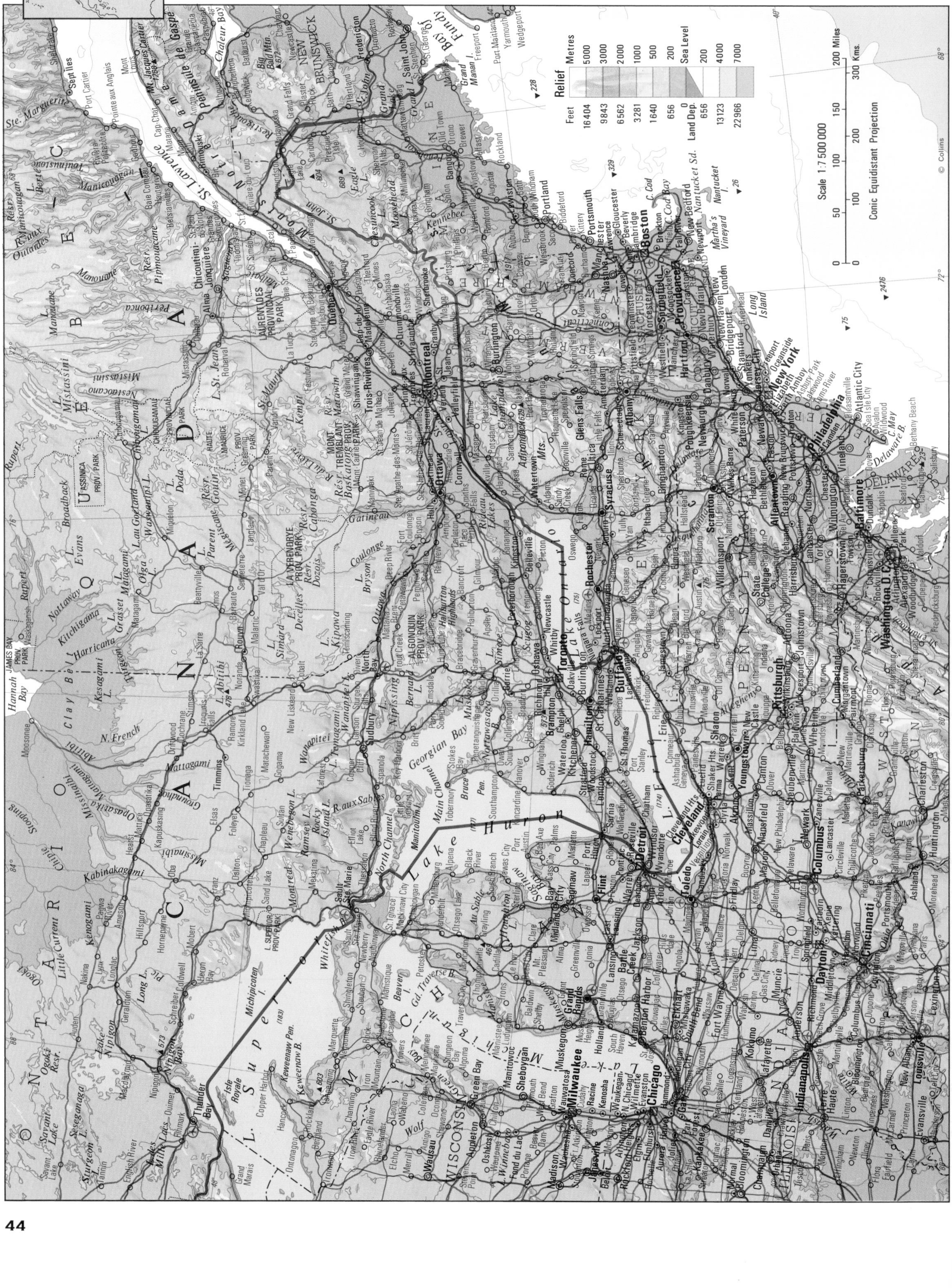

Relief

Feet	Metres
16 404	5000
9843	3000
6562	2000
3281	1000
1640	500
656	200
0	Sea Level
Land Dep.	
656	200
13 123	4000

Scale 1:12 500 000

| 0 | 100 | 200 | 300 | 400 Miles |
| 0 | 100 | 200 | 300 | 400 | 500 | 600 Kms. |

Lambert Azimuthal Equal Area Projection

Scale 1:7 500 000

| 0 | 40 | 80 Miles |
| 0 | 40 | 80 | 120 Kms. |

© Collins ◇ Longman Atlases Cbi

© Collins

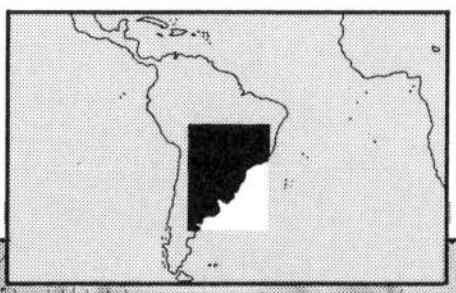

46

Relief

Feet	Metres
16 404	5000
9843	3000
6562	2000
3281	1000
1640	500
656	200
0	Sea Level
Land Dep.	
656	200
13 123	4000

Scale 1:12 500 000

0   100   200   300   400   500 Miles
0   100 200 300 400 500 600 700 800 Kms.

Lambert Azimuthal Equal Area Projection

wn
w Amsterdam
Paramaribo
Nieuw
Nickerie   Albina St. Laurent
Afobaka   du Maroni
W.J. Van   Cayenne
Blommesteln Meer   Kaw   C. Orange
SURINAM   GUIANA   St. Georges
              (Fr.)
                        Camopi
Tumuc Humac Mts.   Amapá   C. Norte

AMAPÁ
Mérirumá   Serra do Navio   Araguari
              Pto. Grande
              Macapá   Ilha   Estuario do
                             Caviana   Rio Amazonas
                                        (Amazon Delta)
Obidos   Monte   Prainha   I. Grande   Chaves
Farô   Alegre   do Gurupá
LITIGATED   Pôrto de Moz   I. de Marajó   Salinópolis
 AREA   Gurupá   Muaná   Bragança
Juruti   Santarém   Icoraci   Capanema   Viseu
Parintins   Cametá   Belém
         Belterra   Baião   Abaetetuba Acará   Turiaçu
                                                    Cururupu
                                         Guimarães
              Altamira   São Luís
PARA   Represa de   Viana   Rosário   Tutóia
Itaituba   Tucuruí   Tucuruí   Itapecuru   Parnaíba   Camocim
                                                Mirim   Granja
Bacabal   Graiaú Bacabal Caroatá Piracuruca   Antônio Bezerra
                                     Pedreiras   União   Sobral   Fortaleza
                          Marabá   Codó   Campo LITIGATED   Parangaba
Tocantinópolis   Imperatriz   Negrão   Caxias   Maior   AREA   Ipu   Baturité   Aracati
                                 Barra do   Teresina   Iguatu   Areia Branca
                                 Corda   Colinas   Crateús   Senador   Mossoró
         Tocantinópolis   MARANHÃO   Pompeu   Macau
Pôrto Franco   Amarante   Açu   Natal
         Carolina   Loreto Represa da Boa   Floriano   RIO GRANDE
              Riachão Esperança   Oeiras   Iguatu   DO NORTE
Conceição   Piacá   Picos   Crato   Caicó   Pombal
do Araguaia   Juazeiro   Patos Guarabira
Araguacema   São João   do Norte   PARAÍBA   João
                        Sta.   do Piauí PIAUÍ   Serra Talhada Campina Grande Pessoa
              Pedro   Filomena   Paulistana   Salgueiro   Pesqueira Caruaru Itabaiana
A   Z   Afonso   PERNAMBUCO   Olinda
              Chapada   Perolina   Arcoverde   Belo   Palmares   Recife
                                                                         Jardim
TOCANTINS   das   Remanso   Garanhuns   Palmeira
         Pto. Nacional   Balsas   Mangabeiras   Juàzeiro   Paulo Afonso dos Índios Viçosa Rio
Sta. Isabel   Parnaguá   ALAGOAS Largo
do Morro   Represa   Propriá   Arapiraca   Maceió
                                      Barra   Xique Xique de Sobradinho   SERGIPE Penedo
         Peixe   Senhor do Bonfim   Quemadas   Pedrinhas
                        Parnã   Jacobina   Aracaju
MATO GROSSO   Campos   BAHIA Barreiras   Serrinha   Estância
         Sta. Isabel   Belos   Ibotirama   Feira de   Alagoinhas
Diamantino   Carinhanha   Santana
                        Posse   Planalto   Cachoeira   Santo Amaro
GROSSO   Aruanã   Niquelândia   Brasiliano   Maragogipe Salvador
Cuiabá   Aragarças   Nazaré
Planalto do   Uruaçu   Serra Geral de Goiás   Brumado   Valença
                        Goiás   (Brazilian Highlands)   Jequié
         Rondonópolis   GOIÁS   DIST.(FED) Formosa   Vitória da   Ibicaraí Ilhéus
Mato Grosso   Anápolis   Brasília   Conquista   Monte Azul   Itabuna
         Alto Araguaia   Goiânia   Luziânia   MINAS GERAIS   Itapetinga   Salto da   Canavieiras
                                                              Divisa

Equator

18
4402   4235

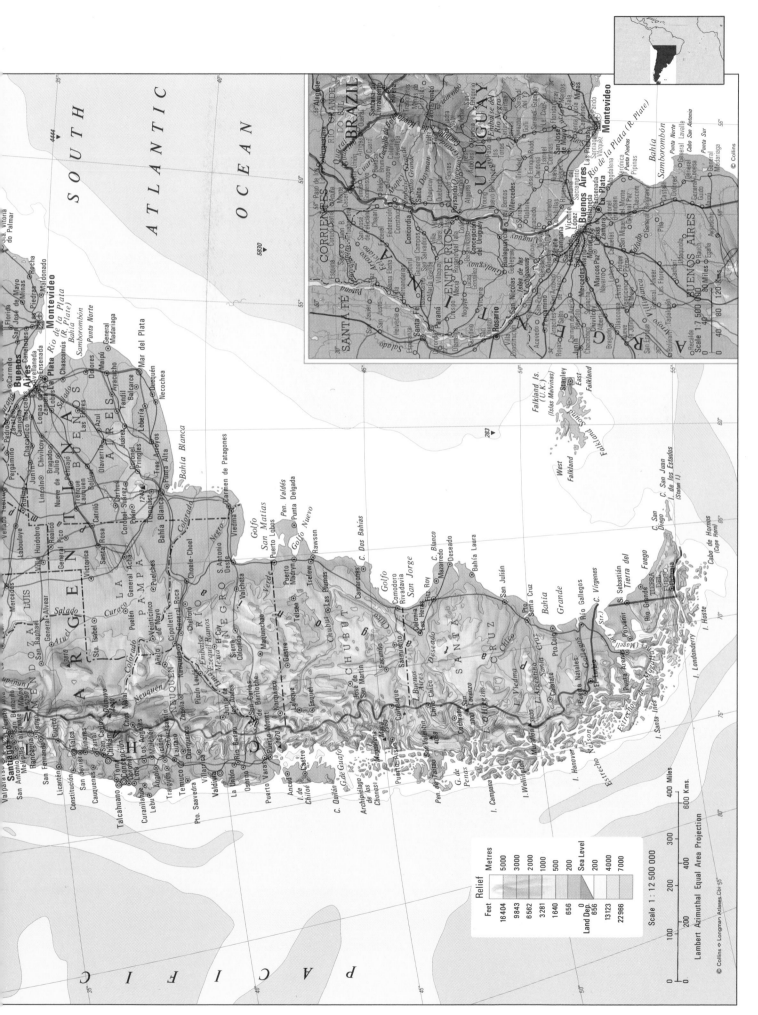

SOUTH   ATLANTIC   OCEAN

PACIFIC

OCEAN

BRAZIL

URUGUAY

Montevideo

Buenos Aires
La Plata

ARGENTINA

CHILE

Santiago

Montevideo
Buenos Aires
La Plata
Rio de la Plata (R. Plate)

SANTA FE
CORRIENTES
ENTRE RIOS
Paraná
Rosario
Santa Fe
BUENOS AIRES

Scale 1:7 500 000

| 0 | 40 | 80 | Miles |
| 0 | 40 | 80 | 120 Kms. |

© Collins

Mar del Plata
Bahía Blanca
Punta Alta
Carmen de Patagones
Viedma
Golfo San Matías
Pen. Valdés
Punta Delgada
Golfo Nuevo
Puerto Madryn
Rawson
Trelew
C. Dos Bahías
Camarones
Golfo San Jorge
Comodoro Rivadavia
C. Blanco
Deseado
Mazaredo
Bahía Laura
San Julián
Pto. Santa Cruz
Bahía Grande
Río Gallegos

Falkland Is.
(Islas Malvinas)
Stanley
East Falkland
West Falkland
Falkland Sound

C. San Diego
I. de los Estados
(Staten I.)

TIERRA DEL FUEGO
Ushuaia
Cabo de Hornos
(Cape Horn)

Estrecho de Magellan

Relief

Feet	Metres
16404	5000
9843	3000
6562	2000
3281	1000
1640	500
656	200
0	Sea Level
Land Dep.	656	200
13123	4000
22966	7000

Scale 1 : 12 500 000

| 0 | 100 | 200 | 300 | 400 Miles |
| 0 | 200 | 400 | 600 Kms. |

Lambert Azimuthal Equal Area Projection

© Collins ◇ Longman Atlases Cbi·95

49

NORTHERN AFRICA

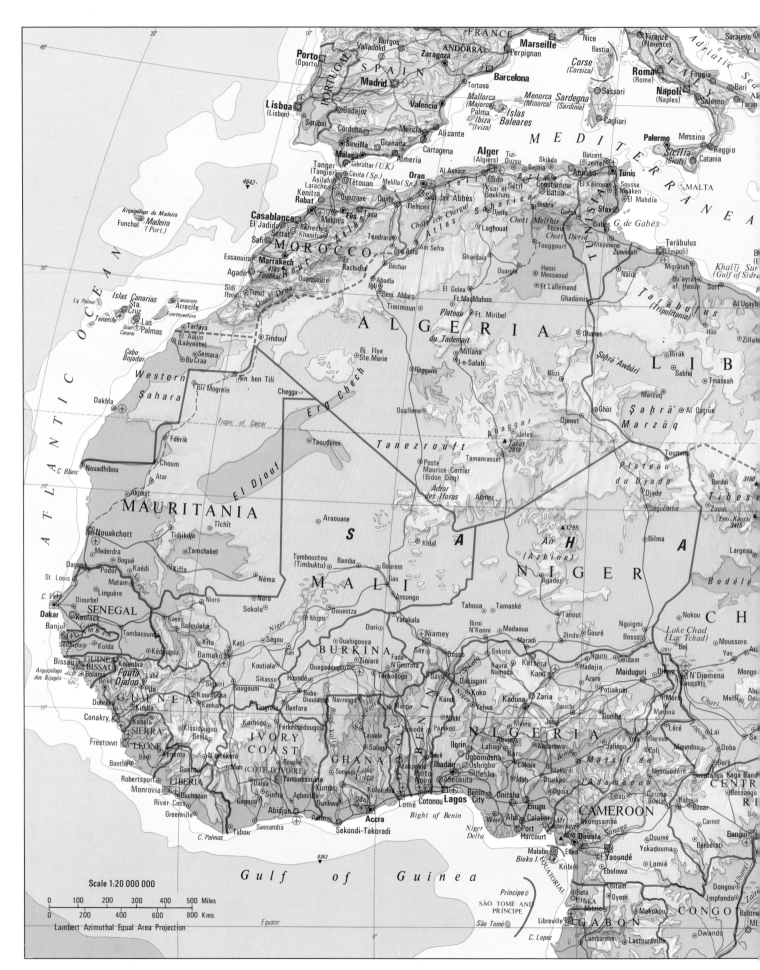

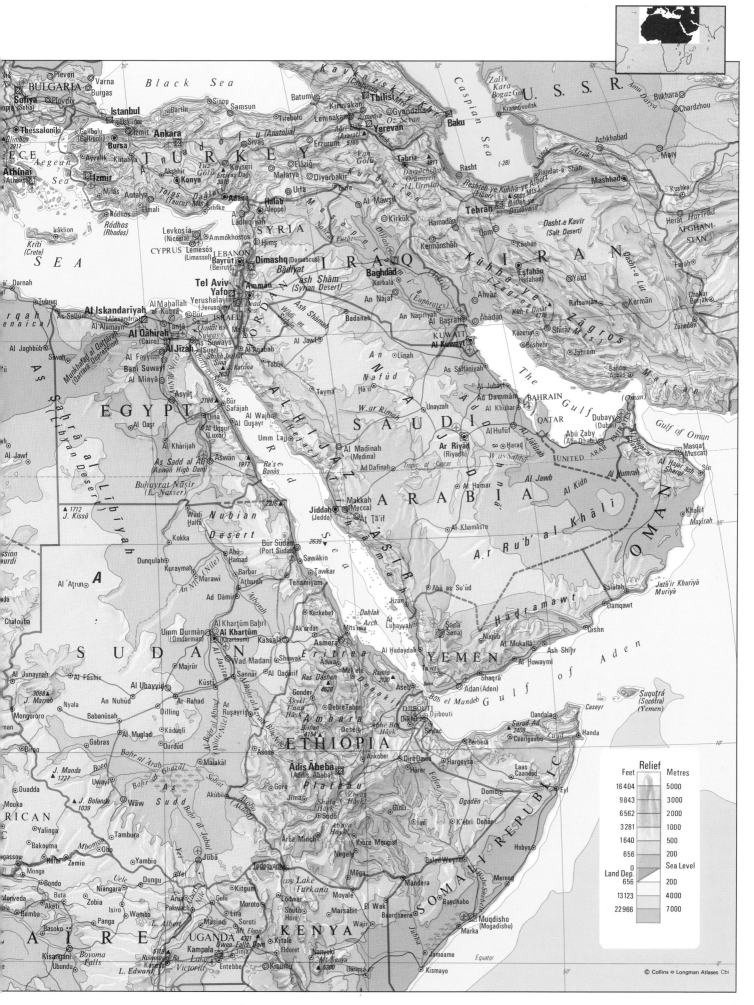

BULGARIA

Black Sea

Istanbul

TURKEY

Ankara

GREECE

Athinai
(Athens)

SEA

Kríti
(Crete)

EGYPT

Aş Saḥrā al Lībīyah (Libyan Desert)

SUDAN

Al Khartūm
(Khartoum)

ETHIOPIA

Ādis Ābeba
(Addis Ababa)

ZAIRE

UGANDA

KENYA

SYRIA

Dimashq (Damascus)

LEBANON

Bayrūt (Beirut)

Tel Aviv-
Yafo

ISRAEL

JORDAN

IRAQ

Baghdad

U.S.S.R.

Tbilisi

Yerevan

Baku

Caspian Sea

IRAN

Tehrān

AFGHANI-
STAN

SAUDI

ARABIA

Al Hijāz

Makkah (Mecca)

Jiddah
(Jedda)

Al Kuwayt

KUWAIT

BAHRAIN

QATAR

UNITED ARAB
EMIRATES

Dubayy (Dubai)

Abū Ẓaby
(Abu Dhabi)

Gulf of Oman

OMAN

Masqaṭ
(Muscat)

Ar Rub' al Khālī

Ar Riyāḍ
(Riyadh)

YEMEN

Ṣan'ā
(Sana)

Gulf of Aden

DJIBOUTI

Djibouti

SOMALI REPUBLIC

Muqdisho
(Mogadishu)

Suquṭrá
(Socotra)
(Yemen)

CYPRUS

Tropic of Cancer

Equator

Relief		
Feet		Metres
16404		5000
9843		3000
6562		2000
3281		1000
1640		500
656		200
0		Sea Level
Land Dep.		
656		200
13123		4000
22966		7000

© Collins ◊ Longman Atlases Cbi

CENTRAL AND EAST AFRICA

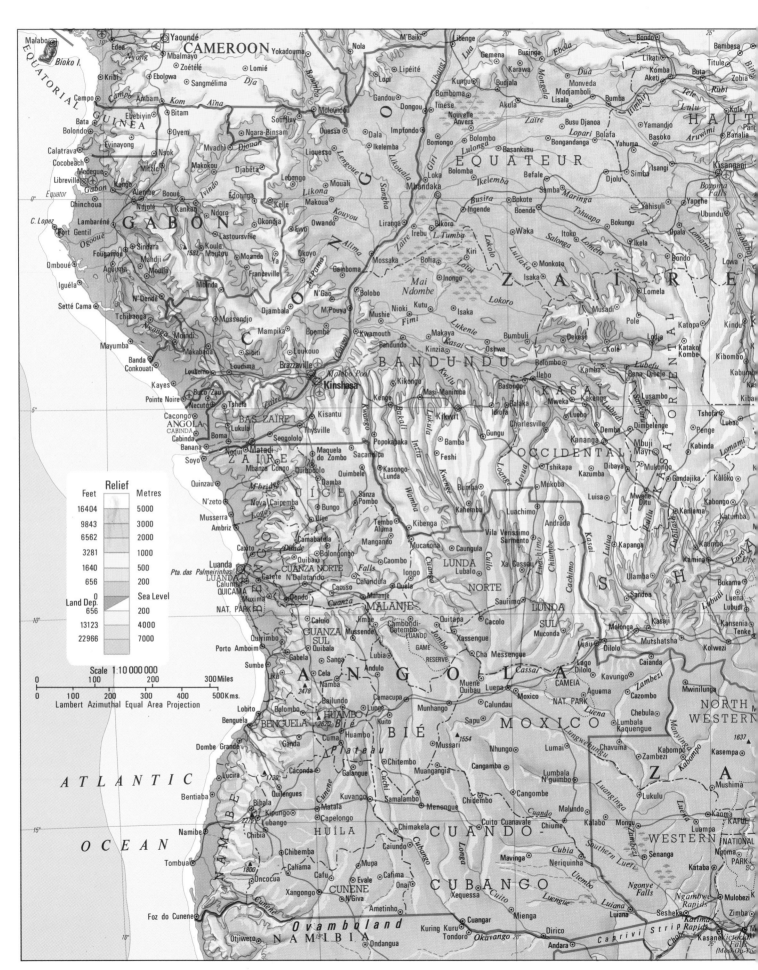

Relief

Feet	Metres
16404	5000
9843	3000
6562	2000
3281	1000
1640	500
656	200
0	Sea Level

Land Dep.

656	200
13123	4000
22966	7000

Scale 1:10 000 000

0   100   200   300 Miles
0 100 200 300 400 500 Kms.
Lambert Azimuthal Equal Area Projection

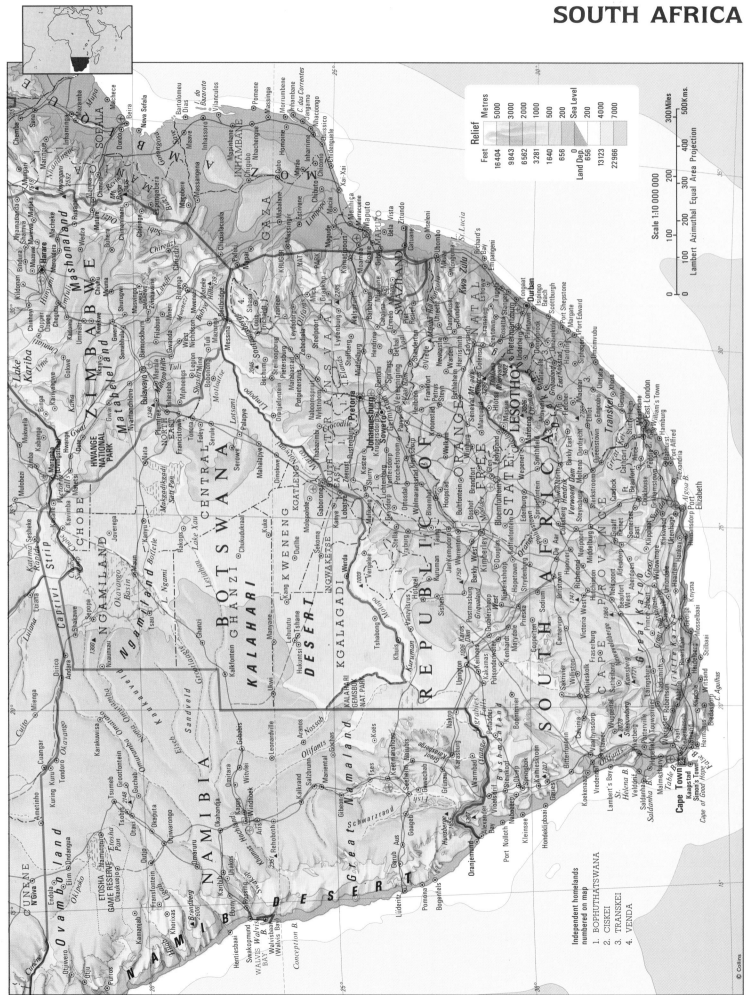

SOUTH AFRICA

54

Introduction

The Index includes an alphabetical list of selected names appearing on the maps. Each entry consists of the name followed by a page reference and the name's location on the map, given by latitude and longitude co-ordinates. Most features are indexed to the largest scale map on which they appear, however when the name applies to countries or other extensive features it is generally indexed to the map on which it appears in its entirety. Areal features are generally indexed using co-ordinates which indicate the centre of the feature. The latitude and longitude indicated for a point feature gives the location of the point on the map. In the case of rivers the mouth or confluence is always taken as the point of reference.

Names in the Index are generally in the local language and where a conventional English version exists, this is cross referenced to the entry in the local language. Names of features which extend across the boundaries of more than one country are usually named in English if no single official name exists. Names in languages not written in the Roman alphabet have been transliterated using the official system of the country if one exists, e.g. Pinyin system for China, otherwise the systems recognised by the United States Board on Geographical Names have been used.

Names abbreviated on the maps are given in full in the Index.

Abbreviations of Geographical Terms

b., B.	bay, Bay
c., C.	cape, Cape
d.	internal division e.g. county, region, state.
des.	desert
est.	estuary
f.	physical feature e.g. valley, plain, geographic district or region
g., G.	gulf, Gulf
i., I., is., Is.	island, Island, islands, Islands
l., L.	lake, Lake
mtn., Mtn.	mountain, Mountain
mts., Mts.	mountains, Mountains
pen., Pen.	peninsula, Peninsula
Pt.	Point
r.	river
resr., Resr.	reservoir, Reservoir
Sd.	Sound
str., Str.	strait, Strait

A

Aachen 16 50.46N 6.06E
Aarau 16 47.24N 8.04E
Aare r. 16 47.37N 8.13E
Aba 50 5.06N 7.21E
Abā as Su'ūd 24 17.28N 44.06E
Ābādān 24 30.21N 48.15E
Abadla 50 31.01N 2.45W
Abakan 23 53.43N 91.25E
Ābaya Hāyk' l. 51 6.20N 38.00E
Abbeville 12 50.06N 1.51E
Abbotsbury 9 50.40N 2.36W
Abéché 51 13.49N 20.49E
Åbenrå 19 55.02N 9.26E
Aberayron 9 52.15N 4.16W
Aberdare 9 51.43N 3.27W
Aberdare Range mts. 53 0.20S 36.40E
Aberdeen 11 57.08N 2.07W
Aberdovey 9 52.33N 4.03W
Aberfeldy 11 56.37N 3.54W
Abergavenny 9 51.49N 3.01W
Abersoch 8 52.50N 4.31W
Aberystwyth 9 52.25N 4.06W
Ābhē bid Hāyk' l. 51 11.06N 41.50E
Abidjan 50 5.19N 4.01W
Abilene Tex. 40 32.27N 99.45W
Abingdon 9 51.40N 1.17W
Abitibi r. 44 51.03N 80.55W
Abitibi, L. 44 48.42N 79.45W
Abou Deïa 50 11.20N 19.20E
Aboyne 11 57.05N 2.48W
Abrantes 13 39.28N 8.12W
Abruzzi d. 14 42.05N 13.45E
Abu Dhabi see Abū Ẓaby 24
Abū Ḥamad 51 19.32N 33.20E
Abuja 50 9.12N 7.11E
Abunã 46 9.41S 65.20W
Abū Ẓaby 24 24.27N 54.23E
Åby 19 58.40N 16.11E
Abyaḍ, Al Baḥr al r. 24 15.38N 32.31E
Acámbaro 42 20.01N101.42W
Acapulco 42 16.51N 99.56W
Acatlán 42 18.12N 98.02W
Accra 50 5.33N 0.15W
Accrington 8 53.46N 2.22W
Achill I. 10 53.57N 10.00W
Achinsk 22 56.10N 90.10E
Aconcagua mtn. 48 32.39S 70.00W
Acqui 14 44.41N 8.28E
Acraman, L. 36 32.02S135.26E
Adamaoua, Massif de l' mts. 50 7.05N 12.00E
Adams N.Y. 44 43.49N 76.01W
Adams, Mt. 40 46.13N121.29W
'Adan 24 12.50N 45.00E
Adana 21 37.00N 35.19E
Adapazari 21 40.45N 30.23E
Adda r. 14 45.08N 9.55E
Ad Dafīnah 24 23.18N 41.58E
Ad Dāmir 51 17.37N 33.59E
Ad Dammām 24 26.23N 50.08E
Ad Darb 24 17.44N 42.15E
Ad Dawḥah 24 25.15N 51.34E
Addis Ababa see Ādīs Ābeba 51
Adelaide 36 34.56S138.36E
Aden see 'Adan 24
Aden, G. of 24 13.00N 50.00E
Adendorp 54 32.18S 24.31E
Adige r. 14 45.10N 12.20E
Adirondack Mts. 44 44.00N 74.00W
Ādīs Ābeba 51 9.03N 38.42E
Adiyaman 21 37.46N 38.15E
Admiralty Is. 30 2.10S147.00E
Adour r. 12 43.28N 1.35W
Adra 13 36.43N 3.03W
Adrano 14 37.39N 14.49E
Adriatic Sea 14 42.30N 16.00E
Ādwa 51 14.12N 38.56E
Aegean Sea 15 39.00N 25.00E
Afghanistan 25 32.45N 65.00E
Afmadow 53 0.27N 42.05E
Afyon 21 38.46N 30.32E
Agadez 50 17.00N 7.56E
Agadir 50 30.26N 9.36W
Agana 30 13.28N144.45E
Agboville 50 5.55N 4.15W
Agde 12 43.19N 3.28E
Agen 12 44.12N 0.38E
Aghada 10 51.50N 8.13W
Āgra 25 27.11N 78.01E
Agra r. 13 42.12N 1.43W
Agreda 13 41.51N 1.55W
Agri r. 15 40.13N 16.45E
Ağri 21 39.44N 43.03E
Ağri Daği mtn. 21 39.45N 44.15E
Agrigento 14 37.19N 13.36E
Aguascalientes 42 21.51N102.18W
Águeda r. 13 41.00N 6.56W
Aguilas 13 37.25N 1.35W
Agulhas, C. 54 34.50S 20.00E
Agulhas Negras mtn. 45 22.20S 44.43W
Ahaggar mts. 50 24.00N 5.50E
Ahaura 29 42.21S171.33E
Ahlen 16 51.46N 7.53E
Ahmadābād 25 23.02N 72.37E
Ahvāz 24 31.17N 48.44E
Aigues-Mortes 12 43.34N 4.11E
Ailsa Craig i. 11 55.15N 5.07W
Ain r. 12 45.47N 5.12E
Aïna r. 52 0.38N 12.47E
Aïn ben Tili 50 26.00N 9.32W
Aïn Sefra 50 32.45N 0.35W
Aïr mts. 50 18.30N 8.30E
Airdrie 11 55.52N 3.59W
Aire 12 43.39N 0.15W
Aire r. 8 53.42N 0.54W
Aisne r. 12 49.27N 2.55E
Aix-en-Provence 12 43.31N 5.27E
Aix-les-Bains 12 45.42N 5.55E
Aíyina i. 15 37.43N 23.30E
Aíyion 15 38.15N 22.05E
Ajaccio 12 41.55N 8.43E
Ajmer 25 26.27N 74.38E
Akashi 28 34.38N134.59E
Aketi 52 2.46N 23.51E
Akhḍar, Al Jabal al mts. 51 32.10N 22.00E
Akhelóös 15 38.20N 21.04E
Akhisar 15 38.54N 27.49E
Akita 26 39.44N140.05E
Akjoujt 50 19.45N 14.23W
Aklavik 38 68.12N135.00W
Ākobo r. 51 8.30N 33.15E
Akola 25 20.44N 77.00E
Akpatok I. 39 60.30N 68.30W
Akron Ohio 44 41.04N 81.31W
Aksaray 21 38.22N 34.02E
Akşehir 21 38.22N 31.24E
Aksu 25 42.10N 80.00E
Aktogay 22 46.57N 79.40E
Akūbū r. see Ākobo r. 51
Akxokesay 25 36.48N 91.06E
Alabama d. 41 33.00N 87.00W
Alabama r. 41 31.05N 87.55W
Alakurtti 20 67.00N 30.23E
Al 'Alamayn 51 30.50N 28.57E
Alamosa 40 37.28N105.54W
Alanya 21 36.32N 32.02E
Al' Aqabah 24 29.32N 35.00E
Alaşehir 15 38.22N 28.29E
Alaska d. 38 65.00N153.00W
Alaska, G. of 38 58.45N145.00W
Alaska Range mts. 38 62.10N152.00W
Al 'Aṭrun 51 18.11N 26.36E
Alazani r. 21 41.06N 46.40E
Alba 14 44.42N 8.02E
Albacete 13 39.00N 1.52W
Alba-lulia 17 46.04N 23.33E
Albania 15 41.00N 20.00E
Albany r. 39 52.10N 82.00W
Albany Ga. 41 31.37N 84.10W
Albany N.Y. 44 42.39N 73.45W
Albany Oreg. 40 44.38N123.07W
Al Başrah 24 30.33N 47.50E
Al Bayḍā' 51 32.50N 21.50E
Albemarle Sd. 41 36.10N 76.00W
Alberche r. 13 40.00N 4.45W
Albert, L. 53 1.45N 31.00E
Alberta d. 38 55.00N115.00W
Albert Nile r. 53 3.30N 32.00E
Albi 12 43.56N 2.08E
Ålborg 19 57.03N 9.56E
Alborz, Reshteh-ye Kūhhā-ye mts. 24 36.00N 52.30E
Albuquerque 40 35.05N106.38W
Alburquerque 13 39.13N 6.59W
Albury 37 36.03S146.53E
Alcácer do Sal 13 38.22N 8.30W
Alcamo 14 37.59N 12.58E
Alcañiz 13 41.03N 0.09W
Alcaudete 13 37.35N 4.05W
Alcázar de San Juan 13 39.24N 3.12W
Alcira 13 39.10N 0.27W
Alcoy 13 38.42N 0.29W
Alcudia 13 39.51N 3.09E
Aldan 23 58.44N125.22E
Aldan r. 23 63.30N130.00E
Aldeburgh 9 52.09N 1.35E
Alderney i. 9 49.42N 2.11W
Aldershot 9 51.15N 0.47W
Aldridge 9 52.36N 1.55W
Alegrete 49 29.46S 55.46W
Aleksandrovsk Sakhalinskiy 23 50.55N142.12E
Alençon 12 48.25N 0.05E
Aleppo see Ḥalab 24
Alès 12 44.08N 4.05E
Alessandria 14 44.54N 8.37E
Ålesund 18 62.28N 6.11E
Aleutian Is 30 52.00N176.00W
Aleutian Range mts. 38 58.00N156.00W
Alexander Archipelago is. 38 56.30N134.30W
Alexander Bay town 54 28.36S 16.26E
Alexandria B.C. 38 52.38N122.27W
Alexandria Ont. 44 45.18N 74.39W
Alexandria see Al Iskandarīyah 51
Alexandria Va. 44 38.48N 77.03W
Alexandroúpolis 15 40.50N 25.53E
Al Fāshir 51 13.37N 25.22E
Al Fayyūm 51 29.19N 30.50E
Alfiós r. 15 37.37N 21.27E
Alford 11 57.14N 2.42W
Algeciras 13 36.08N 5.27W
Alger 50 36.50N 3.00E
Algeria 50 28.00N 2.00E
Alghero 14 40.33N 8.20E
Algiers see Alger 50
Algoa B. 54 33.50S 26.00E
Al Ḥajar ash Sharqī mts. 51 23.00N 59.00E
Al Ḥamar 24 22.26N 46.12E
Al Ḥudaydah 24 14.50N 42.58E
Al Hufūf 24 25.20N 49.34E
Al Ḥuwaymī 24 14.05N 47.44E
Aliákmon r. 15 40.30N 22.38E
Alicante 13 38.21N 0.29W
Alice Springs town 34 23.42S133.52E
Alima r. 52 1.36S 16.35E
Alingsås 19 57.56N 12.31E
Al Iskandarīyah 51 31.13N 29.55E
Aliwal North 54 30.41S 26.41E
Al Jaghbūb 51 29.42N 24.38E
Al Jawb f. 24 23.00N 50.00E
Al Jawf 24 29.49N 39.52E
Al Jazīrah f. 51 14.30N 33.00E
Al Jīzah 51 30.01N 31.12E
Al Jubayl 24 27.59N 49.40E
Al Junaynah 51 13.27N 22.30E
Al Khābūrah 24 23.58N 57.10E
Al Khamāsīn 24 20.29N 44.49E
Al Khārijah 51 25.27N 30.32E
Al Kharṭūm 51 15.33N 32.35E
Al Kharṭūm Baḥrī 51 15.39N 32.34E
Al Khubar 51 26.18N 50.06E
Al Kidn des. 24 22.20N 54.20E
Alkmaar 16 52.37N 4.44E
Al Kuwayt 24 29.20N 48.00E
Allāhābād 25 25.27N 81.51E
Allakaket 38 66.30N152.45W
Allegheny r. 44 40.27N 80.00W
Allegheny Mts. 41 38.30N 80.00W
Allen, Lough 10 54.07N 8.04W
Allentown 44 40.37N 75.30W
Aller r. 16 52.57N 9.11E
Alliance Nebr. 40 42.08N103.00W
Allier r. 12 46.58N 3.04E
Alloa 11 56.07N 3.49W
Al Luḥayyah 51 15.43N 42.42E
Alma-Ata 22 43.19N 76.55E
Almadén 13 38.47N 4.50W
Al Madīnah 24 24.30N 39.35E
Al Manāmah 24 26.12N 50.36E
Almansa 13 38.52N 1.06W
Almanzora r. 13 37.16N 1.49W
Al Mawşil 24 36.21N 43.08E
Almazán 13 41.29N 2.31W
Almeirim 13 39.12N 8.37W
Almelo 16 52.21N 6.40E
Almería 13 36.50N 2.26W
Älmhult 19 56.33N 14.08E
Al Minyā 51 28.06N 30.45E
Al Muglad 51 11.01N 27.50E
Al Mukallā 24 14.34N 49.09E
Al Mukhā 24 13.19N 43.15E
Almuñécar 13 36.44N 3.41W
Alnwick 8 55.25N 1.41W
Alofi 30 19.03S169.55W
Alónnisos i. 15 39.08N 23.50E
Alpes Maritimes mts. 12 44.07N 7.08E
Alpine 40 30.22N103.40W
Alps mts. 12 46.00N 7.30E
Al Qaḍārif 51 14.02N 35.24E
Al Qāhirah 51 30.03N 31.15E
Al Qaşr 51 25.42N 28.53E
Al Qaṭrūn 50 24.55N 14.38E
Al Quşayr 51 26.04N 34.15E
Als i. 19 54.59N 9.55E
Alsace d. 12 48.25N 7.40E
Alsasua 13 42.54N 2.10W
Alston 11 54.48N 2.26W
Alta 18 70.00N 23.15E
Alta r. 18 69.50N 23.30E
Altai mts. 26 46.30N 93.30E
Altamura 15 40.50N 16.32E
Altanbulag 26 50.18N106.30E
Altea 13 38.37N 0.03W
Altenburg 16 50.59N 12.27E
Altnaharra 11 58.16N 4.26W
Alto Araguaia 47 17.19S 53.10W
Alton 9 51.08N 0.59W
Altoona 44 40.30N 78.24W
Al Ubayyiḍ 51 13.11N 30.10E
Al' Uqaylah 50 30.15N 19.12E
Al Uqşur 51 25.41N 32.24E
Alva 40 36.48N 98.40W
Alvarado 42 18.49N 95.46W
Älvdalen 19 61.14N 14.02E
Älvsbyn 18 65.39N 20.59E
Al Wajh 24 26.16N 36.28E
Alyaty 21 39.59N 49.20E
Amadeus, L. 32 24.50S130.45E
Amadjuak L. 39 65.00N 71.00W
Amagasaki 28 34.43N135.25E
Åmål 19 59.03N 12.42E
Amaliás 15 37.48N 21.21E
Amamula 53 0.17S 27.49E
Amares 13 41.38N 8.21W
Amarillo 40 35.14N101.50W
Amasya 21 40.37N 35.50E
Amazon r. see Amazonas r. 47
Amazonas r. 47 2.00S 52.00W
Ambāla 25 30.23N 76.46E
Ambarchik 23 69.39N162.27E
Amberg 16 49.27N 11.52E
Amble 8 55.20N 1.34W
Ambleside 8 54.26N 2.58W
Amboise 12 47.25N 1.00E
Ambriz 52 7.54S 13.12E
Amdo 25 32.22N 91.07E
Amersfoort 16 52.10N 5.23E
Amga 23 60.51N131.59E
Amga r. 23 62.40N135.20E
Amgu 26 45.48N137.36E
Amgun r. 23 53.10N139.47E
Amhara Plateau f. 51 10.00N 37.00E
Amiata mtn. 14 42.53N 11.37E
Amiens 12 49.54N 2.18E
Amlwch 8 53.24N 4.21W
'Ammān 24 31.57N 35.56E
Ammanford 9 51.48N 4.00W
Ammassalik 39 65.40N 38.00W
Ammókhostos 24 35.07N 33.57E
Amorgós i. 15 36.50N 25.55E
Ampala 43 13.16N 87.39W
Amrāvati 25 20.56N 77.45E
Amritsar 25 31.38N 74.53E
Amsterdam 16 52.22N 4.54E
Amu Darya r. 22 43.50N 59.00E
Amundsen G. 38 70.30N122.00W
Amur r. 23 53.17N140.00E
Anabar r. 23 72.40N113.30E
Anaconda 40 46.09N112.56W
Anadolu f. 21 38.00N 33.00E
Anadyr r. 23 65.00N176.00E
Anáfi i. 15 36.21N 25.50E
Anambas, Kepulauan is. 27 3.00N106.10E
Anápolis 47 16.19S 48.58W
Anār 24 30.54N 55.18E
Anatolia f. see Anadolu f. 21
Añatuya 48 28.26S 62.48W
Anchorage 38 61.10N150.00W
Ancón 46 11.50S 77.10W
Ancona 14 43.37N 13.33E
Andalusia 41 31.20N 86.30W
Andaman Islands 25 12.00N 92.45E
Andaman Sea 25 10.00N 95.00E
Andara 54 18.04S 21.26E
Andelot 12 48.15N 5.18E
Andenes 18 69.18N 16.10E
Anderson r. 38 69.45N129.00W
Andes mts. 49 32.40S 70.00W
Andhra Pradesh d. 25 17.00N 79.00E
Andizhan 22 40.48N 72.23E
Andorra town 12 42.30N 1.31E
Andorra 12 42.30N 1.32E
Andover 9 51.13N 1.29W
Andria 14 41.13N 16.18E
Andropov 20 58.01N 38.52E
Ándros i. 15 37.50N 24.50E
Andros I. 43 24.30N 78.00W
Andújar 13 38.02N 4.03W
Andulo 52 11.28S 16.43E
Aneto, Pico de mtn. 13 42.40N 0.19E
Angara r. 23 58.00N 93.00E
Angarsk 23 52.31N103.55E
Angaston 35 34.30S139.03E
Ånge 18 62.31N 15.40E
Ängelholm 19 56.15N 12.50E
Ångerman r. 18 63.00N 17.43E
Angers 12 47.29N 0.32W
Ångesån r. 18 66.22N 22.58E
Anglesey i. 8 53.16N 4.25W
Angoche 53 16.10S 39.57E
Angola 52 11.00S 18.00E
Angoulême 12 45.40N 0.10E
Anguilla i. 43 18.14N 63.05W
Angumu 53 0.10S 27.38E
Anholt i. 19 56.42N 11.34E
Aniak 38 61.32N159.40W
Ankara 21 39.55N 32.50E
Ānkober 51 9.32N 39.43E
Annaba 50 36.55N 7.47E
An Najaf 24 31.59N 44.19E
Annam Highlands see Annamitique, Chaîne mts. 27
Annamitique, Chaîne mts. 27 17.00N106.00E
Annan 11 54.59N 3.16W
Annan r. 11 54.58N 3.16W
Annandale f. 11 55.12N 3.25W
Anna Plains 32 19.18S121.34E
Annapurna mtn. 25 28.34N 83.50E
Ann Arbor 44 42.18N 83.43W
Annecy 12 45.54N 6.07E
Anniston 41 33.58N 85.50W
Annonay 12 45.15N 4.40E
An Nuhūd 51 12.41N 28.28E
Anoka 41 45.11N 93.20W
Anqing 26 30.40N117.03E
Ansbach 16 49.18N 10.36E
Anshan 26 41.06N122.58E
Anstruther 11 56.14N 2.42W
Antakya 21 36.12N 36.10E
Antalya 21 36.53N 39.42E
Antananarivo 53 18.55S 47.31E
Antequera 13 37.01N 4.34W
Antibes 12 43.35N 7.07E
Anticosti, Île d' i. 39 49.20N 63.00W
Antigua 42 14.33N 90.42W
Antigua i. 43 17.09N 61.49W
Antipodes Is. 30 49.42S178.50E
Antofagasta 48 23.39S 70.24W
Antrain 12 48.28N 1.30W
Antrim 10 54.43N 6.14W
Antrim d. 10 54.58N 6.20W
Antrim, Mts. of 10 55.00N 6.10W
Antwerpen 16 51.13N 4.25E
Anvik 38 62.38N160.20W
Anxi Gansu 26 40.32N 95.57E
Anyang 26 36.05N114.20E
Anzio 14 41.27N 12.37E
Aomori 26 40.50N140.43E
Aosta 14 45.43N 7.19E
Apalachee B. 41 29.30N 84.00W
Aparri 27 18.22N121.40E
Apeldoorn 16 52.13N 5.57E
Apia 30 13.48S171.45W
Apostle Is. 41 47.00N 90.30W
Apóstoles 48 27.55S 55.45W
Appalachian Mts. 41 39.30N 78.00W
Appennino mts. 14 42.00N 13.30E
Appleby 8 54.35N 2.29W
Appleton 41 44.17N 88.24W
Apucarana 45 23.34S 51.28W
Apure r. 46 7.40N 66.30W
Aquidauana 48 20.27S 55.45W
Aquila 42 18.30N103.50W
Aquitaine d. 12 44.40N 0.00
'Arab, Baḥr al r. 51 9.02N 29.28E
Arabian Sea 24 15.00N 64.00E
Aracaju 47 10.54S 37.07W
Araçatuba 45 21.12S 50.24W
Arafura Sea 27 9.00S133.00E
Aragarças 47 15.55S 52.12W
Aragón r. 13 42.20N 1.45W
Araguaia r. 47 5.20S 48.30W
Araguari r. 47 1.15N 50.05W
Arāk 24 34.06N 49.44E
Arakan Yoma mts. 25 19.30N 94.30E
Araks r. 21 40.00N 48.28E
Aral Sea see Aralskoye More sea 22
Aralsk 22 46.56N 61.43E
Aralskoye More sea 22 45.00N 60.00E
Aramac 34 22.59S145.14E
Aranda de Duero 13 41.40N 3.41W
Aran I. 10 53.07N 9.38W
Aran Is. 10 53.07N 9.38W
Aranjuez 13 40.02N 3.37W
Araouane 50 18.53N 3.31W
Araraquara 45 21.46S 48.08W
Ararat 36 37.20S143.00E
Ararat mtn. see Ağri Daği mtn. 21
Aras r. Turkey see Araks r. 21
Araxá 45 19.37S 46.50W
Arbatax 14 39.56N 9.41E
Arbroath 11 56.34N 2.35W
Arcachon 12 44.40N 1.11W
Arctic Bay town 39 73.05N 85.20W
Arctic Red r. 38 67.26N133.48W
Arctic Red River town 38 67.27N133.46W
Arda r. 15 41.39N 26.30E
Ardabīl 24 38.15N 48.18E
Ardara 10 54.46N 8.25W
Ardèche r. 12 44.31N 4.40E
Ardennes mts. 16 50.10N 5.30E
Ardila r. 13 38.10N 7.30W
Ardmore 10 51.58N 7.43W
Ardnamurchan, Pt. of 11 56.44N 6.14W
Ardrossan 11 55.38N 4.49W
Ards Pen. 10 54.30N 5.30W
Åre 18 63.25N 13.05E
Arecibo 43 18.29N 66.44W
Arena, Pt. 40 38.58N123.44W
Arendal 19 58.27N 8.48E
Arequipa 46 16.25S 71.32W
Arès 12 44.47N 1.08W
Arévalo 13 41.03N 4.43W
Arezzo 14 43.27N 11.52E
Arganda 13 40.19N 3.26W
Argelès-sur-Mer 12 42.33N 3.01E
Argens r. 12 43.10N 6.45E
Argentan 12 48.45N 0.01W
Argentina 49 36.00S 63.00W
Argentino, L. 49 50.15S 72.25W
Argenton 12 46.36N 1.30E
Argeş r. 15 44.13N 26.22E
Árgos 15 37.37N 22.45E
Argostólion 15 38.10N 20.30E
Århus 19 56.09N 10.13E
Ariano 14 41.04N 15.00E
Arica 48 18.29S 70.20W
Arima 46 10.38N 61.17W
Arinos r. 47 10.20S 57.35W
Aris 54 22.48S 17.10E
Arisaig 11 56.55N 5.51W
Ariza 13 41.19N 2.03W
Arizona d. 40 34.00N112.00W
Arkaig, Loch 11 56.58N 5.08W
Arkansas d. 41 35.00N 92.00W
Arkansas r. 41 33.50N 91.00W
Arkansas City 41 37.03N 97.02W
Arkhangel'sk 20 64.32N 41.10E
Árki i. 15 37.22N 26.45E
Arklow 10 52.47N 6.10W
Arlberg Pass 16 47.00N 10.05E
Arles 12 43.41N 4.38E
Arlington Va. 44 38.52N 77.05W
Arlon 16 49.41N 5.49E
Armadale 33 32.10S115.57E
Armagh 10 54.21N 6.41W
Armagh d. 10 54.16N 6.35W
Armavir 21 44.59N 41.10E
Armenia 46 4.32N 75.40W
Armidale 37 30.32S151.40E
Arnaud r. 39 60.00N 69.45W
Årnes 19 60.09N 11.28E
Arnhem 16 52.00N 5.55E
Arnhem, C. 34 12.10S137.00E
Arnhem B. 34 12.20S136.12E
Arnhem Land f. 34 13.10S134.30E
Arno r. 14 43.43N 10.17E
Ar Rahad 51 12.42N 30.33E
Arran i. 11 55.35N 5.14W
Arras 12 50.17N 2.46E
Arrecife 50 28.57N 13.32W
Ar Riyāḍ 24 24.39N 46.44E
Arrochar 11 56.12N 4.44W
Arrow, Lough 10 54.03N 8.20W
Ar Rub' al Khālī des. 24 19.00N 50.30E
Ar Ruşayriş 51 11.52N 34.23E
Árta 15 39.10N 20.57E
Artesia 40 32.51N104.24W
Arthur's Pass 29 42.50S171.45E
Artillery L. 38 63.09N107.52W
Artvin 21 41.12N 41.48E
Aru, Kepulauan is. 27 6.00S134.30E
Arua 53 3.02N 30.56E
Aruanã 47 14.54S 51.05W
Aruba i. 43 12.30N 70.00W
Arunachal Pradesh d. 25 28.40N 94.60E
Aruwimi r. 52 1.20N 23.36E
Arvagh 10 53.56N 7.35W
Arvidsjaur 18 65.35N 19.07E
Arzignano 14 45.31N 11.20E
Asahi dake mtn. 26 43.42N142.54E
Asansol 25 23.41N 86.59E
Aschaffenburg 16 49.58N 9.10E
Aschersleben 16 51.46N 11.28E
Ascoli Piceno 14 42.52N 13.36E
Āseb 51 13.01N 42.47E
Åseda 19 57.10N 15.20E
Ashbourne 10 53.31N 6.25W
Ashburton r. 32 21.15S115.00E
Ashburton 29 43.54S171.46E
Ashby de la Zouch 9 52.45N 1.29W
Ashcroft 38 50.43N121.17W
Asheville 41 35.35N 82.35W
Ashford Kent 9 51.08N 0.53E
Ashington 8 55.11N 1.34W
Ash Shiḥr 24 14.45N 49.36E
Ashton 54 33.49S 20.04E
Asinara i. 14 41.04N 8.18E
'Asīr f. 24 19.00N 42.00E
Askeaton 10 52.36N 9.00W
Askersund 19 58.53N 14.54E
Askim 19 59.35N 11.10E
Āsmera 51 15.20N 38.58E
Aspiring, Mt. 29 44.20S168.45E
As Saffānīyah 24 28.00N 48.48E
As Sallūm 51 31.31N 25.09E
Assam d. 25 26.30N 93.00E
Assen 16 53.00N 6.34E
Assiniboia 38 49.38N105.59W
Assis 45 22.37S 50.25W
As Suways 51 29.59N 32.33E
Asti 14 44.54N 8.13E
Astipálaia i. 15 36.35N 26.25E
Astorga 13 42.30N 6.02W
Astoria 40 46.12N123.50W
Astrakhan 21 46.22N 48.00E
Asunción 45 25.15S 57.40W
Aswān 51 24.05N 32.56E
Aswan High Dam see As Sadd al 'Ālī 51
Asyūṭ 51 27.14N 31.07E
Atacama, Desierto des. 48 20.00S 69.00W
Atacama Desert see Atacama, Desierto des. 48
Atar 50 20.32N 13.08W
Atasu 22 48.42N 71.38E
'Aṭbarah 51 17.42N 34.00E
'Aṭbarah r. 51 17.47N 34.00E
Athabasca 38 54.44N113.15W
Athabasca r. 38 58.30N111.00W
Athabasca, L. 38 59.30N109.00W
Athenry 10 53.18N 8.45W
Athens see Athínai 15
Athens Ga. 41 33.57N 83.24W
Atherton 34 17.15S145.29E
Athínai 15 37.59N 23.42E
Athlone 10 53.26N 7.57W
Atholl, Forest of 11 56.50N 3.55W
Áthos mtn. 15 40.09N 24.19E
Atlanta Ga. 41 33.45N 84.23W
Atlantic City 44 39.22N 74.26W
Atlas Saharien mts. 50 34.20N 2.00E
Atlin 38 59.35N133.42W
Atrak r. Iran see Atrek r. 24
Ätran r. 19 56.53N 12.30E
Atrek r. 24 37.23N 54.00E
Aṭ Ṭā'if 24 21.15N 40.21E
Aubagne 12 43.17N 5.35E
Aube r. 12 48.30N 3.37E
Aubin 12 44.32N 2.14E
Aubusson 12 45.57N 2.11E
Auch 12 43.40N 0.36E
Auchterarder 11 56.18N 3.43W
Auckland 29 36.55S174.45E
Auckland Is. 30 50.35S166.00E
Aude r. 12 43.13N 2.20E
Augrabies Falls f. 54 28.33S 20.27E
Augsburg 16 48.21N 10.54E
Augusta Ga. 41 33.29N 82.00W
Aulnay 12 46.02N 0.22W
Aulne r. 12 48.30N 4.11W
Aumale 12 49.46N 1.45E
Aurich 16 53.28N 7.29E
Aurillac 12 44.56N 2.26E
Aus 54 26.41S 16.14E
Austin Minn. 41 43.40N 92.58W
Austin Tex. 40 30.18N 97.47W
Australia 27

Australian Alps *mts.* 35 36.30S148.30E
Australian Capital Territory *d.* 37 35.30S149.00E
Austria 16 47.30N 14.00E
Autun 12 46.58N 4.18E
Auxerre 12 47.48N 3.35E
Aux Sables *r.* 44 46.13N 82.04W
Avallon 12 47.30N 3.54E
Avanos 21 38.44N 34.51E
Avarua Rarotonga 30 21.12S159.46W
Aveiro 13 40.40N 8.35W
Avellaneda 49 34.40S 58.20W
Avellino 14 40.55N 14.46E
Aversa 14 40.58N 14.12E
Avesta 19 60.09N 16.12E
Aveyron *r.* 12 44.09N 1.10E
Avezzano 14 42.03N 13.26E
Aviemore 11 57.12N 3.50W
Avignon 12 43.56N 4.48E
Ávila 13 40.39N 4.42W
Avilés 13 43.35N 5.57W
Avon *r.* Australia 33 31.40S116.07E
Avon *d.* 9 51.35N 2.40W
Avon *r.* Dorset 9 50.43N 1.45W
Avon *r.* Glos. 9 52.00N 2.10W
Avonmouth 9 51.30N 2.42W
Avranches 12 48.42N 1.21W
Awe, Loch 11 56.18N 5.24W
Axel Heiberg I. 39 79.30N 90.00W
Axim 50 4.53N 2.14W
Axiós *r.* 15 40.31N 22.43E
Axminster 9 50.47N 3.01W
Ayaguz 22 47.59N 80.27E
Aydin 15 37.52N 27.50E
Ayers Rock *see* Uluru 34
Áyios Evstrátios *i.* 15 39.30N 25.00E
Aylesbury 9 51.48N 0.49W
Aylsham 8 52.48N 1.16E
Ayr 11 55.28N 4.37W
Ayr *r.* 11 55.28N 4.38W
Ayre, Pt. of 8 54.25N 4.22W
Ayvalik 15 39.19N 26.42E
Azbine *mts. see* Aïr *mts.* 50
Azov, Sea of *see* Azovskoye More 21
Azovskoye More *sea* 21 46.00N 36.30E
Azraq, Al Baḩr al *r.* 51 15.45N 32.25E
Azuaga 13 38.16N 5.40W
Azul 49 36.46S 59.50W

B

Baardheere 53 2.18N 42.18E
Babanūsah 51 11.20N 27.48E
Babar, Kepulauan *is.* 27 8.00S129.30E
Bab el Mandeb *str.* 51 13.00N 43.10E
Bacan *i.* 27 0.73S127.63E
Bacău 17 46.32N 26.59E
Baccarat 12 48.27N 6.45E
Badajoz 13 38.53N 6.58W
Badalona 13 41.27N 2.15E
Badanah 24 30.59N 41.02E
Baden 16 48.01N 16.14E
Baden-Baden 16 48.45N 8.15E
Badgastein 16 47.07N 13.09E
Bādiyat ash Shām *des.* 24 32.00N 39.00E
Badu I. 34 10.07S142.08E
Baffin *d.* 39 66.00N 72.00W
Baffin B. 39 74.00N 70.00W
Baffin I. 39 68.50N 70.00W
Bāfq 24 31.35N 55.21E
Bafra 21 41.34N 35.56E
Bagamoyo 53 6.26S 38.55E
Bagé 45 31.22S 54.06W
Baghdād 24 33.20N 44.26E
Bagheria 14 38.05N 13.30E
Baghlān 25 36.11N 68.44E
Bahamas 43 23.30N 75.00W
Bahāwalpur 25 29.24N 71.41E
Bahi 53 5.59S 35.15E
Bahía, Islas de la *is.* 43 16.10N 86.30W
Bahía Blanca 45 38.45S 62.15W
Bahrain 24 26.00N 50.35E
Baião 47 2.41S 49.41W
Bailundo 52 12.13S 15.46E
Baing 27 10.15S120.34E
Baird Mts. 38 67.35N161.30W
Baja 17 46.12N 18.58E
Baja California *pen.* 42 30.00N115.00W
Bakali *r.* 52 3.58S 17.10E
Baker Mont. 40 46.23N104.16W
Baker Oreg. 40 44.46N117.50W
Baker, Mt. 40 48.48N121.10W
Bakersfield 40 35.25N119.00W
Bakouma 51 5.42N 22.47E
Baku 21 40.22N 49.53E
Bala 8 52.54N 3.36W
Balaklava 21 44.31N 33.35E
Balakovo 20 52.04N 47.46E
Balama 53 13.19S 38.35E
Balashov 21 51.30N 43.10E
Balasore 25 21.30N 86.56E
Balboa 43 8.37N 79.33W
Balbriggan 10 53.36N 6.12W
Balcarce 49 37.52S 58.15W
Balclutha 29 46.16S169.46E
Baleares, Islas *is.* 13 39.30N 2.30E
Bali *i.* 27 8.20S115.07E
Balikesir 15 39.38N 27.51E
Balkan Mts. *see* Stara Planina *mts.* 15
Balkhash 22 46.51N 75.00E
Ballachulish 11 56.40N 5.08W
Ballantrae 11 55.06N 5.01W
Ballarat 36 37.36S143.58E
Ballater 11 57.03N 3.03W
Ballenas, Bahía de *b.* 42 26.40N113.30W
Ballina 10 54.08N 9.10W
Ballinasloe 10 53.20N 8.15W
Ballycastle 10 55.12N 6.15W
Ballyclare 10 54.45N 6.00W
Ballyconnell 10 54.06N 7.37W
Ballydehob 10 51.34N 9.28W
Ballygar 10 53.32N 8.20W
Ballygawley 10 54.28N 7.03W
Ballykelly 10 55.03N 7.00W
Ballymena 10 54.52N 6.17W
Ballymoney 10 55.04N 6.31W
Ballyshannon 10 54.30N 8.11W
Ballyvaughan 10 53.06N 9.09W
Ballyvourney 10 51.57N 9.10W
Balombo 52 12.20S 14.45E
Balsas *r.* 42 18.10N102.05W
Baltic Sea 19 57.00N 20.00E
Baltimore Md. 44 39.17N 76.37W
Baluchistan *f.* 25 28.00N 66.00E
Bamako 50 12.40N 7.59W
Bamberg 16 49.54N 10.53E
Bambesa 52 3.27N 25.43E
Bampton Devon 9 51.00N 3.29W
Banaba *i.* 30 0.52S169.35E
Banagher 10 53.12N 8.00W
Banalia 52 1.33N 25.23E
Banās, Ra's *c.* 24 23.54N 35.48E
Banbridge 10 54.21N 6.17W
Banbury 9 52.04N 1.21W
Banchory 11 57.03N 2.30W
Banda 52 3.47S 11.04E
Banda, Laut *sea* 27 5.00S128.00E
Banda Aceh 27 5.35N 95.20E
Bandar 'Abbās 24 27.10N 56.15E
Bandar-e Torkeman 51 36.55N 54.05E
Bandar Seri Begawan 27 4.56N114.58E
Banda Sea *see* Banda, Laut *sea* 27
Bandawe 53 11.57S 34.11E
Bandeira *mtn.* 45 20.25S 41.45W
Bandirma 15 40.22N 28.00E
Bandon 10 51.45N 8.45W
Bandon *r.* 10 51.43N 8.38W
Bandundu 52 3.20S 17.24E
Bandung 27 6.57S107.34E
Banff 11 57.40N 2.31W
Bangalore 25 12.58N 77.35E
Banghāzī 50 32.07N 20.05E
Bangka *i.* 27 2.20S106.10E
Bangkok 27 13.44N100.30E
Bangladesh 25 24.30N 90.00E
Bangor U.K. 8 53.13N 4.09W
Bangor U.K. 10 54.40N 5.41W
Bangor Maine 44 44.49N 68.47W
Bangui 50 4.23N 18.37E
Bangweulu, L. 53 11.15S 29.45E
Banī Suwayf 51 29.05N 31.05E
Banjarmasin 27 3.22S114.36E
Banjul 50 13.28N 16.39W
Ban Kantang 27 7.25N 99.35E
Banks I. N.W.T. 38 73.00N122.00W
Banks Pen. 29 43.45S173.10E
Banks Str. 35 40.37S148.07E
Bannockburn 11 56.06N 3.55W
Bantry 10 51.41N 9.27W
Bantry B. 10 51.40N 9.40W
Baoji 26 34.20N107.17E
Baoshan 26 25.07N 99.08E
Baotou 26 40.35N109.59E
Baraawe 53 1.02N 44.02E
Baradine *r.* 37 30.17S148.27E
Baranoa 46 10.50N 74.55W
Barbacena 45 21.13S 43.47W
Barbados 43 13.20N 59.40W
Barbastro 13 42.02N 0.07E
Barberton 54 25.46S 31.02E
Barbezieux 12 45.28N 0.09W
Barbuda *i.* 43 17.41N 61.48W
Barcaldine 34 23.31S145.15E
Barcellona 14 38.10N 15.13E
Barcelona 13 41.25N 2.10E
Bardai 50 21.21N 16.56E
Bardsey *i.* 8 52.45N 4.48W
Bareilly 25 28.21N 79.25E
Barents Sea 20 73.00N 40.00E
Bari 15 41.08N 16.52E
Barito *r.* 27 3.35S114.35E
Barking 9 51.32N 0.05E
Barkly East 54 30.58S 27.33E
Barkly Tableland *f.* 34 19.00S136.40E
Barkly West 54 28.32S 24.29E
Bar-le-Duc 12 48.46N 5.10E
Barlee, L. 33 29.30S119.30E
Barlee Range *mts.* 32 23.40S116.00E
Barletta 14 41.20N 16.15E
Barmouth 8 52.44N 4.03W
Barnard Castle *town* 8 54.33N 1.55W
Barnaul 22 53.21N 83.15E
Barnet 9 51.39N 0.11W
Barnsley 8 53.33N 1.29W
Barnstaple 9 51.05N 4.03W
Baro 50 8.34N 6.26E
Barra *i.* 11 56.59N 7.28W
Barra Mansa 45 22.35S 44.12W
Barrancabermeja 46 7.06N 73.54W
Barrancas 46 8.45N 62.13W
Barranqueras 45 27.30S 58.55W
Barranquilla 46 11.10N 74.50W
Barreiras 47 12.09S 44.58W
Barreiro 13 38.40N 9.05W
Barreiros 47 8.49S 35.12W
Barrême 16 43.57N 6.22E
Barretos 45 20.37S 48.38W
Barrhead 11 55.47N 4.24W
Barrie 44 44.24N 79.40W
Barrier Range *mts.* 36 31.25S141.25E
Barrington Tops *mts.* 37 32.30S151.28E
Barrow *r.* 10 52.17N 7.00W
Barrow 38 71.16N156.50W
Barrow Creek *town* 34 21.32S133.53E
Barrow I. 32 21.40S115.27E
Barrow-in-Furness 8 54.08N 3.15W
Barry 9 51.23N 3.19W
Barstow 40 34.55N117.01W
Bar-sur-Aube 12 48.14N 4.43E
Basel 16 47.33N 7.36E
Basilan *i.* 27 6.40N122.10E
Basildon 9 51.34N 0.25E
Basingstoke 9 51.15N 1.05W
Basoko 52 1.20N 23.36E
Basongo 52 4.23S 20.28E
Bassein 25 16.46N 94.45E
Basse-Terre 43 16.00N 61.43W
Bass Str. 35 39.45S146.00E
Bastia 12 42.41N 9.26E
Bastogne 16 50.00N 5.43E
Batang 26 30.02N 99.01E
Batangas 27 13.46N121.01E
Bath 9 51.22N 2.22W
Bathgate 11 55.44N 3.38W
Bathurst, C. 38 70.30N128.00W
Bathurst I. 39 76.00N100.00W
Bathurst Inlet *town* 38 66.48N108.00W
Batley 8 53.43N 1.38W
Baton Rouge 41 30.30N 91.10W
Battle 9 50.55N 0.30E
Battle Creek *town* 44 42.20N 85.11W
Batu *mtn.* 24 6.55N 39.46E
Batu, Kepulauan *is.* 27 0.30S 98.20E
Batumi 21 41.37N 41.36E
Baugé 12 47.33N 0.06W
Bauru 45 22.19S 49.07W
Bayan Har Shan *mts.* 26 34.00N 97.20E
Bayburt 21 40.15N 40.16E
Bay City Mich. 44 43.35N 83.52W
Bayern *d.* 16 48.30N 11.30E
Bayeux 12 49.16N 0.42W
Baykal, Ozero *l.* 23 53.30N108.00E
Bay of Plenty *d.* 29 38.00S177.10E
Bayonne 12 43.30N 1.28W
Bayreuth 16 49.56N 11.35E
Bayrūt 24 33.52N 35.30E
Baza 13 37.30N 2.45W
Bazas 12 44.26N 0.13W
Beachy Head 9 50.43N 0.15E
Beaufort Sea 38 72.00N141.00W
Beaufort West 54 32.20S 22.34E
Beauly 11 57.29N 4.29W
Beauly *r.* 11 57.29N 4.25W
Beaumont Tex. 41 30.04N 94.06W
Beaune 12 47.02N 4.50E
Beauvais 12 49.26N 2.05E
Beccles 9 52.27N 1.33E
Béchar 50 31.35N 2.17W
Bedford 9 52.08N 0.29W
Bedford, C. 34 15.14S145.21E
Bedford Levels *f.* 9 52.35N 0.08W
Bedfordshire *d.* 9 52.04N 0.28W
Bedlington 8 55.08N 1.34W
Beeston 8 52.55N 1.11W
Befale 52 0.27N 21.01E
Beg, Lough 10 54.47N 6.29W
Begna *r.* 19 60.32N 10.00E
Beijing 26 39.55N116.25E
Beira 54 9.49S 34.52E
Beirut *see* Bayrūt 24
Beitbridge 54 22.10S 30.01E
Beja 13 38.01N 7.52W
Béjar 13 40.24N 5.45W
Bela 25 26.14N 66.19E
Belalcázar 13 38.35N 5.10W
Belang 27 0.58N124.56E
Belau 30 7.30N134.30E
Belaya *r.* 22 55.40N 52.30E
Belcher Is. 39 56.00N 79.00W
Belcoo 10 54.18N 7.53W
Belém 47 1.27S 48.29W
Belen 40 34.39N106.48W
Belén, Cuchilla de *mts.* 49 30.49S 56.28W
Belfast 10 54.36N 5.57W
Belfast Lough 10 54.42N 5.45W
Belfort 12 47.38N 6.52E
Belgium 16 51.00N 4.30E
Belgorod 21 50.38N 36.36E
Belgrade *see* Beograd 17
Belitung *i.* 27 3.00S108.00E
Belize Belize 43 17.29N 88.20W
Belize C. America 43 17.00N 88.30W
Bellary 25 15.11N 76.54E
Belle Île 12 47.20N 3.10W
Belle Isle, Str. of 39 51.35N 56.30W
Belleville 44 44.10N 77.23W
Bell Ville 49 32.35S 62.41W
Belmopan 43 17.25N 88.46W
Belmullet 10 54.14N 10.00W
Belo Horizonte 45 19.45S 43.54W
Beloye More *sea* 20 65.30N 38.00E
Belozersk 20 60.00N 37.49E
Beltsy 17 47.45N 27.59E
Benalla 37 36.35S145.58E
Benavente 13 42.00N 5.40W
Benbecula *i.* 11 57.26N 7.18W
Ben Cruachan *mtn.* 11 56.26N 5.18W
Bend 40 44.04N121.20W
Bendigo 36 36.48S144.21E
Bengal, B. of 25 20.00N 90.00E
Benghazi *see* Banghāzī 50
Bengkulu 27 3.46S102.18E
Benguela 52 12.34S 13.24E
Ben Hope *mtn.* 11 58.24N 4.36W
Beni *r.* 48 10.23S 65.24W
Benidorm 13 38.33N 0.09W
Benin 50 9.30N 2.15E
Benin, Bight of 50 5.30N 3.00E
Benin City 50 6.19N 5.41E
Ben Lomond *mtn.* 11 56.12N 4.38W
Ben Macdhui *mtn.* 11 57.04N 3.40W
Ben More *mtn.* Central 11 56.23N 4.31W
Ben More *mtn.* Strath. 11 56.26N 6.02W
Ben More Assynt *mtn.* 11 58.07N 4.52W
Ben Nevis *mtn.* 11 56.48N 5.00W
Benoni 54 26.12S 28.18E
Bentinck I. 34 17.04S139.30E
Benue *r.* 50 7.52N 6.45E
Ben Wyvis *mtn.* 11 57.40N 4.35W
Benxi 26 41.21N123.47E
Beograd 17 44.49N 20.28E
Berbera 51 10.28N 45.02E
Berbérati 50 4.19N 15.51E
Berdyansk 21 46.45N 36.47E
Bergama 15 39.08N 27.10E
Bergamo 14 45.42N 9.40E
Bergen 19 60.23N 5.20E
Bergen op Zoom 16 51.30N 4.17E
Bergerac 12 44.50N 0.29E
Bering Sea 38 65.00N170.00W
Bering Str. 38 65.00N170.00W
Berkshire *d.* 9 51.25N 1.03W
Berkshire Downs *hills* 9 51.32N 1.36W
Berlin 16 52.32N 13.25E
Bermejo *r.* Tucumán 48 26.47S 58.30W
Bern 16 46.57N 7.26E
Berne *see* Bern 12
Berwick-upon-Tweed 8 55.46N 2.00W
Besançon 12 47.14N 6.02E
Bessarabia *f.* 17 46.30N 28.40E
Betanzos 13 43.17N 8.13W
Bethal 54 26.26S 29.27E
Bethel Alas. 38 60.48N161.46W
Beverly Mass. 44 42.33N 70.53W
Bexhill 9 50.51N 0.29E
Bexley 9 51.26N 0.10E
Beyla 50 8.42N 8.39W
Bezhetsk 20 57.49N 36.40E
Bezhitsa 20 53.19N 34.17E
Béziers 12 43.21N 3.13E
Bhāgalpur 25 25.15N 87.00E
Bhamo 25 24.10N 97.30E
Bhopāl 25 23.16N 77.24E
Bhuj 25 23.16N 69.40E
Bhutan 25 27.15N 91.00E
Biarritz 12 43.29N 1.33W
Bicester 9 51.53N 1.09W
Biddeford 44 43.30N 70.26W
Bideford 9 51.01N 4.13W
Biel 12 47.09N 7.16E
Bié Plateau *f.* 52 13.00S 16.00E
Biggar 11 55.38N 3.31W
Bighorn *r.* 40 46.05N107.20W
Big Snowy Mtn. 40 46.46N109.31W
Bihać 14 44.49N 15.53E
Bihār 25 24.30N 86.00E
Bihor *mtn.* 17 46.26N 22.43E
Bijagós, Arquipélago dos *is.* 50 11.30N 16.00W
Bīkaner 25 28.42N 73.25E
Bikin 23 46.52N134.15E
Bikoro 52 0.45S 18.09E
Bilāspur Madhya P. 25 22.05N 82.09E
Bilbao 13 43.15N 2.56W
Billingham 8 54.36N 1.18W
Billings 40 45.47N108.30W
Bill of Portland *c.* 9 50.32N 2.28W
Biloxi 41 30.30N 88.53W
Bima *r.* 52 3.24N 25.10E
Bindura 54 17.18S 31.20E
Binga 54 17.38S 27.19E
Bingen 16 49.58N 7.55E
Binghamton 44 42.08N 75.54W
Biograd 14 43.56N 15.27E
Birhan *mtn.* 51 11.00N 37.50E
Birkenhead 8 53.24N 3.01W
Birmingham U.K. 9 52.30N 1.55W
Birmingham Ala. 41 33.30N 86.55W
Birr 10 53.06N 7.56W
Biscay, B. of 12 45.30N 4.00W
Bishop Auckland 8 54.40N 1.40W
Bishop's Stortford 9 51.53N 0.09E
Biskra 50 34.48N 5.40E
Bismarck 40 46.50N100.48W
Bismarck Sea 30 4.00S147.00E
Bissau 50 11.52N 15.39W
Bitam 52 2.05N 11.30E
Bitburg 16 49.58N 6.31E
Bitlis 21 38.23N 42.04E
Bitola 15 41.02N 21.21E
Bitterfontein 54 31.02S 18.14E
Biumba 53 1.38S 30.02E
Biwa ko *l.* 28 35.10N136.00E
Biysk 22 52.35N 85.16E
Black *r.* Ark. 41 35.30N 91.20W
Blackall 34 24.25S145.28E
Blackburn 8 53.44N 2.30W
Black Mts. 9 51.52N 3.09W
Blackpool 8 53.48N 3.03W
Black Sea 24 43.00N 33.00E
Blacksod B. 10 54.04N 10.00W
Black Volta *r.* 50 8.14N 2.11W
Blackwater *r.* Waterford 10 51.58N 7.52W
Blaenau Ffestiniog 8 53.00N 3.57W
Blair Athol 34 22.42S147.33E
Blair Atholl 11 56.46N 3.51W
Blairgowrie 11 56.36N 3.21W
Blanc, Mont *mtn.* 12 45.50N 6.52E
Blanca, Bahía *b.* 49 39.20S 62.00W
Blanche, L. 36 29.15S139.40E
Blandford Forum 9 50.52N 2.10W
Blarney 10 51.56N 8.34W
Blavet *r.* 12 47.43N 3.18W
Blaye 12 45.08N 0.40W
Blenheim 29 41.32S173.58E
Bletchley 9 51.59N 0.45W
Bloemfontein 54 29.07S 26.14E
Blois 12 47.36N 1.20E
Bloody Foreland *c.* 10 55.09N 8.17W
Bloomington Ill. 41 40.29N 89.00W
Bloomington Ind. 44 39.10N 86.31W
Blue Mts. 40 45.00N118.00W
Blue Nile *r. see* Azraq, Al Baḩr al *r.* 51
Blue Stack Mts. 10 54.44N 8.09W
Blumenau 45 26.55S 49.07W
Blyth Northum. 8 55.07N 1.29W
Boa Vista 46 2.51N 60.43W
Bobo-Dioulasso 50 11.11N 4.18W
Bochum 16 51.28N 7.11E
Bodélé *f.* 50 16.50N 17.10E
Boden 18 65.50N 21.42E
Bodmin 9 50.28N 4.44W
Bodmin Moor 9 50.35N 4.35W
Bodö 18 67.18N 14.26E
Boende 52 0.15S 20.49E
Boggeragh Mts. 10 52.03N 8.53W
Bognor Regis 9 50.47N 0.40W
Bogor 27 6.34S106.45E
Bogotá 46 4.38N 74.05W
Bohol *i.* 27 9.45N124.10E
Boise 40 43.38N116.12W
Boké 50 10.57N 14.13W
Bokungu 52 0.44S 22.28E
Bolama 50 11.35N 15.30W
Bolbec 12 49.34N 0.28E
Bolivia 48 17.00S 65.00W
Bologna 14 44.30N 11.20E
Bolomba 52 0.30N 19.13E
Bolsover 8 53.14N 1.18W
Bolton 8 53.35N 2.26W
Bolu 21 40.45N 31.38E
Bolvadin 21 38.43N 31.02E
Bolzano 14 46.30N 11.20E
Boma 52 5.50S 13.03E
Bombay 25 18.58N 72.50E
Bombo 53 0.34N 32.32E
Bomi 26 29.50N 95.45E
Bomokandi *r.* 53 3.37N 26.09E
Bomongo 52 1.30N 18.21E
Bonar-Bridge *town* 11 57.53N 4.21W
Bonavista 39 48.38N 53.08W
Bo'ness 11 56.01N 3.36W
Bonin Is. 30 27.00N142.10E
Bonn 16 50.44N 7.06E
Bontang 27 0.05N117.31E
Boothia, G. of 39 70.00N 90.00W
Booué 52 0.00 11.58E
Borås 19 57.43N 12.55E
Bordeaux 12 44.50N 0.34W
Borden I. 38 78.30N111.00W
Borders *d.* 11 55.30N 2.53W
Bordertown 36 36.18S140.49E
Bordö *i.* 18 62.10N 7.13W
Borger 40 35.39N101.24W
Borisov 17 54.09N 28.30E
Borlänge 19 60.29N 15.25E
Borneo *i.* 27 1.00N114.00E
Bornholm *i.* 19 55.10N 15.00E
Borzya 23 50.24N116.35E
Boscastle 9 50.42N 4.42W
Bosna *r.* 15 45.04N 18.27E
Bosporus *str. see* Istanbul Boğazi *str.* 15
Bossangoa 50 6.29N 17.27E
Bosso 50 13.43N 13.19E
Bosten Hu *l.* 25 42.00N 87.00E
Boston U.K. 8 52.59N 0.02W
Boston U.S.A. 44 42.21N 71.04W
Botany B. 37 34.04S151.08E
Bothnia, G. of 18 63.30N 20.30E
Botswana 54 22.00S 24.15E
Bouaflé 50 7.01N 5.47W
Bouaké 50 7.42N 5.00W
Bouar 50 5.58N 15.35E
Bougouni 50 11.25N 7.28W
Boulder 40 40.02N105.16W
Boulogne 12 50.43N 1.37E
Bourem 50 16.59N 0.20W
Bourg 12 46.12N 5.13E
Bourges 12 47.05N 2.23E
Bourgogne *d.* 12 47.10N 4.20E
Bournemouth 9 50.43N 1.53W
Boussac 12 46.22N 2.13E
Bouvard, C. 33 32.40S115.34E
Bowen 34 20.00S148.15E
Boyle 10 53.58N 8.19W
Boyne *r.* 10 53.43N 6.17W
Boyoma Falls *f.* 52 0.18N 25.32E
Bozeman 40 45.40N111.00W
Brač *i.* 15 43.20N 16.38E
Bracadale, Loch 11 57.22N 6.30W
Bräcke 18 62.44N 15.30E
Bradano *r.* 15 40.23N 16.52E
Bradford 8 53.47N 1.45W
Braemar 11 57.01N 3.24W
Braga 13 41.32N 8.26W
Brahmaputra *r.* 25 23.50N 89.45E
Braintree 9 51.53N 0.32E
Brandberg *mtn.* 54 21.08S 14.35E
Brande 19 55.57N 9.07E
Brandenburg 16 52.25N 12.34E
Brandfort 54 28.41S 26.27E
Brandon 39 49.50N 99.57W
Brandon Mtn. 10 52.14N 10.15W
Brasília 47 15.45S 47.57W
Braşov 17 45.40N 25.35E
Bratislava 17 48.10N 17.10E
Bratsk 23 56.20N101.15E
Braunschweig 16 52.15N 10.30E
Bray 10 53.12N 6.07W
Bray Head Kerry 10 51.53N 10.26W
Brazilian Highlands *see* Brasil, Planalto *mts.* 47
Brazos *r.* 41 28.55N 95.20W
Brazzaville 52 4.14S 15.10E
Breadalbane *f.* 11 56.30N 4.20W
Brechin 11 56.44N 2.40W
Brecon 9 51.57N 3.23W
Brecon Beacons *mts.* 9 51.53N 3.27W
Breda 16 51.35N 4.46E
Bredasdorp 54 34.31S 20.03E
Bregenz 16 47.31N 9.46E
Bremen 16 53.05N 8.48E
Bremerhaven 16 53.33N 8.35E
Brenner Pass 16 47.00N 11.30E
Brenta *r.* 16 45.25N 12.15E
Brescia 16 45.33N 10.12E
Bressay *i.* 11 60.08N 1.05W
Bressuire 12 46.50N 0.28W
Brest France 12 48.23N 4.30W
Brest U.S.S.R. 17 52.08N 23.40E
Brett, C. 29 35.15S174.20E
Briançon 12 44.53N 6.39E
Bridgend 9 51.30N 3.35W
Bridgeport Conn. 44 41.12N 73.12W
Bridgetown 43 13.06N 59.37W
Bridgnorth 9 52.33N 2.25W
Bridgwater 9 51.08N 3.00W
Bridlington 8 54.06N 0.11W
Brig 16 46.19N 8.00E
Brigg 8 53.33N 0.30W
Bright 37 36.42S146.58E
Brighton 9 50.50N 0.09W
Brindisi 15 40.38N 17.57E
Brisbane 37 27.30S153.00E
Bristol 9 51.26N 2.35W
Bristol Channel 9 51.17N 3.20W
British Columbia *d.* 38 55.00N125.00W
British Virgin Is. 43 18.30N 64.30W
Britstown 54 30.34S 23.30E
Brive 12 45.09N 1.32E
Brixham 9 50.24N 3.31W
Brno 16 49.11N 16.39E
Broadway 9 52.02N 1.51W
Brockton 44 42.05N 71.01W
Brodick 11 55.34N 5.09W
Bromley 9 51.24N 0.02E
Bromsgrove 9 52.20N 2.03W
Brooks Range *mts.* 38 68.50N152.00W
Broom, Loch 11 57.52N 5.07W
Broome 32 17.58S122.15E
Brora 11 58.01N 3.52W
Brough England 8 54.32N 2.19W
Brough Scotland 11 60.29N 1.12W
Bruges *see* Brugge 16
Brugge 16 51.13N 3.14E
Brunei 27 4.56N114.58E
Brunswick Ga. 41 31.09N 81.21W
Bruny I. 35 43.15S147.16E
Brussels *see* Bruxelles 16
Bruxelles 16 50.50N 4.23E
Bryansk 20 53.15N 34.09E
Bua *r.* 53 12.42S 34.15E
Bucaramanga 46 7.08N 73.10W
Buchan Ness *c.* 11 57.28N 1.47W
Bucharest *see* Bucureşti 17
Buckhaven and Methil 8 56.11N 3.03W
Buckie 11 57.40N 2.58W
Buckingham 9 52.00N 0.59W
Buckinghamshire *d.* 9 51.50N 0.48W
Bucureşti 17 44.25N 26.06E
Budapest 17 47.30N 19.03E
Bude 9 50.49N 4.33W
Budjala 52 2.38N 19.48E
Buenaventura 46 3.54N 77.02W
Buenos Aires 49 34.40S 58.25W
Buffalo N.Y. 44 42.52N 78.55W
Buffalo Wyo. 40 44.21N106.40W
Builth Wells 9 52.09N 3.24W
Bujumbura 53 3.22S 29.21E
Bukama 52 9.16S 25.52E
Bukavu 53 2.30S 28.49E
Bukhara 22 39.47N 64.26E
Bukoba 53 1.20S 31.49E
Bula 27 3.07S130.27E
Bulawayo 54 20.10S 28.43E
Bulgaria 15 42.30N 25.00E
Buller *r.* 29 41.45S171.35E
Buller, Mt. 37 37.11S146.26E
Bulloo *r.* 36 28.43S142.27E
Buncrana 10 55.08N 7.27W
Bundaberg 34 24.50S152.21E
Bundoran 10 54.28N 8.17W
Bunia 53 1.30N 30.10E
Burdur 21 37.44N 30.17E
Burg 16 52.17N 11.51E
Burgas 15 42.30N 27.29E
Burgos 13 42.21N 3.41W
Burgsvik 19 57.03N 18.16E
Burias *i.* 27 12.50N123.10E
Burkina 50 12.15N 1.30W
Burlington 44 43.19N 79.48W
Burma 25 21.45N 97.00E
Burnham-on-Sea 9 51.15N 3.00W
Burnie 35 41.03S145.55E
Burnley 8 53.47N 2.15W
Buronga 36 34.08S142.11E
Burra 36 33.40S138.57E
Burren Junction 37 30.08S148.59E
Burriana 13 39.54N 0.05W
Bursa 15 40.11N 29.04E
Būr Safājah 51 26.44N 33.56E
Būr Sa'īd 51 31.17N 32.18E
Būr Sūdān 51 19.39N 37.01E
Burton upon Trent 8 52.58N 1.39W
Buru *i.* 27 3.30S126.30E
Burundi 53 3.00S 30.00E
Bururi 53 3.58S 29.35E
Bury G.M. 8 53.36N 2.19W
Bury St. Edmunds 9 52.15N 0.42E
Būshehr 24 28.57N 50.52E
Bushmanland *f.* 54 29.25S 19.40E
Businga 52 3.16N 20.55E
Busira *r.* 52 0.05N 18.18E
Buta 52 2.50N 24.50E
Butare 53 2.38S 29.43E
Bute *i.* 11 55.51N 5.07W
Bute, Sd. of 11 55.44N 5.10W
Butiaba 53 1.48N 31.15E
Buton *i.* 27 5.00S122.50E
Butte Mont. 40 46.00N112.31W
Buttevant 10 52.14N 8.41W
Butt of Lewis *c.* 11 58.31N 6.15W
Butuan 27 8.56N125.31E
Buxton 8 53.16N 1.54W
Buzi *r.* 54 19.52S 34.00E
Bydgoszcz 17 53.16N 17.33E

C

Cabimas 46 10.26N 71.27W
Cabinda 52 5.34S 12.12E
Cabot Str. 39 47.00N 59.00W
Cabrera, Sierra *mts.* 13 42.10N 6.30W
Cabriel *r.* 13 39.13N 1.07W
Cáceres 13 39.29N 6.23W
Cachimo *r.* 52 7.02S 21.13E
Cachoeira do Sul 45 30.03S 52.52W
Cacín *r.* 13 37.10N 4.01W
Cacolo 52 10.09S 19.15E
Cader Idris *mtn.* 9 52.40N 3.55W
Cadí, Serra del *mts.* 13 42.12N 1.35E
Cadiz 27 10.57N123.18E
Cádiz 13 36.32N 6.18W
Caen 12 49.11N 0.22W
Caernarfon 8 53.08N 4.17W
Caerphilly 9 51.34N 3.13W
Cagliari 14 39.14N 9.07E
Caguas 43 18.08N 66.00W
Caha Mts. 10 51.44N 9.45W
Cahersiveen 10 51.51N 10.14W
Cahir 10 52.23N 7.56W
Cahora Bassa Dam 53 15.36S 32.41E
Cahore Pt. 10 52.34N 6.12W
Cahors 12 44.28N 0.26E
Cahuapanas 46 5.15S 77.00W
Caibarién 43 22.31N 79.28W
Caicos Is. 43 21.30N 72.00W
Cairngorms *mts.* 11 57.04N 3.30W
Cairns 34 16.51S145.43E
Cairo *see* Al Qāhirah 51
Cairo Ill. 41 37.02N 89.02W
Cajamarca 46 7.09S 78.32W
Calabar 50 4.56N 8.22E
Calabozo 46 8.58N 67.28W
Calabria *d.* 15 39.00N 16.30E
Calahorra 13 42.18N 1.58W
Calais 7 50.57N 1.52E
Calamocha 13 40.54N 1.18W
Călăraşi 17 44.11N 27.21E
Calatayud 13 41.21N 1.39W
Calbayog 27 12.04N124.58E
Calcutta 25 22.32N 88.22E
Caledon *r.* 54 30.27S 26.12E
Calf of Man *i.* 8 54.03N 4.49W
Calgary 38 51.05N114.05W
Cali 46 3.24N 76.30W
Caliente 40 37.36N114.31W
California *d.* 40 37.00N120.00W
California, Golfo de *g.* 42 28.30N112.30W
Callander 11 56.15N 4.13W
Callao 48 12.05S 77.08W
Caltagirone 14 37.14N 14.30E
Calulo 52 10.05S 14.56E
Calvi 12 42.34N 8.44E
Calvinia 54 31.29S 19.44E
Cam *r.* 9 52.34N 0.21E
Camacupa 52 12.01S 17.22E
Camagüey 43 21.25N 77.55W
Camarón, C. 43 15.59N 85.00W
Camberley 9 51.21N 0.45W
Cambodia 27 12.45N105.00E
Camborne 9 50.12N 5.19W
Cambrai 12 50.10N 3.14E
Cambrian Mts. 9 52.33N 3.33W
Cambridge 9 52.13N 0.08E
Cambridge G. 32 15.00S128.05E
Cambridgeshire *d.* 9 52.15N 0.05E
Cambundi-Catembo 52 10.09S 17.35E
Camden U.K. 9 51.33N 0.10W
Camden N.J. 44 39.57N 75.07W
Camelford 9 50.37N 4.41W
Cameron Mts. 29 45.50S167.00E
Cameroon 50 5.30N 12.15E
Cameroun, Mont *mtn.* 50 4.20N 9.05E
Campana 49 34.10S 58.57W
Campbell, C. 29 41.45S174.15E
Campbelltown 37 34.04S150.49E
Campbeltown 11 55.25N 5.36W
Campeche 42 19.50N 90.30W
Campeche, Bahía de *b.* 42 19.30N 94.00W
Camperdown 36 38.15S143.14E
Campina Grande 47 7.15S 35.50W
Campinas 45 22.54S 47.06W
Campobasso 14 41.34N 14.39E
Campo Gallo 48 26.35S 62.50W
Campo Grande 48 20.24S 54.35W
Campos 45 21.45S 41.18W
Canada 38 60.00N105.00W
Canadian *r.* 41 35.20N 95.40W
Çanakkale 15 40.09N 26.26E
Çanakkale Boğazi *str.* 15 40.15N 26.30E
Canal du Midi 12 43.18N 2.00E
Canarias, Islas *is.* 50 29.00N 15.00W
Canaveral, C. 41 28.28N 80.28W
Canberra 37 35.18S149.08E
Candeleda 13 40.10N 5.14W
Cangamba 52 13.40S 19.50E
Cangzhou 26 38.15N116.58E
Çankiri 21 40.35N 33.37E
Canna *i.* 11 57.03N 6.30W
Cannes 12 43.33N 7.00E
Cannich 11 57.20N 4.45W
Cannock 9 52.42N 2.02W
Canōas 45 29.55S 51.10W
Canon City 40 38.27N105.14W
Cantabria, Sierra de *mts.* 13 42.40N 2.30W
Canterbury *d.* 29 43.30S172.00E
Canterbury 9 51.17N 1.05E
Canterbury Bight 29 44.15S172.00E
Can Tho 27 10.03N105.40E
Canton *see* Guangzhou 26
Canton Ohio 44 40.48N 81.23W
Caombo 52 8.45S 16.50E
Cape Barren I. 35 40.25S148.15E
Cape Breton I. 39 46.00N 61.00W
Cape Cod B. 44 41.50N 70.17W
Capelongo 52 14.55S 15.03E
Cape Town 54 33.55S 18.27E
Cape York Pen. 34 12.40S142.20E
Capri *i.* 14 40.33N 14.13E
Caprivi Strip *f.* 54 17.50S 23.10E
Caracas 46 10.35N 66.56W
Caravaca 13 38.06N 1.51W
Carcassonne 12 43.13N 2.21E
Carcross 38 60.11N134.41W
Cárdenas 43 23.02N 81.12W
Cardenete 13 39.46N 1.42W
Cardiff 9 51.28N 3.11W
Cardigan 9 52.06N 4.41W
Carentan 12 49.18N 1.14W
Carhaix 12 48.16N 3.35W
Carhué 49 37.11S 62.45W
Caribbean Sea 43 15.00N 75.00W
Caribou Mts. 38 58.30N115.00W
Carlingford 10 54.03N 6.12W
Carlingford Lough 10 54.03N 6.09W
Carlisle 8 54.54N 2.55W
Carlow 10 52.50N 6.46W
Carlow *d.* 10 52.43N 6.50W
Carmarthen 9 51.52N 4.20W
Carmarthen B. 9 52.30N 4.30W
Carmel Head 8 53.24N 4.35W
Carmila 34 21.55S149.25E
Carmona 13 37.28N 5.38W
Carndonagh 10 55.15N 7.15W
Carnegie, L. 32 26.15S123.00E
Carnew 10 52.43N 6.31W
Carnot 50 4.59N 15.56E
Carnoustie 11 56.30N 2.44W
Carolina 43 18.23N 65.57W
Caroline Is. 30 5.00N147.00E
Carpathians *mts.* 17 48.45N 23.45E
Carpaţii Meridionali *mts.* 17 45.35N 24.40E
Carpentaria, G. of 34 14.00S139.00E
Carpentras 12 44.03N 5.03E
Carra, Lough 10 53.41N 9.15W
Carrara 14 44.04N 10.06E
Carrauntoohil *mtn.* 10 52.00N 9.45W
Carrickfergus 10 54.43N 5.49W
Carrickmacross 10 53.58N 6.43W
Carrick-on-Shannon 10 53.57N 8.06W
Carrick-on-Suir 10 52.21N 7.26W
Carrowmore Lough 10 54.11N 9.47W
Çarşamba 21 41.13N 36.43E
Carson City 40 39.10N119.46W
Carstairs 11 55.42N 3.41W
Cartagena Colombia 46 10.24N 75.33W
Cartagena Spain 13 37.36N 0.59W
Carterton 29 41.01S175.31E
Caruarú 47 8.15S 35.55W
Carvoeiro 46 1.24S 61.59W
Casablanca 50 33.39N 7.35W
Cascade Pt. 29 44.01S168.22E
Cascade Range *mts.* 40 44.00N121.30W
Caserta 14 41.06N 14.21E
Cashel Tipperary 10 52.31N 7.54W
Caspe 13 41.14N 0.03W
Casper 40 42.50N106.20W
Caspian Depression *see* Prikaspiyskaya Nizmennost *ost* 21
Caspian Sea 21 42.00N 51.00E
Castaños 42 26.48N101.26W
Castelo Branco 13 39.50N 7.30W
Casterton 36 37.35S141.25E
Castilla y León *d.* 13 41.50N 4.15W
Castlebar 10 53.52N 9.19W
Castleblayney 10 54.08N 6.46W
Castle Douglas 11 54.56N 3.56W
Castleford 8 53.43N 1.21W
Castlemaine 36 37.05S144.19E
Castlerea 10 53.45N 8.30W
Castletown 8 54.04N 4.38W
Castres 12 43.36N 2.14E
Castries 43 14.01N 60.59W
Casula 53 15.26S 33.32E
Cataluña *d.* 13 42.00N 2.00E
Catamarca 48 28.30S 65.45W
Catanduanes *i.* 27 13.45N124.20E
Catanduva 45 21.03S 49.00W
Catania 14 37.31N 15.05E
Catete 52 9.09S 13.40E
Catterick 8 54.23N 1.38W
Caucasus Mts. *see* Kavkazskiy Khrebet *mts.* 21
Cavan 10 54.00N 7.22W
Cavan *d.* 10 53.58N 7.10W
Caxambu 45 21.59S 44.54W
Caxias do Sul 45 29.14S 51.10W
Caxito 52 8.32S 13.38E
Cayenne 47 4.55N 52.18W
Cayman Is. 43 19.00N 81.00W
Cazombo 52 11.54S 22.56E
Cebu *i.* 27 10.15N123.45E
Cecina 14 43.18N 10.30E
Cedar City 40 37.40N113.04W
Cedar Falls *town* 41 42.34N 92.26W
Cedar Rapids *town* 41 41.59N 91.31W
Ceduna 36 32.07S133.42E
Ceerigaabo 51 10.40N 47.20E
Cefalù 14 38.01N 14.03E
Celaya 42 20.32N100.48W
Celebes *i. see* Sulawesi *i.* 27
Celebes Sea 27 3.00N122.00E
Celle 16 52.37N 10.05E
Celtic Sea 7 50.00N 8.00W
Cemaes Head 9 52.08N 4.42W
Central *d.* 11 56.10N 4.20W
Central African Republic 50 6.30N 20.00E
Central Auckland *d.* 29 36.45S174.45E
Centralia Ill. 41 38.32N 89.08W
Central Siberian Plateau *see* Srednе Sibirskoyf. *f.* 23
Cerignola 14 41.17N 15.53E
Cerro de Pasco 46 10.43S 76.15W
Cessnock 37 32.51S151.21E
Cetinje 15 42.24N 18.55E
Ceuta 13 35.53N 5.19W
Cévennes *mts.* 12 44.25N 4.05E
Chad 50 13.00N 19.00E
Chad, L. 50 13.30N 14.00E

Challans 12 46.51N 1.52W
Châlons-sur-Marne 12 48.58N 4.22E
Chalon-sur-Saône 12 46.47N 4.51E
Chambéry 12 45.34N 5.55E
Chambeshi r. 53 11.15S 30.37E
Chamonix 12 45.55N 6.52E
Champaign 41 40.07N 88.14W
Champlain, L. 44 44.45N 73.15W
Chandeleur Is. 41 29.50N 88.50W
Chandigarh 25 30.44N 76.47E
Changchun 26 43.51N125.15E
Changde 26 29.00N111.35E
Chang Jiang r. 26 31.40N121.15E
Changsha 26 28.09N112.59E
Channel Is. 9 49.28N 2.13W
Chanthaburi 27 12.35N102.05E
Chapala, Lago de l. 42 20.00N103.00W
Chapayevsk 20 52.58N 49.44E
Chard 9 50.52N 2.59W
Chardzhou 22 39.00N 63.34E
Charente r. 12 45.57N 1.00W
Charleroi 16 50.25N 4.27E
Charleston S.C. 41 32.48N 79.58W
Charleston W.Va. 44 38.23N 81.40W
Charlotte N.C. 41 35.05N 80.50W
Charlottesville 41 38.02N 78.29W
Charlottetown 39 46.14N 63.09W
Charlton 36 36.18S143.27E
Charolles 12 46.26N 4.17E
Chartres 12 48.27N 1.30E
Châteaubriant 12 47.43N 1.22W
Châteaudun 12 48.04N 1.20E
Châteauroux 12 46.49N 1.41E
Château-Thierry 12 49.03N 3.24E
Châtellerault 12 46.49N 0.33E
Chatham 9 51.23N 0.32E
Chatham Is. 30 44.00S176.35W
Châtillon-sur-Seine 16 47.52N 4.35E
Chattahoochee r. 41 30.52N 84.57W
Chattanooga 41 35.01N 85.18W
Chatteris 9 52.27N 0.03E
Chaumont 12 48.07N 5.08E
Cheboksary 20 56.08N 47.12E
Cheboygan 44 45.40N 84.28W
Chegutu 54 18.09S 30.07E
Chelmsford 9 51.44N 0.28E
Cheltenham 9 51.53N 2.07W
Chelyabinsk 22 55.10N 61.25E
Chemba 53 17.11S 34.53E
Chemnitz 16 50.50N 12.55E
Chên, Gora mtn. 23 65.30N141.20E
Chengdu 26 30.41N104.05E
Chepstow 9 51.38N 2.40W
Cher r. 12 47.12N 2.04E
Cherbourg 12 49.38N 1.37W
Cheremkhovo 23 53.08N103.01E
Cherepovets 20 59.05N 37.55E
Cherkassy 21 49.27N 32.04E
Cherkessk 21 44.14N 42.05E
Chernigov 17 51.30N 31.18E
Chernovtsy 17 48.19N 25.52E
Chernyakhovsk 19 54.38N 21.49E
Chertsey 9 51.23N 0.27W
Cherwell r. 9 51.44N 1.15W
Chesapeake B. 41 38.40N 76.25W
Chesham 9 51.43N 0.38W
Cheshire d. 8 53.14N 2.30W
Chesil Beach f. 9 50.37N 2.33W
Chester 8 53.12N 2.53W
Chesterfield 8 53.14N 1.26W
Chetumal 43 18.30N 88.17W
Cheyenne Wyo. 40 41.08N104.50W
Chiai 26 23.29N120.27E
Chiang Mai 26 18.48N 98.59E
Chiavari 14 44.19N 9.19E
Chiba 28 35.36N140.07E
Chibemba 52 15.43S 14.07E
Chibia 52 15.10S 13.32E
Chibuto 54 24.41S 33.32E
Chicago 41 41.50N 87.45W
Chichester 9 50.50N 0.47W
Chicoutimi-Jonquière 44 48.26N 71.04W
Chieti 14 42.22N 14.12E
Chigubo 54 22.38S 33.18E
Chihuahua 42 28.40N106.06W
Chikwawa 53 16.00S 34.54E
Chilapa 42 17.38N 99.11W
Chile 48 32.30S 71.00W
Chillán 49 36.36S 72.07W
Chiloé, Isla de i. 49 43.00S 73.00W
Chilpancingo 42 17.33N 99.30W
Chiltern Hills 9 51.40N 0.53W
Chilumba 53 10.25S 34.18E
Chilwa, L. 53 15.15S 35.45E
Chimbote 46 9.04S 78.34W
Chimkent 22 42.16N 69.25E
Chimoio 54 19.04S 33.29E
China 26 33.00N103.00E
Chinandega 43 12.35N 87.10W
Chinati Peak 40 30.05N104.30W
Chinchoua 52 0.00 9.48E
Chindio 53 17.46S 35.23E
Chindwin r. 25 21.30N 95.12E
Chinga 53 15.14S 38.40E
Chingola 53 12.29S 27.53E
Chin Hills 26 22.30N 93.30E
Chinhoyi 54 17.22S 30.10E
Chipata 53 13.37S 32.40E
Chipera 53 15.20S 32.35E
Chipinge 54 20.12S 32.38E
Chippenham 9 51.27N 2.07W
Chipping Norton 9 51.56N 1.32W
Chir r. 21 48.34N 42.53E
Chiredzi r. 54 21.10S 31.50E
Chiromo 53 16.28S 35.10E
Chisasibi 39 53.50N 79.01W
Chistopol 20 55.25N 50.38E
Chita 23 52.03N113.35E
Chitipa 53 9.41S 33.19E
Chitral 25 35.52N 71.58E
Chittagong 25 22.20N 91.50E
Chiumbe r. 52 6.37S 21.04E
Chiuta, L. 53 14.45S 35.50E
Chivhu 54 19.01S 30.53E
Chobe r. 54 17.48S 25.12E
Chojnice 17 53.42N 17.32E
Cholet 12 47.04N 0.53W
Choma 53 16.51S 27.04E
Chomutov 16 50.28N 13.25E
Ch'ŏngjin 26 41.55N129.50E
Chongquing 26 29.31N106.35E
Chorley 8 53.39N 2.39W
Chorzów 17 50.19N 18.56E
Christchurch New Zealand 29 43.33S172.40E
Christchurch U.K. 9 50.44N 1.47W
Christianshåb 39 68.50N 51.00W
Christmas I. 27 10.30S105.40E
Christmas I. see Kiritimati i. 31
Chu r. 22 45.00N 67.30E
Chudleigh 9 50.35N 3.36W
Chudovo 20 59.10N 31.41E
Chuiquimula 43 15.52N 89.50W
Chuna r. 23 58.00N 94.00E
Chunya 53 8.31S 33.28E
Chuquicamata 48 22.20S 68.56W
Chur 12 46.52N 9.32E
Churchill 39 58.45N 94.00W
Churchill r. Man. 39 58.20N 94.15W
Churchill r. Nfld. 39 53.20N 60.00W
Churchill, C. 39 58.50N 93.00W
Churchill L. 38 56.00N108.00W
Churchill Peak mtn. 38 58.10N125.00W
Church Stretton 9 52.32N 2.49W
Ciénaga 46 11.11N 74.15W
Cienfuegos 43 22.10N 80.27W
Cieza 13 38.14N 1.25W
Cimarron r. 41 36.15N 96.55W
Cinca r. 13 41.22N 0.20E
Cincinnati 44 39.10N 84.30W
Cirencester 9 51.43N 1.59W
Ciudad Bolívar 46 8.06N 63.36W
Ciudad Camargo 42 27.41N105.10W
Ciudad de México 42 19.25N 99.10W
Ciudadela 13 40.00N 3.50E
Ciudad Guayana 46 8.22N 62.40W
Ciudad Guerrero 42 28.33N107.28W
Ciudad Juárez 42 31.42N106.29W
Ciudad Madero 42 22.19N 97.50W
Ciudad Real 13 38.59N 3.55W
Ciudad Victoria 42 23.43N 99.10W
Civray 12 46.09N 0.18E
Çivril 21 38.18N 29.43E
Cizre 21 37.21N 42.11E
Clacton on Sea 9 51.47N 1.10E
Clara 10 53.21N 7.37W
Clare d. 10 52.52N 8.55W
Clare r. 10 53.17N 9.04W
Claremorris 10 53.44N 9.00W
Clarence r. 29 42.10S173.55E
Clarence Str. 32 12.00S131.00E
Clarke I. 35 40.30S148.10E
Clayton r. 36 29.06S137.59E
Clear I. 10 51.26N 9.30W
Cleethorpes 8 53.33N 0.02W
Clermont-Ferrand 12 45.47N 3.05E
Clevedon 9 51.26N 2.52W
Cleveland d. 8 54.37N 1.08W
Cleveland Ohio 44 41.30N 81.41W
Cleveland Hills 8 54.25N 1.10W
Cleveleys 8 53.52N 3.01W
Clew B. 10 53.50N 9.47W
Clifden 10 53.29N 10.02W
Clinton 29 46.13S169.23E
Cloghan Offaly 10 53.13N 7.54W
Clogher Head Kerry 10 52.09N 10.28W
Clonakilty 10 51.37N 8.54W
Clones 10 54.11N 7.16W
Clonmel 10 52.21N 7.44W
Cloud Peak mtn. 40 44.23N107.11W
Cloughton 8 54.20N 0.27W
Clovis N.Mex. 40 34.14N103.13W
Clowne 8 53.18N 1.16W
Clutha r. 29 46.18S169.05E
Clwyd d. 8 53.07N 3.20W
Clwyd r. 8 53.19N 3.30W
Clyde r. 11 55.58N 4.53W
Clydebank 11 55.53N 4.23W
Coast Mts. 38 55.30N128.00W
Coast Range mts. 40 40.00N123.00W
Coatbridge 11 55.52N 4.02W
Coatzacoalcos 42 18.10N 94.25W
Cobán 42 15.28N 90.20W
Cobar 37 31.32S145.51E
Cobh 10 51.50N 8.18W
Cobija 48 11.02S 68.44W
Cobourg 44 43.58N 78.11W
Coburg 16 50.15N 10.58E
Cochabamba 48 17.24S 66.09W
Cochrane Ont. 44 49.04N 81.02W
Cockburn 36 32.05S141.00E
Coco r. 43 14.58N 83.15W
Cod, C. 44 41.42N 70.15W
Coen 34 13.56S143.12E
Coghinas r. 14 40.57N 8.50E
Cognac 12 45.42N 0.19W
Coimbatore 25 11.00N 76.57E
Coimbra 13 40.12N 8.25W
Coín 13 36.40N 4.45W
Colchester 9 51.54N 0.55E
Coldstream 11 55.39N 2.15W
Coleraine 10 55.08N 6.40W
Colesberg 54 30.43S 25.05E
Colima 42 19.14N103.41W
Coll i. 11 56.38N 6.34W
Collingwood 29 40.41S172.41E
Collin Top mtn. 10 54.58N 6.08W
Colne r. Essex 9 51.50N 0.59E
Colo r. 37 33.26S150.53E
Cologne see Köln 16
Colombia 46 4.00N 72.30W
Colombo 25 6.55N 79.52E
Colón 46 9.21N 79.54W
Colonsay i. 11 56.04N 6.13W
Colorado r. Argentina 49 39.50S 62.02W
Colorado r. Ariz. 40 32.00N114.58W
Colorado d. 40 39.00N106.00W
Colorado r. Tex. 41 28.30N 96.00W
Colorado Plateau f. 40 35.45N112.00W
Colorado Springs town 40 38.50N104.40W
Columbia r. 40 46.10N123.30W
Columbia S.C. 41 34.00N 81.00W
Columbus Ga. 41 32.28N 84.59W
Columbus Ohio 44 39.59N 83.03W
Colville r. 38 70.06N151.30W
Colwyn Bay town 8 53.18N 3.43W
Comayagua 43 14.30N 87.39W
Comeragh Mts. 10 52.17N 7.34W
Commonwealth Territory d. 37 35.00S151.00E
Como 14 45.48N 9.04E
Como, Lago di l. 14 46.05N 9.17E
Comodoro Rivadavia 49 45.50S 67.30W
Comoros 53 12.15S 44.00E
Conakry 50 9.30N 13.43W
Concarneau 12 47.53N 3.55W
Concepción 49 36.50S 73.03W
Conception, Pt. 40 34.27N120.26W
Conchos r. 42 29.34N104.30W
Concord N.H. 44 43.12N 71.32W
Confolens 12 46.01N 0.40E
Congleton 8 53.10N 2.12W
Congo r. see Zaïre r. 52
Coningsby 8 53.07N 0.09W
Coniston 8 54.22N 3.06W
Conn, Lough 10 54.01N 9.15W
Connah's Quay town 8 53.13N 3.03W
Connecticut d. 44 41.45N 72.45W
Connecticut r. 44 41.17N 72.21W
Connemara f. 10 53.32N 9.56W
Conon r. 11 57.33N 4.33W
Consett 8 54.52N 1.50W
Constance, L. see Bodensee 16
Constanţa 15 44.10N 28.31E
Constantina 13 37.54N 5.36W
Contas r. 47 14.15S 39.00W
Cook Is. 30 15.00S160.00W
Cookstown 10 54.39N 6.46W
Cook Str. 29 41.15S174.30E
Cooktown 34 15.29S145.15E
Coolgardie 33 31.01S121.12E
Coonabarabran 37 31.16S149.18E
Copán ruins 43 14.52N 89.10W
Copenhagen see København 19
Copiapó 48 27.22S 70.20W
Copper Belt f. 53 12.40S 28.00E
Coppermine r. 38 67.54N115.10W
Coquimbo 48 29.58S 71.21W
Coral Bay town 32 23.02S113.48E
Coral Sea 34 14.30S149.30E
Corangamite, L. 36 38.10S143.25E
Corbeil 12 48.37N 2.29E
Corby 9 52.29N 0.41W
Córdoba Argentina 48 31.25S 64.10W
Córdoba Spain 13 37.53N 4.46W
Corfu i. see Kérkira i. 15
Corinto 43 12.29N 87.14W
Cork 10 51.54N 8.28W
Cork d. 10 52.00N 8.40W
Corner Brook town 39 48.58N 57.58W
Cornwall d. 9 50.26N 4.40W
Cornwallis I. 39 75.00N 95.00W
Coromandel 29 36.46S175.30E
Coronation G. 38 68.00N112.00W
Corpus Christi 41 27.47N 97.26W
Corrib, Lough 10 53.26N 9.14W
Corrientes 48 27.30S 58.48W
Corse i. 12 42.00N 9.10E
Corse, Cap c. 12 43.00N 9.21E
Corsham 9 51.25N 2.11W
Corsica i. see Corse i. 12
Corte 12 42.18N 9.08E
Coruche 13 38.58N 8.31W
Corumbá 48 19.00S 57.27W
Corwen 8 52.59N 3.23W
Cosenza 14 39.17N 16.14E
Cosne 12 47.25N 2.55E
Costa Brava f. 13 41.30N 3.00E
Costa del Sol f. 13 36.30N 4.00W
Costa Rica 43 10.00N 84.00W
Côte d'Azur f. 12 43.20N 6.45E
Cotonou 50 6.24N 2.31E
Cotopaxi mtn. 46 0.40S 78.28W
Cotswold Hills 9 51.50N 2.00W
Cottbus 16 51.43N 14.21E
Coulonge r. 44 45.51N 76.45W
Coupar Angus 11 56.33N 3.17W
Coutances 12 49.03N 1.29W
Coventry 9 52.25N 1.31W
Covington Ky. 44 39.04N 84.30W
Cowdenbeath 11 56.07N 3.21W
Cowes 9 50.45N 1.18W
Cowra 37 33.50S148.45E
Coxim 48 18.28S 54.37W
Cradock 54 32.10S 25.35E
Craigavon 10 54.28N 6.25W
Craignure 11 56.28N 5.42W
Crail 11 56.16N 2.38W
Crailsheim 16 49.09N 10.06E
Cranbrook 38 49.29N115.48W
Cranston 44 41.47N 71.26W
Crawley 9 51.07N 0.10W
Cremona 14 45.08N 10.03E
Cres i. 14 44.50N 14.20E
Crest 12 44.44N 5.02E
Creston Iowa 41 41.04N 94.20W
Crete i. see Kriti i. 15
Creus, Cabo de c. 13 42.20N 3.19E
Creuse r. 12 47.00N 0.35E
Crewe 8 53.06N 2.28W
Crianlarich 11 56.23N 4.37W
Criccieth 8 52.55N 4.15W
Crieff 11 56.23N 3.52W
Crimea pen. see Krym pen. 21
Crinan 11 56.06N 5.34W
Cristóbal Colón mtn. 46 10.53N 73.48W
Crocodile r. Trans. 54 24.11S 26.48E
Cromarty 11 57.40N 4.02W
Cromarty Firth est. 11 57.41N 4.10W
Cromer 8 52.56N 1.18E
Cromwell 29 45.03S169.14E
Crookhaven 10 51.29N 9.45W
Croom 10 52.31N 8.43W
Crosby 8 54.11N 4.34W
Crotone 15 39.05N 17.06E
Crowl Creek r. 37 31.58S144.53E
Crowsnest Pass 38 49.40N114.41W
Croydon 9 51.23N 0.06W
Cuamba 53 14.48S 36.32E
Cuangar 52 17.34S 18.39E
Cuango r. see Kwango r. 52
Cuanza r. 52 9.20S 13.09E
Cua Rao 26 19.16N104.27E
Cuba 43 22.00N 79.00W
Cubango r. see Okavango r. 52
Cubia r. 52 16.00S 21.46E
Cuchi r. 52 15.23S 17.12E
Cúcuta 46 7.55N 72.31W
Cuddalore 25 11.43N 79.46E
Cuenca 46 2.54S 79.00W
Cuernavaca 42 18.57N 99.15W
Cuiabá r. 48 18.00S 57.25W
Cuillin Hills 11 57.12N 6.13W
Cuito r. 52 18.01S 20.50E
Culiacán 42 24.50N107.23W
Cullen 11 57.41N 2.50W
Cullera 13 39.10N 0.15W
Cullin Sd. 11 57.03N 6.13W
Culloden Moor 11 57.29N 3.55W
Culver, Pt. 33 32.52S124.41E
Cumberland r. 41 37.16N 88.25W
Cumberland, L. 41 37.00N 85.00W
Cumberland Sd. 39 65.00N 65.30W
Cumbernauld 11 55.57N 4.00W
Cumbria d. 8 54.30N 3.00W
Cumbrian Mts. 8 54.32N 3.05W
Cumnock 11 55.27N 4.15W
Cunene r. 52 17.15S 11.50E
Cuneo 14 44.22N 7.32E
Cupar 11 56.19N 3.01W
Curaçao i. 46 12.15N 69.00W
Curicó 49 34.59S 71.14W
Curitiba 45 25.24S 49.16W
Currane, Lough 10 51.50N 10.07W
Curvelo 45 18.45S 44.27W
Cushendall 10 55.06N 6.05W
Cuttack 25 20.30N 85.50E
Cuxhaven 16 53.52N 8.42E
Cuzco 46 13.32S 71.57W
Cwmbran 9 51.39N 3.01W
Cyclades is. see Kikládhes is. 15
Cyprus 24 35.00N 33.00E
Cyrenaica f. see Barqah f. 51
Czechoslovakia 16 49.30N 15.00E

D

Dacca see Dhaka 25
Dachau 16 48.15N 11.26E
Dagana 50 16.31N 15.30W
Da Hinggan Ling mts. 26 50.00N122.10E
Dajing 26 28.25N121.10E
Dakar 50 14.38N 17.27W
Dakhla 50 23.43N 15.57W
Dal r. 19 60.38N 17.27E
Dalbeattie 11 54.55N 3.49W
Dalby 35 27.11S151.12E
Dalian 26 38.49N121.48E
Dalkeith 11 55.54N 3.04W
Dallas Tex. 41 32.47N 96.48W
Dalmally 11 56.25N 4.58W
Dalmellington 11 55.19N 4.24W
Daloa 50 6.56N 6.28W
Dalrymple, Mt. 34 21.02S148.38E
Dalwhinnie 11 56.56N 4.15W
Damascus see Dimashk 24
Damāvand, Qolleh-ye mtn. 24 35.47N 52.04E
Damba 52 6.44S 15.17E
Dampier 32 20.40S116.42E
Da Nang 27 16.04N108.13E
Danbury Conn. 44 41.24N 73.26W
Dande r. 52 8.30S 13.23E
Dandong 26 41.10N124.25E
Danlí 43 14.02N 86.30W
Dannevirke 29 40.12S176.08E
Danube r. 17 45.26N 29.38E
Danville Va. 41 36.34N 79.25W
Dārān 24 33.00N 50.27E
Dardanelles see Çanakkale Boğazi str. 15
Dar es Salaam 53 6.51S 39.18E
Darfield 29 43.29S172.07E
Dargaville 29 35.57S173.53E
Dargo 37 37.30S147.16E
Darhan 26 49.34N106.23E
Darién, Golfo del g. 46 9.20N 77.30W
Darjeeling 25 27.02N 88.16E
Darling r. 36 34.05S141.57E
Darling Downs f. 35 28.00S149.45E
Darlington 8 54.33N 1.33W
Darmstadt 16 49.52N 8.30E
Dartmoor Forest hills 9 50.33N 3.55W
Dartmouth 9 50.21N 3.35W
Daru 34 9.04S143.12E
Darwen 8 53.42N 2.29W
Darwin 34 12.23S130.44E
Dasht-e Kavīr des. 24 34.40N 55.00E
Dasht-e Lūt des. 24 31.30N 58.00E
Dasht-e Mārgow des. 24 30.45N 63.00E
Datong 26 40.10N113.15E
Dauphin 39 51.09N100.05W
Dauphiné, Alpes du mts. 12 44.35N 5.45E
Davao 27 7.05N125.38E
Davenport 41 41.40N 90.36W
Daventry 9 52.16N 1.10W
Davis Str. 39 66.00N 58.00W
Davos 16 46.47N 9.50E
Dawlish 9 50.34N 3.28W
Dawna Range mts. 27 17.00N 98.00E
Dawson 38 64.04N139.24W
Dawson Creek town 38 55.44N120.15W
Dawson Range f. 38 62.40N139.00W
Dax 12 43.43N 1.03W
Dayton Ohio 44 39.45N 84.10W
Daytona Beach town 41 29.11N 81.01W
Dead Sea 24 31.25N 35.30E
Deal 9 51.13N 1.25E
Dearborn 44 42.18N 83.14W
Death Valley f. 40 36.00N116.45W
Deauville 12 49.21N 0.04E
Decatur Ill. 41 39.44N 88.57W
Deccan f. 25 18.30N 77.30E
Děčín 16 50.48N 14.15E
Dedza 53 14.20S 34.24E
Dee r. D. and G. 11 54.50N 4.05W
Dee r. Grampian 11 57.07N 2.04W
Dee r. Wales 8 53.13N 3.05W
Dehra Dūn 25 30.19N 78.02E
Dej 17 47.08N 23.55E
Dekese 52 3.25S 21.24E
Delano 40 35.45N119.16W
Delaware d. 44 39.10N 75.30W
Delaware r. 44 39.20N 75.25W
Delft 16 52.01N 4.23E
Delhi 25 28.40N 77.13E
Delicias 42 28.10N105.30W
Del Rio 40 29.23N100.56W
Delta Utah 40 39.22N112.35W
Demba 52 5.28S 22.14E
Denakil f. 51 13.00N 41.00E
Denbigh 8 53.11N 3.25W
Den Helder 16 52.58N 4.46E
Denia 13 38.51N 0.07E
Deniliquin 37 35.33S144.58E
Denizli 21 37.46N 29.05E
Denman 37 32.23S150.42E
Denmark 19 55.50N 10.00E
Denver 40 39.45N104.58W
Derbent 21 42.03N 48.18E
Derby 8 52.55N 1.28W
Derbyshire d. 8 52.55N 1.28W
Derg, Lough Donegal 10 54.37N 7.55W
Derg, Lough Tipperary 10 52.57N 8.18W
Derrynasaggart Mts. 10 51.58N 9.15W
Derryveagh Mts. 10 55.00N 8.07W
Derwent r. Cumbria 8 54.38N 3.34W
Derwent r. N. Yorks. 8 53.44N 0.57W
Deseado r. 49 47.45S 65.50W
Des Moines Iowa 41 41.35N 93.35W
Dessau 16 51.51N 12.15E
Dete 54 18.39S 26.49E
Detroit 44 42.23N 83.05W
Deutsche Bucht b. 16 54.00N 8.15E
Deva 17 45.54N 22.55E
Deventer 16 52.15N 6.10E
Deveron r. 11 57.40N 2.30W
Devizes 9 51.21N 2.00W
Devon d. 9 50.50N 3.40W
Devon I. 39 75.00N 86.00W
Dewsbury 8 53.42N 1.38W
Dey-Dey L. 35 29.12S131.02E
Dhaka 25 23.43N 90.25E
Dhodhekánisos is. 15 37.00N 27.00E
Dholpur 25 26.42N 77.54E
Diamantino 45 14.25S 56.29W
Dibaya 52 6.31S 22.57E
Dickinson 40 46.54N102.48W
Didcot 9 51.36N 1.14W
Dieppe 12 49.55N 1.05E
Digne 12 44.05N 6.14E
Dijlah r. 24 31.00N 47.27E
Dijon 12 47.20N 5.02E
Dikili 15 39.05N 26.52E
Dikwa 50 12.01N 13.55E
Dili 27 8.35S125.35E
Dillon 40 45.14N112.38W
Dilolo 52 10.39S 22.20E
Dimashk 24 33.30N 36.19E
Dimbelenge 52 5.32S 23.04E
Dimitrovgrad 15 42.01N 25.34E
Dinan 12 48.27N 2.02W
Dinant 16 50.16N 4.55E
Dingle 10 52.09N 10.17W
Dingwall 11 57.35N 4.26W
Diourbel 50 14.30N 16.10W
Dipolog 27 8.34N123.28E
Dirē Dawa 51 9.35N 41.50E
Disappointment, L. 32 23.30S122.55E
Disaster B. 37 37.20S149.58E
Disko i. 39 69.45N 53.00W
Diss 9 52.23N 1.06E
Diyarbakir 21 37.55N 40.14E
Dja r. 52 1.38N 16.03E
Djado 50 21.00N 12.20E
Djambala 52 2.33S 14.38E
Djelfa 50 34.43N 3.14E
Djibouti 51 12.00N 42.50E
Djibouti town 51 11.35N 43.11E
Djolu 52 0.35N 22.28E
Djugu 53 1.55N 30.31E
Dnepr r. 17 50.00N 31.00E
Dnepropetrovsk 21 48.29N 35.00E
Dnestr r. 17 46.21N 30.20E
Dno 20 57.50N 30.00E
Doboj 17 44.44N 18.02E
Doce r. 45 19.32S 39.57W
Dodecanese is. see Dhodhekánisos is. 15
Dodge City 40 37.45N100.02W
Dodoma 53 6.10S 35.40E
Doha see Ad Dawḩah 24
Dokkum 16 53.20N 6.00E
Dole 12 47.05N 5.30E
Dolgellau 9 52.44N 3.53W
Dolomiti mts. 14 46.25N 11.50E
Dombås 19 62.05N 9.08E
Dombe Grande 52 13.00S 13.06E
Dominica 43 15.30N 61.30W
Dominican Republic 43 18.00N 70.00W
Don r. U.S.S.R. 21 47.06N 39.16E
Don r. England 8 53.41N 0.50W
Don r. Scotland 11 57.10N 2.05W
Donaghadee 10 54.39N 5.33W
Donald 36 36.25S143.04E
Donau r. Germany see Danube r. 16
Doncaster 8 53.31N 1.09W
Donegal 10 54.39N 8.06W
Donegal d. 10 54.52N 8.00W
Donegal Pt. 10 52.43N 9.38W
Donetsk 21 48.00N 37.50E
Dongchuan 26 26.10N103.02E
Donggala 27 0.48S119.45E
Donington 8 52.55N 0.12W
Doon, Loch 11 55.15N 4.23W
Dorchester 9 50.52N 2.28W
Dordogne r. 12 45.03N 0.34W
Dordrecht 16 51.48N 4.40E
Dori 50 14.03N 0.02W
Dorking 9 51.14N 0.20W
Dornie 11 57.16N 5.31W
Dornoch 11 57.52N 4.02W
Dornoch Firth est. 11 57.50N 4.04W
Dorset d. 9 50.48N 2.25W
Dortmund 16 51.32N 7.27E
Douai 12 50.22N 3.05E
Douala 50 4.05N 9.43E
Douarnenez 12 48.05N 4.20W
Doubs r. 12 46.57N 5.03E
Douentza 50 14.58N 2.48W
Douglas 8 54.09N 4.29W
Doumé 50 4.16N 13.30E
Dounreay 11 58.35N 3.42W
Dourados 48 22.09S 54.52W
Douro r. 13 41.10N 8.40W
Dove r. Derbys. 8 52.50N 1.35W
Dover 9 51.07N 1.19E
Dovey r. 9 52.33N 3.56W
Dowa 53 13.40S 33.55E
Down d. 10 54.20N 6.00W
Downham Market 9 52.36N 0.22E
Downpatrick 10 54.21N 5.43W
Downpatrick Head 10 54.20N 9.22W
Dowra 10 54.11N 8.02W
Drachten 16 53.06N 6.05E
Draguignan 12 43.32N 6.28E
Drakensberg mts. 54 30.00S 29.05E
Dráma 15 41.09N 24.11E
Drammen 19 59.44N 10.15E
Drava r. 17 45.34N 18.56E
Dresden 16 51.03N 13.45E
Dreux 12 48.44N 1.23E
Drina r. 17 44.53N 19.20E
Drogheda 10 53.42N 6.23W
Droitwich 9 52.16N 2.10W
Dronne r. 12 45.02N 0.09W
Drumheller 38 51.28N112.40W
Drum Hills 10 52.03N 7.42W
Drummondville 44 45.52N 72.30W
Drummore 11 54.41N 4.54W
Drymen 11 56.04N 4.27W
Dua r. 52 3.12N 20.55E
Dubai see Dubayy 24
Dubawnt r. 39 62.50N102.00W
Dubayy 24 25.13N 55.17E
Dubbo 37 32.16S148.41E
Dubica 16 45.11N 16.48E
Dublin 10 53.21N 6.18W
Dublin d. 10 53.20N 6.18W
Dubrovnik 15 42.40N 18.07E
Dubuque 41 42.31N 90.41W
Dudinka 23 69.27N 86.13E
Dudley 9 52.30N 2.05W
Duero r. Spain see Douro r. 13
Dufftown 11 57.27N 3.09W
Duisburg 16 51.26N 6.45E
Dukou 26 26.33N101.44E
Duleek 10 53.39N 6.24W
Dülmen 16 51.51N 7.16E
Duluth 41 46.50N 92.10W
Dumbarton 11 55.57N 4.35W
Dumfries 11 55.04N 3.37W
Dumfries and Galloway d. 11 55.05N 3.40W
Duna r. Hungary see Danube r. 17
Dunărea r. Romania see Danube r. 17
Dunav r. Bulgaria see Danube r. 17
Dunav r. Yugo. see Danube r. 17
Dunbar 11 56.00N 2.31W
Dunblane 11 56.12N 3.59W
Dunboyne 10 53.26N 6.30W
Duncansby Head 11 58.39N 3.01W
Dundalk 10 54.01N 6.25W
Dundee 11 56.28N 3.00W
Dunedin 29 45.52S170.30E
Dunedoo 37 32.00S149.25E
Dunfermline 11 56.04N 3.29W
Dungannon 10 54.31N 6.47W
Dungarvan 10 52.06N 7.39W
Dungeness c. 9 50.55N 0.58E
Dungiven 10 54.56N 6.56W
Dungu 53 3.40N 28.40E
Dunkeld 11 56.34N 3.36W
Dunkerque 12 51.02N 2.23E
Dunkirk see Dunkerque 12
Dunkwa 50 5.59N 1.45W
Dun Laoghaire 10 53.17N 6.09W
Dunleer 10 53.49N 6.24W
Dunmahon 10 52.09N 7.23W
Dunnet Head 11 58.40N 3.23W
Dunoon 11 55.57N 4.57W
Duns 11 55.47N 2.20W
Dunshaughlin 10 53.30N 6.34W
Dunstable 9 51.53N 0.32W
Dunstan Mts. 29 44.45S169.45E
Durance r. 12 43.55N 4.48E
Durango 42 24.01N104.00W
Durban 54 29.50S 30.59E
Düren 16 50.48N 6.30E
Durham 8 54.47N 1.34W
Durham d. 8 54.42N 1.45W
Durmitor mtn. 15 43.08N 19.03E
Durness 11 58.33N 4.45W
Durrow 10 52.51N 7.25W
Dursey Head 10 51.35N 10.15W
D'Urville I. 29 40.45S173.50E
Dushanbe 22 38.38N 68.51E
Düsseldorf 16 51.13N 6.47E
Dvina r. 22 57.03N 24.02E
Dyfed d. 9 52.00N 4.17W
Dzerzhinsk R.S.F.S.R. 20 56.15N 43.30E
Dzhambul 22 42.50N 71.25E
Dzhankoy 21 45.42N 34.23E

E

Eabamet L. 41 51.30N 87.55W
Eagle Pass town 40 28.44N100.31W
Ealing 9 51.31N 0.20W
Earn r. 11 56.21N 3.18W
Earn, Loch 11 56.23N 4.12W
Easingwold 8 54.08N 1.11W
Easky 10 54.17N 8.58W
Eastbourne 9 50.46N 0.18E
East C. 29 37.45S178.30E
East China Sea 26 29.00N125.00E
Easter I. see Pascua, Isla de i. 31
East Grinstead 9 51.08N 0.01W
East Kilbride 11 55.46N 4.09W
East Lansing 44 42.45N 84.30W
Eastleigh 9 50.58N 1.21W
East London 54 33.00S 27.54E
Eastmain 39 52.15N 78.30W
Eastmain r. 39 52.15N 78.30W
Easton Penn. 44 40.41N 75.13W
East Retford 8 53.19N 0.55W
East Sussex d. 9 50.56N 0.12E
Eau-Claire, Lac à l' l. 39 56.10N 74.30W
Ebbw Vale 9 51.47N 3.12W
Ebola r. 52 3.12N 21.00E
Ebolowa 52 2.56N 11.11E
Ebro r. 13 40.43N 0.54E
Ecclefechan 8 55.03N 3.18W
Echuca 37 36.10S144.20E
Écija 13 37.33N 5.04W
Ecuador 46 1.40S 79.00W
Eddystone Pt. 35 40.58S148.12E
Edea 52 3.47N 10.15E
Eden 37 37.04S149.54E
Eden r. Cumbria 8 54.57N 3.02W
Edenderry 10 53.21N 7.05W
Ederny 10 54.32N 7.40W
Édhessa 15 40.47N 22.03E
Edinburgh 11 55.57N 3.13W
Edirne 15 41.40N 26.35E
Edmonton 38 53.34N113.25W
Edmundston 44 47.22N 68.20W
Edremit 15 39.35N 27.02E
Edward, L. 53 0.30S 29.30E
Edwards Plateau f. 40 30.30N100.30W
Egersund 19 58.27N 6.00E
Egmont, Mt. 29 39.20S174.05E
Eğridir 21 37.52N 30.51E
Egypt 51 26.30N 29.30E
Eidsvold 34 25.23S151.08E
Eigg i. 11 56.53N 6.09W
Eighty Mile Beach f. 32 19.00S121.00E
Eil, Loch 11 56.51N 5.12W
Eildon, L. 37 37.10S146.00E
Eindhoven 16 51.26N 5.30E
Eisenach 16 50.59N 10.19E
Eisenhut mtn. 16 47.00N 13.45E
Eisleben 16 51.32N 11.33E
Ejin Qi 26 41.50N100.50E
Eksjö 19 57.40N 14.47E
El Aaiún 50 27.10N 13.11W
Elands r. Trans. 54 24.52S 29.20E
El Arenal 13 39.30N 2.45E
El Asnam 50 36.20N 1.30E
Elâzig 21 38.41N 39.14E
Elba i. 14 42.47N 10.17E
Elbe r. 16 53.33N 10.00E
Elbert, Mt. 40 39.05N106.27W
Elbeuf 12 49.17N 1.01E
Elbistan 21 38.14N 37.11E
Elbrus mtn. 21 43.21N 42.29E
Elburz Mts. see Alborz, Reshteh-ye Kūhhā-ye ye 51
Elche 13 38.16N 0.41W
Elcho I. 34 11.55S135.45E
Elde r. 16 53.17N 12.40E
El Dorado Ark. 41 33.12N 92.40W
Elektrostal 20 55.46N 38.30E
El Ferrol 13 43.29N 8.14W
Elgin 11 57.39N 3.20W
El Golea 50 30.35N 2.51E
Elkhart Ind. 44 41.52N 85.56W
Elkins W.Va. 44 38.55N 79.51W
Elko 40 40.50N115.46W
Ellen, Mt. 40 38.06N110.50W
Ellesmere I. 39 78.00N 82.00W
Ellesmere Port 8 53.17N 2.55W
Ellon 11 57.22N 2.05W
Elmalı 21 36.43N 29.56E
Elmshorn 16 53.46N 9.40E
Eloy 40 32.45N111.33W
El Paso 40 31.45N106.30W
El Real 43 8.06N 77.42W
El Salvador 43 13.30N 89.00W
Elvas 13 38.53N 7.10W
Elverum 19 60.53N 11.34E
Ely Nev. 40 39.15N114.53W
Elyria 44 41.22N 82.06W
Emba r. 21 46.38N 53.00E
Embleton 8 55.30N 1.37W
Embu 53 0.32S 37.28E
Emden 16 53.23N 7.13E
Emory Peak mtn. 40 29.15N103.19W
Empangeni 54 28.45S 31.54E
Empedrado 48 27.59S 58.47W
Emporia Kans. 41 38.24N 96.10W
Ems r. 16 53.14N 7.25E
Emyvale 10 54.20N 6.59W
Encarnación 45 27.20S 55.50W
Endicott Mts. 38 68.00N152.00W
Enfield 9 51.40N 0.05W
Engels 21 51.30N 46.07E
Enggano i. 27 5.20S102.15E
England 8 53.00N 2.00W
English Channel 9 50.15N 1.00W
Enkhuizen 16 52.42N 5.17E
Enköping 19 59.38N 17.04E
Enna 14 37.34N 14.15E
Ennis 10 52.51N 9.00W
Enniscorthy 10 52.30N 6.35W
Enniskillen 10 54.21N 7.40W
Ennistymon 10 52.56N 9.18W
Enschede 16 52.13N 6.54E
Ensenada Argentina 49 34.51S 57.55W
Ensenada Baja Calif. Norte 42 31.53N116.35W
Entebbe 53 0.08N 32.29E
Enugu 50 6.20N 7.29E
Epernay 16 49.02N 3.58E
Épinal 12 48.10N 6.28E
Epping 9 51.42N 0.07E
Epsom 9 51.20N 0.16W
Equatorial Guinea 52 2.00N 10.00E
Erdre r. 12 47.27N 1.34W
Erechim 45 27.35S 52.15W
Ereğli Konya 21 37.30N 34.02E
Ereğli Zonguldak 21 41.17N 31.26E
Erenhot 26 43.48N112.00E
Erfurt 16 50.58N 11.02E
Ergani 21 38.17N 39.44E
Erie 44 42.07N 80.05W
Erie, L. 44 42.15N 81.00W
Eriskay i. 11 57.04N 7.17W
Eritrea f. 51 15.30N 38.00E
Ermelo 54 26.30S 29.59E
Errigal Mtn. 10 55.02N 8.08W
Erzincan 21 39.44N 39.30E
Erzurum 21 39.57N 41.17E
Esbjerg 19 55.28N 8.27E
Escondido r. 43 11.58N 83.45W
Escuintla 42 14.18N 90.47W
Eşfahān 24 32.42N 51.40E
Esher 9 51.23N 0.22W
Eshowe 54 28.53S 31.29E
Esk r. N. Yorks. 8 54.29N 0.37W
Eskilstuna 19 59.22N 16.30E
Eskimo Point town 39 61.10N 94.15W
Eskişehir 21 39.46N 30.30E
Esperance 33 33.49S121.52E
Espíritu Santo i. 30 15.50S166.50E
Espungabera 54 20.28S 32.48E
Esquel 49 42.55S 71.20W
Essen 16 51.27N 6.57E
Essex d. 9 51.46N 0.30E
Estepona 13 36.26N 5.09W
Estevan 38 49.09N103.00W
Eston 8 54.34N 1.07W
Estoril 13 38.42N 9.23W
Estremoz 13 38.50N 7.35W
Étaples 12 50.31N 1.39E
Ethiopia 51 10.00N 39.00E
Etive, Loch 11 56.27N 5.15W
Etna, Monte mtn. 14 37.43N 14.59E
Etosha Pan f. 54 18.50S 16.20E
Euboea see Évvoia i. 15
Eucla 33 31.40S128.51E
Euclid 44 41.34N 81.33W
Eugene 40 44.03N123.07W
Euphrates r. see Nahr al Furāt r. 24
Eureka Calif. 40 40.49N124.10W
Euroa 37 36.46S145.35E
Europa, Picos de mts. 13 43.10N 4.40W
Euskirchen 16 50.40N 6.47E
Evale 52 16.24S 15.50E
Evansville 44 38.00N 87.33W
Everard, C. 37 37.50S149.16E
Everest, Mt. 25 27.59N 86.56E
Evesham 9 52.06N 1.57W
Evje 19 58.36N 7.51E
Évora 13 38.34N 7.54W
Évreux 12 49.03N 1.11E
Évvoia i. 15 38.30N 23.50E
Ewe, Loch 11 57.48N 5.38W
Exe r. 9 50.40N 3.28W
Exeter 9 50.43N 3.31W
Exmoor Forest hills 9 51.08N 3.45W
Exmouth 9 50.37N 3.24W
Eye 9 52.19N 1.09E
Eyemouth 11 55.52N 2.05W
Eyre, L. 36 28.30S137.25E

F

Fåborg 19 55.06N 10.15E
Faenza 16 44.17N 11.52E
Fagernes 19 60.59N 9.17E
Fairbanks 38 64.50N147.50W
Fairborn 44 39.48N 84.03W
Fair Isle 11 59.32N 1.38W
Faisalābād 25 31.25N 73.05E
Faizābād 25 37.05N 70.40E
Fakenham 8 52.50N 0.51E
Falaise 12 48.54N 0.11W
Falcarragh 10 55.08N 8.06W
Falkenberg 19 56.54N 12.28E
Falkirk 11 56.00N 3.48W
Falkland Is. 49 51.45S 59.00W
Fall River town 44 41.43N 71.08W
Falmouth 9 50.09N 5.05W
Falster i. 19 54.48N 11.58E
Falun 19 60.36N 15.38E
Fannich, Loch 11 57.38N 5.00W
Faradje 53 3.45N 29.43E
Fareham 9 50.52N 1.11W
Farewell, C. 29 40.30S172.35E
Fargo 41 46.52N 96.59W
Farnborough 9 51.17N 0.46W

Farne Is. 8 55.38N 1.36W
Farnham 9 51.13N 0.49W
Faro 13 37.01N 7.56W
Faroe Is. 18 62.00N 7.00W
Fårösund 19 57.52N 19.03E
Farrell 44 41.13N 80.31W
Farsund 19 58.05N 6.48E
Farvel, Kap c. 39 60.00N 44.20W
Făurei 17 45.04N 27.15E
Fauske 18 67.17N 15.25E
Favignana i. 14 37.57N 12.19E
Faxe r. 18 63.15N 17.15E
Fayetteville N.C. 41 35.03N 78.53W
Fdérik 50 22.30N 12.30W
Feale r. 10 52.28N 9.37W
Fécamp 12 49.45N 0.23E
Federal States of Micronesia 30 10.00N155.00E
Feeagh, Lough 10 53.56N 9.35W
Fehmarn i. 16 54.30N 11.05E
Feira 53 15.30S 30.27E
Feldkirch 16 47.15N 9.38E
Felixstowe 9 51.58N 1.20E
Feodosiya 21 45.03N 35.23E
Fergana 22 40.23N 71.19E
Fergus Falls town 41 46.18N 96.00W
Fermanagh d. 10 54.21N 7.40W
Fermoy 10 52.08N 8.17W
Ferrara 14 44.49N 11.38E
Ferret, Cap c. 12 44.42N 1.16W
Fès 50 34.05N 5.00W
Feshi 52 6.08S 18.12E
Fetlar i. 11 60.37N 0.52W
Fife d. 11 56.10N 3.10W
Fife Ness c. 11 56.17N 2.36W
Figeac 12 44.32N 2.01E
Figueira da Foz 13 40.09N 8.51W
Figueres 13 42.16N 2.57E
Fiji 30 18.00S178.00E
Filey 8 54.13N 0.18W
Findhorn r. 11 57.38N 3.37W
Findlay 44 41.02N 83.40W
Finisterre, Cabo de c. 13 42.54N 9.16W
Finland 20 64.30N 27.00E
Finland, G. of 19 59.30N 24.00E
Finlay r. 38 56.30N124.40W
Finn r. 10 54.50N 7.30W
Firenze 14 43.46N 11.15E
Firth of Clyde est. 11 55.35N 4.53W
Firth of Forth est. 11 56.05N 3.00W
Firth of Lorn est. 11 56.20N 5.40W
Firth of Tay est. 11 56.24N 3.08W
Fishguard 9 51.59N 4.59W
Fitzroy Crossing 32 18.13S125.33E
Fizi 53 4.18S 28.56E
Flagstaff 40 35.12N111.38W
Flåm 19 60.50N 7.07E
Flamborough Head 8 54.06N 0.05W
Flannan Is. 11 58.16N 7.40W
Flathead L. 40 47.50N114.05W
Fleetwood 8 53.55N 3.01W
Flen 19 59.04N 16.35E
Flensburg 16 54.47N 9.27E
Flinders r. 34 17.30S140.45E
Flinders I. Tas. 35 40.00S148.00E
Flinders Ranges mts. 36 31.25S138.45E
Flin Flon 39 54.47N101.51W
Flint U.K. 8 53.15N 3.07W
Flint U.S.A. 44 43.03N 83.40W
Flint r. Ga. 41 30.52N 84.35W
Flinton 35 27.54S149.34E
Florence see Firenze 14
Florence, L. 36 28.52S138.08E
Flores i. 27 8.40S121.20E
Flores, Laut sea 27 7.00S121.00E
Flores Sea see Flores, Laut sea 27
Florianópolis 45 27.35S 48.34W
Florida d. 41 29.00N 82.00W
Flórina 15 40.48N 21.25E
Florö 19 61.36N 5.00E
Flushing see Vlissingen 16
Focşani 17 45.40N 27.12E
Foggia 14 41.28N 15.33E
Foix 12 42.57N 1.35E
Folkestone 9 51.05N 1.11E
Fond du Lac 38 59.20N107.09W
Fontainebleau 12 48.24N 2.42E
Fontenay 12 46.28N 0.48W
Forbes 37 33.24S148.03E
Foreland Pt. 9 51.15N 3.47W
Forest of Bowland hills 8 53.57N 2.30W
Forest of Dean f. 9 51.48N 2.32W
Forfar 11 56.38N 2.54W
Formby Pt. 8 53.34N 3.07W
Formentera i. 13 38.41N 1.30E
Formosa see Taiwan 26
Forres 11 57.37N 3.38W
Fort Albany 39 52.15N 81.35W
Fortaleza 47 3.45S 38.35W
Fort Augustus 11 57.09N 4.41W
Fort Beaufort 54 32.46S 26.36E
Fort Chipewyan 38 58.46N111.09W
Fort Collins 40 40.35N105.05W
Fort-de-France 43 14.36N 61.05W
Fort Frances 39 48.37N 93.23W
Fort Good Hope 38 66.16N128.37W
Forth r. 11 56.06N 3.48W
Fort Lauderdale 41 26.08N 80.08W
Fort Maguire 53 13.38S 34.59E
Fort McMurray 38 56.45N111.27W
Fort McPherson 38 67.29N134.50W
Fort Myers 41 26.39N 81.51W
Fort Nelson 38 58.48N122.44W
Fort Norman 38 64.55N125.29W
Fort Portal 53 0.40N 30.17E
Fort Randall 38 55.10N162.47W
Fort Reliance 38 62.45N109.08W
Fort Resolution 38 61.10N113.39W
Fortrose 11 57.34N 4.09W
Fort St. John 38 56.14N120.55W
Fort Scott 41 37.52N 94.43W
Fort Severn 39 56.00N 87.40W
Fort Simpson 38 61.46N121.15W
Fort Smith 41 35.22N 94.27W
Fort Smith d. 38 63.30N118.00W
Fort Vermilion 38 58.22N115.59W
Fort Wayne 44 41.05N 85.08W
Fort William 11 56.49N 5.07W
Fort Worth 41 32.45N 97.20W
Fort Yukon 38 66.35N145.20W
Fougères 12 48.21N 1.12W
Foula i. 11 60.08N 2.05W
Foulness I. 9 51.35N 0.55E
Foulwind, C. 29 41.45S171.30E
Foveaux Str. 29 46.40S168.00E
Fowey 9 50.20N 4.39W
Foxe Channel 39 65.00N 80.00W
Foxton 29 40.27S175.18E
Foyle r. 10 55.00N 7.20W
Foyle, Lough 10 55.05N 7.10W
Foz do Iguaçu 45 25.33S 54.31W
Franca 45 20.33S 47.27W
France 12 47.00N 2.00E
Franceville 52 1.38S 13.31E
Francistown 54 21.12S 27.29E
Frankfort 54 27.15S 28.30E
Frankfurt Brandenburg 16 52.20N 14.32E
Frankfurt Hessen 16 50.06N 8.41E
Franz Josef Land is. see Frantsa Iosifa, Zemlya ya 22
Fraser r. B.C. 38 49.05N123.00W
Fraserburg 54 31.55S 21.29E
Fraserburgh 11 57.42N 2.00W
Fredericia 19 55.35N 9.46E
Fredericksburg Va. 41 38.18N 77.30W
Fredericton 44 45.57N 66.40W
Frederikshåb 39 62.05N 49.30W
Frederikshavn 19 57.26N 10.32E
Fredrikstad 19 59.13N 10.57E
Freeport 43 26.40N 78.30W
Freetown 50 8.30N 13.17W
Freiburg 16 48.00N 7.52E
Fréjus 12 43.26N 6.44E
Fremantle 33 32.07S115.44E
Freshford 10 52.44N 7.23W
Fresno 40 36.41N119.57W
Fribourg 16 46.50N 7.10E
Friedrichshafen 16 47.39N 9.29E
Frobisher Bay town 39 63.45N 68.30W
Frohavet est. 18 63.55N 9.05E
Frome 9 51.16N 2.17W
Frome, L. 36 30.48S139.48E
Fröya i. 18 63.45N 8.45E
Frunze 22 42.53N 74.46E
Fuerte r. 42 25.42N109.20W
Fuji san mtn. 28 35.22N138.44E
Fukui 26 36.04N136.12E
Fukuoka 26 33.39N130.21E
Fulda 16 50.35N 9.45E
Funabashi 28 35.42N139.59E
Funchal 50 32.38N 16.54W
Fundy, B. of 44 45.00N 66.00W
Furancungo 53 14.51S 33.38E
Furneaux Group is. 35 40.15S148.15E
Fürstenwalde 16 52.22N 14.04E
Fürth 16 49.28N 11.00E
Fushun 26 41.50N123.55E
Fuyu 26 45.12N124.49E
Fuzhou 26 26.09N119.21E
Fyne, Loch 11 55.55N 5.23W

G

Gabela 52 10.52S 14.24E
Gabès 50 33.52N 10.06E
Gabon 52 0.00 12.00E
Gabon r. 52 0.15N 10.00E
Gaborone 54 24.45S 25.55E
Gadsden 41 34.00N 86.00W
Gaeta 14 41.13N 13.35E
Gagnoa 50 6.04N 5.55W
Gagnon 39 51.55N 68.10W
Gaillac 12 43.54N 1.53E
Gainesville Fla. 41 29.37N 82.31W
Gainsborough 8 53.23N 0.46W
Gairdner, L. 36 31.30S136.00E
Gairloch 11 57.43N 5.40W
Galana r. 53 3.12S 40.09E
Galapagos, Islas is. 31 0.30S 90.30W
Galashiels 11 55.37N 2.49W
Galaţi 17 45.27N 27.59E
Galena Alas. 38 64.43N157.00W
Galesburg 41 40.58N 90.22W
Galle 25 6.01N 80.13E
Gállego r. 13 41.40N 0.55W
Gallipoli 15 40.02N 18.01E
Galloway f. 11 55.00N 4.28W
Gallup 40 35.32N108.46W
Galston 11 55.36N 4.23W
Galty Mts. 10 52.20N 8.10W
Galveston 41 29.17N 94.48W
Galvez 48 32.03S 61.14W
Galway 10 53.17N 9.04W
Galway d. 10 53.25N 9.00W
Gambia 50 13.30N 15.00W
Gambia r. 50 13.28N 15.55W
Gamboma 52 1.50S 15.58E
Ganda 52 12.58S 14.39E
Gandajika 52 6.46S 23.58E
Gander 39 48.58N 54.34W
Gandía 13 38.59N 0.11W
Ganga r. 25 23.22N 90.32E
Ganges r. see Ganga r. 25
Ganzhou 26 25.49N114.50E
Gao 50 16.19N 0.09W
Gap 12 44.33N 6.05E
Gara, Lough 10 53.57N 8.27W
Gard r. 12 43.52N 4.40E
Garda, Lago di l. 14 45.40N 10.40E
Garies 54 30.34S 18.00E
Garissa 53 0.27S 39.49E
Garmisch Partenkirchen 16 47.30N 11.05E
Garonne r. 12 45.00N 0.37W
Garoua 50 9.17N 13.22E
Garron Pt. 10 55.03N 5.57W
Garry L. 39 66.00N100.00W
Garut 27 7.15S107.55E
Garvão 13 37.42N 8.21W
Garve 11 57.37N 4.41W
Garvie Mts. 29 45.15S169.00E
Gary 44 41.34N 87.20W
Gascogne, Golfe de g. 12 44.00N 2.40W
Gascony, G. of see Gascogne, Golfe de 12
Gascoyne r. 32 25.00S113.40E
Gaspé 39 48.50N 64.30W
Gaspé, Péninsule de pen. 44 48.30N 65.00W
Gata, Sierra de mts. 13 40.20N 6.30W
Gatehouse of Fleet 11 54.53N 4.12W
Gateshead 8 54.57N 1.35W
Gatineau r. 44 45.27N 75.40W
Gatton 35 27.32S152.18E
Gavá 13 41.18N 2.00E
Gävle 19 60.40N 17.10E
Gávrion 15 37.52N 24.46E
Gawler 36 34.38S138.44E
Gcuwa 54 32.20S 28.09E
Gdańsk 17 54.22N 18.38E
Gdansk, G. of 17 54.45N 19.15E
Gdov 20 58.48N 27.52E
Gdynia 17 54.31N 18.30E
Geel 16 51.10N 5.00E
Geelong 36 38.10S144.26E
Geidam 50 12.55N 11.55E
Gelsenkirchen 16 51.30N 7.05E
Gemena 52 3.14N 19.48E
Gemlik 21 40.26N 29.10E
General Pico 49 35.38S 63.46W
Geneva see Genève 16
Geneva, L. see Léman, Lac l. 16
Genève 16 46.13N 6.09E
Genoa see Genova 14
Genoa, G. of see Genova, Golfo di g. 14
Genova 14 44.24N 8.54E
Gent 16 51.02N 3.42E
George 54 33.57S 22.27E
George, L. N.S.W. 37 35.07S149.22E
Georgetown Cayman Is. 43 19.20N 81.23W
Georgetown Guyana 46 6.46N 58.10W
George Town Malaysia 27 5.30N100.16E
George Town Tas. 35 41.04S146.48E
Georgia d. 41 33.00N 83.00W
Gera 16 50.51N 12.11E
Geraldine 29 44.05S171.15E
Geraldton 33 28.49S114.36E
Germany 16 51.00N 10.00E
Germiston 54 26.14S 28.10E
Geyve 21 40.32N 30.18E
Ghana 50 8.00N 1.00W
Ghanzi 54 21.42S 21.39E
Ghardaïa 50 32.20N 3.40E
Ghāt 50 24.59N 10.11E
Gibraltar 13 36.07N 5.22W
Gibraltar, Str. of 13 36.00N 5.25W
Gibson Desert 32 23.10S125.35E
Giessen 16 50.35N 8.42E
Gifu 28 35.25N136.45E
Gigha i. 11 55.41N 5.44W
Gijón 13 43.32N 5.40W
Gila r. 40 32.45N114.30W
Gilé 53 16.10S 38.17E
Gilgandra 37 31.42S148.40E
Gilgit 25 35.54N 74.20E
Gill, Lough 10 54.15N 8.14W
Gillingham Kent 9 51.24N 0.33E
Girdle Ness 11 57.06N 2.02W
Giresun 21 40.55N 38.25E
Girona 13 41.59N 2.49E
Gironde r. 12 45.35N 1.00W
Girvan 11 55.15N 4.51W
Gisborne 29 38.41S178.02E
Gisborne d. 29 38.20S177.45E
Gizhiga 23 62.00N160.34E
Gladstone Qld. 34 23.52S151.16E
Glåma r. 19 59.15N 10.55E
Glasgow 11 55.52N 4.15W
Glastonbury 9 51.09N 2.42W
Glazov 20 58.09N 52.42E
Glen Affric f. 11 57.15N 5.03W
Glen Coe f. 11 56.40N 5.03W
Glendale Calif. 40 34.09N118.20W
Glendive 40 47.08N104.42W
Glengarriff 10 51.45N 9.33W
Glen Garry f. Highland 11 57.03N 5.04W
Glen Head 10 54.44N 8.46W
Glen Innes 37 29.42S151.45E
Glen Mòr f. 11 57.15N 4.30W
Glenrothes 11 56.12N 3.10W
Glenshee f. 11 56.45N 3.25W
Głogów 16 51.40N 16.06E
Gloucester 9 51.52N 2.15W
Gloucestershire d. 9 51.45N 2.00W
Goa d. 25 15.30N 74.00E
Goat Fell mtn. 11 55.37N 5.12W
Gobi des. 26 45.00N108.00E
Godalming 9 51.11N 0.37W
Godāvari r. 25 16.40N 82.15E
Godhavn 39 69.20N 53.30W
Godthåb 39 64.10N 51.40W
Göksun 21 38.03N 36.30E
Golden B. 29 40.45S172.50E
Golden Vale f. 10 52.30N 8.07W
Goldsworthy 32 20.20S119.30E
Golspie 11 57.58N 3.58W
Goma 53 1.37S 29.10E
Gombe r. 53 4.43S 31.30E
Gongga Shan mtn. 26 29.30N101.30E
Good Hope, C. of 54 34.21S 18.28E
Goole 8 53.42N 0.52W
Goose L. 40 41.55N120.25W
Göppingen 16 48.43N 9.39E
Gorakhpur 25 26.45N 83.22E
Gore 29 46.06S168.58E
Gori 21 41.59N 44.05E
Gorki see Gor'kiy 20
Gor'kiy 20 56.20N 44.00E
Gorzów Wielkopolski 16 52.42N 15.12E
Gosford 37 33.25S151.18E
Goslar 16 51.54N 10.25E
Gospić 16 44.34N 15.23E
Gosport 9 50.48N 1.08W
Göteborg 19 57.43N 11.58E
Gotha 16 50.57N 10.43E
Gothenburg see Göteborg 19
Gotland i. 19 57.30N 18.33E
Göttingen 16 51.32N 9.57E
Goulburn r. 37 36.08S144.30E
Gourdon 12 44.45N 1.22E
Gouré 50 13.59N 10.15E
Gournay 12 49.29N 1.44E
Gower pen. 9 51.37N 4.10W
Goya 48 29.10S 59.20W
Goyder r. 34 12.38S135.11E
Gozo i. 14 36.03N 14.16E
Grahamstown 54 33.18S 26.30E
Grampian d. 11 57.22N 2.35W
Grampian Mts. 11 56.55N 4.00W
Granada 13 37.10N 3.35W
Granby 44 45.23N 72.44W
Gran Canaria i. 50 28.00N 15.30W
Gran Chaco f. 48 22.00S 60.00W
Grand r. S.Dak. 40 45.40N100.32W
Grand Bahama I. 43 26.35N 78.00W
Grand Canyon f. 40 36.15N113.00W
Grand Cayman i. 43 19.20N 81.30W
Grande r. 48 15.10S 64.55W
Grande r. Minas Gerais 48 20.00S 51.00W
Grande Prairie town 38 55.10N118.52W
Grand Forks 41 47.57N 97.05W
Grand Island town 40 40.56N 98.21W
Grand Junction 40 39.04N108.33W
Grand Manan I. 44 44.38N 66.50W
Grand Rapids town Mich. 44 42.57N 85.40W
Grand St. Bernard, Col du pass 16 45.52N 7.11E
Grand Teton mtn. 40 43.45N110.50W
Grangemouth 11 56.01N 3.44W
Grantham 8 52.55N 0.39W
Grantown-on-Spey 11 57.20N 3.38W
Grants Pass town 40 42.26N123.20W
Granville 12 48.50N 1.35W
Graskop 54 24.55S 30.50E
Grasse 12 43.40N 6.56E
Gravesend 9 51.27N 0.24E
Gray 12 47.27N 5.35E
Grays 9 51.29N 0.20E
Graz 16 47.05N 15.22E
Great Artesian Basin f. 34 26.30S143.02E
Great Australian Bight 33 33.10S129.30E
Great Barrier I. 29 36.15S175.30E
Great Barrier Reef f. 34 16.30S146.30E
Great Basin f. 40 39.00N115.30W
Great Bear L. 38 66.00N120.00W
Great Blasket I. 10 52.05N 10.32W
Great Dividing Range mts. 37 29.00S152.00E
Great Driffield 8 54.01N 0.26W
Greater London d. 9 51.31N 0.06W
Greater Manchester d. 8 53.30N 2.18W
Great Falls town 40 47.30N111.16W
Great Karoo f. 54 32.40S 22.20E
Great Kei r. 54 32.39S 28.23E
Great L. 35 41.50S146.43E
Great Malvern 9 52.07N 2.19W
Great Namaland f. 54 25.30S 17.20E
Great Ouse r. 8 52.47N 0.23E
Great Salt L. 40 41.10N112.40W
Great Sandy Desert 32 20.30S123.35E
Great Slave L. 38 61.30N114.20W
Great Victoria Desert 33 29.00S127.30E
Great Whernside mtn. 8 54.09N 1.59W
Great Yarmouth 9 52.40N 1.45E
Greece 15 39.00N 22.00E
Greeley 40 40.26N104.43W
Green r. 40 38.20N109.53W
Greenhills 33 31.58S117.01E
Greenland 39 68.00N 45.00W
Greenlaw 11 55.43N 2.28W
Greenock 11 55.57N 4.45W
Greensboro N.C. 41 36.03N 79.50W
Greenville S.C. 41 34.52N 82.25W
Grenå 19 56.25N 10.53E
Grenada 43 12.07N 61.40W
Grenoble 12 45.11N 5.43E
Gretna 11 55.00N 3.04W
Grey r. 29 42.28S171.13E
Greymouth 29 42.28S171.12E
Grey Range mts. 35 27.30S143.59E
Greystones 10 53.09N 6.04W
Grim, C. 35 40.45S144.45E
Grimsby 8 53.35N 0.05W
Grodno 17 53.40N 23.50E
Groningen 16 53.13N 6.35E
Groot r. C.P. r. 54 33.58S 25.03E
Groote Eylandt i. 34 14.00S136.40E
Grootfontein 54 19.32S 18.07E
Grossenbrode 16 54.23N 11.07E
Gross Glockner mtn. 16 47.05N 12.50E
Groundhog r. 44 49.43N 81.58W
Groznyy 21 43.21N 45.42E
Guadalajara 42 20.30N103.20W
Guadalcanal i. 30 9.32S160.12E
Guadalete r. 13 36.37N 6.15W
Guadalmena r. 13 38.00N 3.50W
Guadalquivir r. 13 36.50N 6.20W
Guadalupe 42 25.41N100.15W
Guadalupe, Isla de i. 40 29.00N118.25W
Guadarrama r. 13 39.55N 4.10W
Guadarrama, Sierra de mts. 13 41.00N 3.50W
Guadeloupe i. 43 16.20N 61.40W
Guadiana r. 13 37.10N 7.36W
Guadix 13 37.19N 3.08W
Guaíra 48 24.04S 54.15W
Gualeguay 49 33.10S 59.20W
Gualeguaychu 49 33.00S 58.30W
Guam i. 30 13.30N144.40E
Guangxi Zhuangzu d. 26 23.30N109.00E
Guangzhou 26 23.08N113.20E
Guaporé r. 48 12.00S 65.15W
Guarapuava 45 25.22S 51.28W
Guarda 13 40.32N 7.17W
Guardo 13 42.47N 4.50W
Guatemala 43 15.40N 90.00W
Guatemala town 42 14.38N 90.22W
Guaviare r. 46 4.00N 67.35W
Guayaquil 46 2.13S 79.54W
Guaymas 42 27.59N110.54W
Gubin 16 51.59N 14.42E
Guecho 13 43.21N 3.01W
Guéret 12 46.10N 1.52E
Guernsey i. 9 49.27N 2.35W
Guiana 47 3.40N 53.00W
Guiana Highlands 46 4.00N 59.00W
Guildford 9 51.14N 0.35W
Guilin 26 25.20N110.10E
Guinea 50 10.30N 10.30W
Guinea, G. of 50 2.00N 1.00W
Guinea Bissau 50 12.00N 15.30W
Güines 43 22.50N 82.02W
Guingamp 12 48.34N 3.09W
Güiria 46 10.37N 62.21W
Guiyang 26 26.31N106.39E
Gujarat d. 25 22.20N 70.30E
Gulu 53 2.46N 32.21E
Gundagai 37 35.07S148.05E
Gungu 52 5.43S 19.20E
Gunnedah 37 30.59S150.15E
Gürün 21 38.44N 37.15E
Guruve 53 16.42S 30.40E
Guyana 46 4.40N 59.00W
Gwādar 24 25.07N 62.19E
Gwai r. 54 17.59S 26.55E
Gwalior 25 26.12N 78.09E
Gwanda 54 20.59S 29.00E
Gweebarra B. 10 54.52N 8.28W
Gwent d. 9 51.44N 3.00W
Gweru 54 19.25S 29.50E
Gwynedd d. 8 53.00N 4.00W
Gyandzha 21 40.39N 46.20E
Györ 17 47.41N 17.40E

H

Haarlem 16 52.22N 4.38E
Haddington 11 55.57N 2.47W
Hadramawt f. 24 16.30N 49.30E
Hagerstown 44 39.39N 77.43W
Ha Giang 26 22.50N105.00E
Hague, Cap de la c. 12 49.44N 1.56W
Haikou 26 20.03N110.27E
Ḥā'il 24 27.31N 41.45E
Hailsham 9 50.52N 0.17E
Hainan d. 27 19.00N109.30E
Haines Alas. 38 59.11N135.23W
Haiphong 26 20.48N106.40E
Haiti 43 19.00N 73.00W
Hakkâri 21 37.36N 43.45E
Hakodate 26 41.46N140.44E
Ḥalab 24 36.14N 37.10E
Halberstadt 16 51.54N 11.04E
Halden 19 59.09N 11.23E
Haliburton Highlands 44 45.03N 78.03W
Halifax Canada 39 44.38N 63.35W
Halifax U.K. 8 53.43N 1.51W
Halle 16 51.28N 11.58E
Hall's Creek town 32 18.13S127.39E
Hallstavik 19 60.03N 18.36E
Halmahera i. 27 0.45N128.00E
Halmstad 19 56.39N 12.50E
Hälsingborg 19 56.03N 12.42E
Haltwhistle 8 54.58N 2.27W
Hamamatsu 28 34.42N137.44E
Hamar 19 60.48N 11.06E
Hamburg 16 53.33N 10.00E
Hameln 16 52.06N 9.21E
Hamersley Range mts. 32 22.00S118.00E
Hami 26 42.40N 93.30E
Hamilton Canada 44 43.15N 79.51W
Hamilton New Zealand 29 37.46S175.18E
Hamilton U.K. 11 55.46N 4.10W
Hamilton r. 35 27.12S135.28E
Hamilton Ohio 44 39.23N 84.33W
Hammerfest 18 70.40N 23.42E
Hampshire d. 9 51.03N 1.20W
Handa 28 34.53N136.56E
Handeni 53 5.25S 38.04E
Hangzhou 26 30.14N120.08E
Hannibal Mo. 41 39.41N 91.25W
Hannover 16 52.23N 9.44E
Hanoi 26 21.01N105.53E
Hanover 54 31.04S 24.25E
Haparanda 18 65.50N 24.10E
Ḥaraḍ 24 24.12N 49.08E
Harare 54 17.49S 31.04E
Harbin 26 45.45N126.41E
Hardangerfjorden est. 19 60.10N 6.00E
Harding 54 30.34S 29.52E
Hargeysa 51 9.31N 44.02E
Har Hu l. 26 38.20N 97.40E
Hari r. 27 1.00S104.15E
Harlech 8 52.52N 4.08W
Harlow 9 51.47N 0.08E
Harris i. 11 57.50N 6.55W
Harris, Sd. of 11 57.43N 7.05W
Harrisburg Penn. 44 40.16N 76.52W
Harrogate 8 53.59N 1.32W
Harrow 9 51.35N 0.21W
Harstad 18 68.48N 16.30E
Hartford 44 41.45N 72.42W
Hartland Pt. 9 51.01N 4.32W
Hartlepool 8 54.42N 1.11W
Harwich 9 51.56N 1.18E
Haryana d. 25 29.15N 76.30E
Haslemere 9 51.05N 0.41W
Hässleholm 19 56.09N 13.46E
Hastings New Zealand 29 39.39S176.52E
Hastings U.K. 9 50.51N 0.36E
Hatfield 9 51.46N 0.13W
Hattiesburg 41 31.25N 89.19W
Hauge 19 58.18N 6.15E
Haugesund 19 59.25N 5.18E
Hauraki G. 29 36.30S175.00E
Havana see La Habana 43
Havant 9 50.51N 0.59W
Haverfordwest 9 51.48N 4.59W
Haverhill 9 52.06N 0.27E
Havre 40 48.34N109.45W
Hawaii d. 40 21.00N156.00W
Hawaii i. Hawaii 40 19.30N155.30W
Hawaiian Is. 40 21.00N157.00W
Hawea, L. 29 44.30S169.15E
Hawera 29 39.35S174.19E
Hawick 11 55.25N 2.47W
Hawke B. 29 39.18S177.15E
Hawthorne 40 38.13N118.37W
Hay 37 34.31S144.31E
Hayes r. 39 57.00N 92.30W
Hay-on-Wye 9 52.04N 3.09W
Hazelton 38 55.16N127.18W
Hazleton 44 40.58N 75.59W
Heanor 8 53.01N 1.20W
Hebel 37 28.55S147.49E
Hebron 39 58.05N 62.30W
Heerenveen 16 52.57N 5.55E
Hefei 26 31.50N117.16E
Heidelberg 16 49.25N 8.42E
Heilbron 54 27.16S 27.57E
Heilbronn 16 49.08N 9.14E
Hekou 26 22.39N103.57E
Helena 40 46.35N112.00W
Helensburgh 11 56.01N 4.44W
Helmsdale r. 11 58.05N 3.39W
Helsingfors see Helsinki 19
Helsingör 19 56.02N 12.37E
Helsinki 19 60.08N 25.00E
Helston 9 50.07N 5.17W
Hemel Hempstead 9 51.46N 0.28W
Hemsedal 19 60.52N 8.34E
Henares r. 13 40.26N 3.35W
Hendaye 12 43.22N 1.46W
Hengelo 7 52.16N 6.46E
Hengyang 26 26.52N112.35E
Herāt 24 34.20N 62.12E
Hereford 9 52.04N 2.43W
Hereford and Worcester d. 9 52.08N 2.30W
Herford 16 52.07N 8.40E
Hermidale 37 31.33S146.44E
Herne Bay town 9 51.23N 1.10E
Herning 19 56.08N 8.59E
Hertford 9 51.48N 0.05W
Hertfordshire d. 9 51.51N 0.05W
Hexham 8 54.58N 2.06W
Heysham 8 54.03N 2.53W
Heywood 8 53.36N 2.13W
Highland d. 11 57.42N 5.00W
High Peak mtn. 8 53.22N 1.48W
High Wycombe 9 51.38N 0.46W
Hikurangi mtn. 29 37.50S178.10E
Hildesheim 16 52.09N 9.58E
Hillston 37 33.30S145.33E
Hilo Hawaii 40 19.42N155.04W
Hilversum 16 52.14N 5.12E
Himachal Pradesh d. 25 32.05N 77.15E
Himalaya mts. 25 29.00N 84.30E
Ḥimṣ 24 34.44N 36.43E
Hinckley 9 52.33N 1.21W
Hindmarsh, L. 36 36.03S141.53E
Hindu Kush mts. 25 36.40N 70.00E
Hiroshima 26 34.23N132.27E
Hirson 12 49.56N 4.05E
Hispaniola i. 43 19.00N 71.00W
Hitchin 9 51.57N 0.16W
Hjälmaren l. 19 59.15N 15.45E
Hjörring 19 57.28N 9.59E
Hobart 35 42.54S147.18E
Hobyo 51 5.20N 48.30E
Ho Chi Minh 27 10.46N106.43E
Hof 16 50.19N 11.56E
Höfn 18 64.16N 15.10W
Hofors 19 60.33N 16.17E
Hohhot 26 40.42N111.38E
Hokitika 29 42.42S170.59E
Hokkaidō i. 26 43.60N143.00E
Holland Mich. 44 42.46N 86.06W
Holstebro 19 56.21N 8.38E
Holt 8 52.55N 1.04E
Holyhead 8 53.18N 4.38W
Holy I. England 8 55.41N 1.47W
Holy I. Wales 8 53.15N 4.38W
Holywood 10 54.38N 5.50W
Homer Alas. 38 59.40N151.37W
Homer Tunnel 29 44.40S168.15E
Homoine 54 23.45S 35.09E
Honduras 43 14.30N 87.00W
Honfleur 12 49.25N 0.14E
Hong Kong 26 22.15N114.15E
Hongshui He r. 26 23.20N110.04E
Honiton 9 50.48N 3.13W
Honolulu Hawaii 40 21.19N157.50W
Honshū i. 26 36.00N138.00E
Hoopstad 54 27.48S 25.52E
Hoorn 16 52.38N 5.03E
Hoover Dam 40 36.01N114.45W
Hopetoun Vic. 36 35.43S142.20E
Hopetown 54 29.37S 24.04E
Horn, C. see Hornos, Cabo de c. 49
Horncastle 8 53.13N 0.08W
Hornos, Cabo de c. 49 55.47S 67.00W
Hornsea 8 53.55N 0.10W
Horsens 19 55.52N 9.52E
Horsham 9 51.04N 0.20W
Hospitalet de Llobregat 13 41.20N 2.06E
Hotan 25 37.07N 79.57E
Hotazel 54 27.16S 22.57E
Hoting 18 64.07N 16.10E
Houndé 50 11.34N 3.31W
Houston Tex. 41 29.45N 95.25W
Hovd 26 46.40N 90.45E
Hove 9 50.50N 0.10W
Howe, C. 37 37.30S149.59E
Howitt, Mt. 37 37.15S146.40E
Howrah 25 22.35N 88.20E
Hoy i. 11 58.51N 3.17W
Huabei Pingyuan f. 26 36.32N108.14E
Huambo 52 12.47S 15.44E
Huancayo 46 12.05S 75.12W
Huang He r. 26 38.00N118.40E
Huánuco 46 9.55S 76.11W
Hubli 25 15.20N 75.14E
Hucknall 8 53.03N 1.12W
Huddersfield 8 53.38N 1.49W
Hudiksvall 19 61.44N 17.07E
Hudson r. 44 40.42N 74.02W
Hudson B. 39 58.00N 86.00W
Hudson Str. 39 62.00N 70.00W
Hue 27 16.28N107.40E
Huelva 13 37.15N 6.56W
Huelva r. 13 37.25N 6.00W
Huesca 13 42.02N 0.25W
Hughenden 34 20.51S144.12E
Hughes 35 30.40S129.32E
Huiarau Range mts. 29 38.20S177.15E
Huixtla 42 15.09N 92.30W
Hull 44 45.26N 75.45W
Hultsfred 19 57.29N 15.50E
Humansdorp 54 34.02S 24.45E
Humber r. 8 53.40N 0.12W
Humberside d. 8 53.48N 0.35W
Humboldt r. 40 40.02N118.31W
Hün 50 29.06N 15.57E
Hungary 17 47.30N 19.00E
Hŭngnam 26 39.49N127.40E
Hunsrück mts. 16 49.44N 7.05E
Hunstanton 8 52.57N 0.30E
Huntingdon 9 52.20N 0.11W
Huntsville Ala. 41 34.44N 86.35W
Huron, L. 44 44.30N 82.15W
Huskvarna 19 57.48N 14.16E
Husum 16 54.29N 9.04E
Hwange 54 18.20S 26.29E
Hyde 8 53.26N 2.06W
Hyderābād India 25 17.22N 78.26E
Hyderābād Pakistan 25 25.22N 68.22E
Hyères 12 43.07N 6.08E
Hyndman Peak 40 43.46N113.55W
Hythe Kent 9 51.04N 1.05E

I

Ibadan 50 7.23N 3.56E
Ibagué 46 4.25N 75.20W
Ibarra 46 0.23N 78.05W
Ibi 50 8.11N 9.44E
Ibicaraí 47 14.52S 39.37W
Ibina r. 53 1.00N 28.40E
Ibiza i. 13 39.00N 1.23E
Ibotirama 47 12.13S 43.12W
Iceland 18 64.45N 18.00W
Ichinomiya 28 35.18N136.48E
Idah 50 7.05N 6.45E
Idaho d. 40 45.00N115.00W
Ídhra i. 15 37.20N 23.32E
Ierápetra 15 35.00N 25.45E
Iesi 14 43.32N 13.15E
Iesolo 14 45.32N 12.38E
Igoumenítsa 15 39.32N 20.14E
Iguaçu r. 45 25.33S 54.35W
Iguala 42 18.21N 99.31W
Iisalmi 18 63.34N 27.11E
IJsselmeer l. 16 52.45N 5.20E
Ijuí 45 28.23S 53.55W
Ikaría i. 15 37.35N 26.10E
Ikelemba r. 52 0.08N 18.19E
Ilebo 52 4.20S 20.35E
Ilesha Oyo 50 7.38N 4.45E
Ilfracombe 9 51.13N 4.08W
Iligan 27 8.12N124.13E
Ilkley 8 53.56N 1.49W
Illinois d. 41 40.00N 89.00W
Ilminster 9 50.55N 2.56W
Ilorin 50 8.32N 4.34E
Imala 53 14.39S 39.34E
Immingham 8 53.37N 0.12W
Imphāl 25 24.47N 93.55E
Inca 13 39.43N 2.54E
Inch'on 26 37.30N126.38E
India 25 23.00N 78.00E
Indiana d. 44 40.00N 86.15W
Indianapolis 44 39.45N 86.10W
Indian Ocean 27
Indonesia 27 6.00S118.00E
Indore 25 22.43N 75.50E
Indre r. 12 47.16N 0.19W
Indus r. 25 24.20N 67.47E
Inebolu 21 41.57N 33.45E
Ingende 52 0.17S 18.58E
Ingham 34 18.35S146.12E
Ingleborough mtn. 8 54.10N 2.23W
Inhambane 54 23.51S 35.29E
Inisheer i. 10 53.04N 9.32W
Inishmaan i. 10 53.06N 9.36W
Inishmore i. 10 53.08N 9.43W
Inishowen Pen. 10 55.08N 7.20W
Inishturk i. 10 53.43N 10.08W
Inner Hebrides is. 11 56.50N 6.45W
Inner Mongolia d. see Nei Monggol d. 26
Innsbruck 16 47.17N 11.25E
Interlaken 16 46.42N 7.52E
Inuvik 38 68.16N133.40W
Inuvik d. 38 68.00N130.00W
Inveraray 11 56.24N 5.05W
Inverbervie 11 56.51N 2.17W
Invercargill 29 46.26S168.21E
Inverell 37 29.46S151.10E
Invergordon 11 57.42N 4.10W
Inverness 11 57.27N 4.15W
Inverurie 11 57.17N 2.23W
Inzia r. 52 3.47S 17.57E
Ioánnina 15 39.39N 20.49E
Iona i. 11 56.20N 6.25W
Ionian Is. see Iónioi Nísoi is. 15
Ionian Sea 15 38.30N 18.45E
Iónioi Nísoi is. 15 38.45N 20.00E
Íos i. 15 36.42N 25.20E
Iowa d. 41 42.00N 93.00W
Iowa City 41 41.39N 91.30W
Ipiaú 47 14.07S 39.43W
Ipoh 27 4.36N101.02E
Ipswich Australia 37 27.38S152.40E
Ipswich U.K. 9 52.04N 1.09E
Iquitos 46 3.51S 73.13W
Iráklion 15 35.20N 25.08E
Iran 24 32.00N 54.30E
Iraq 24 33.00N 44.00E
Iringa 53 7.49S 35.39E
Irish Sea 10 53.30N 5.40W
Irkutsk 23 52.18N104.15E
Iron Gate f. 17 44.40N 22.30E
Iron Mts. 10 54.10N 7.56W
Irosin 27 12.45N124.02E
Irrapatana 36 29.03S136.28E
Irrawaddy r. 27 15.50N 95.00E
Irtysh r. 22 61.00N 68.40E
Irún 13 43.20N 1.48W
Irvine 11 55.37N 4.40W
Isangi 52 0.48N 24.03E
Isar r. 16 48.48N 12.57E
Ischia i. 14 40.43N 13.54E
Isère r. 12 45.02N 4.54E
Isfahan see Eşfahān 24
Ishim r. 22 57.50N 71.00E
Isiro 53 2.50N 27.40E
Iskenderun 21 36.37N 36.08E
Iskūr r. 15 43.42N 24.27E
Isla r. 11 56.32N 3.22W
Islāmābād 25 33.40N 73.10E
Islands, B. of 29 35.15S174.15E
Islay i. 11 55.45N 6.20W
Isle of Portland f. 9 50.32N 2.25W
Isle of Wight d. 9 50.40N 1.17W
Israel 24 32.00N 35.00E
Issoire 12 45.33N 3.15E
Istanbul 24 41.02N 28.58E
Itabira 45 19.39S 43.14W
Itabuna 47 14.48S 39.18W
Itaituba 47 4.17S 55.59W
Italy 14 43.00N 12.00E
Itapetinga 47 15.17S 40.16W
Itaqui 45 29.07S 56.33W
Ithaca 44 42.26N 76.30W
Itháki 15 38.23N 20.42E
Ituiutaba 45 19.00S 49.25W
Ituri r. 53 1.45N 27.06E
Ivaí r. 45 23.20S 53.23W
Ivalo r. 18 68.43N 27.36E
Ivanhoe 36 32.56S144.22E
Ivanovo R.S.F.S.R. 20 57.00N 41.00E
Ivigtût 39 61.10N 48.00W
Ivindo 52 0.02S 12.13E
Iviza i. see Ibiza i. 13
Ivory Coast 50 7.00N 5.30W
Izhevsk 20 56.49N 53.11E
Izmail 24 45.20N 28.50E
Izmir 24 38.24N 27.09E
Izmit 21 40.48N 29.55E

J

Jabalón r. 13 38.55N 4.07W
Jabalpur 25 23.10N 79.57E
Jaca 13 42.34N 0.33W
Jackson Mich. 44 42.15N 84.24W
Jackson Miss. 41 32.20N 90.11W
Jacksonville Fla. 41 30.20N 81.40W
Jacques Cartier, Mt. 44 49.00N 65.55W
Jacuí r. 45 29.56S 51.13W
Jaffa, C. 36 36.58S139.39E
Jaffna 25 9.38N 80.02E
Jagdalpur 25 19.04N 82.02E
Jaipur 25 26.53N 75.50E
Jakarta 27 6.08S106.45E
Jalapa 42 19.45N 96.48W
Jalón r. 13 41.47N 1.02W
Jamaica 43 18.00N 77.00W
Jamālpur 25 24.55N 89.56E
James r. S.Dak. 41 42.50N 97.15W
James B. 39 53.00N 80.00W
Jammu 25 32.42N 74.52E
Jammu & Kashmir 25 34.45N 76.00E
Jāmnagar 25 22.28N 70.04E
Jämsänkoski 19 61.55N 25.11E
Jamshedpur 25 22.48N 86.11E
Jándula r. 13 38.08N 4.08W
Janesville 41 42.42N 89.02W
Januária 45 15.28S 44.23W
Japan 26 36.00N136.00E
Japan, Sea of 26 40.00N135.00E
Japurá r. 46 3.00S 64.50W
Jardine r. 34 11.07S142.30E
Järvenpää 19 60.28N 25.06E
Jasper 38 52.55N118.05W
Jataí 45 17.58S 51.45W
Játiva 13 39.00N 0.32W
Jaú 45 22.11S 48.35W
Java i. 27
Java Sea see Jawa, Laut sea 27

Lomami r. 52 0.45N 24.10E
Lomas de Zamora 49 34.46S 58.24W
Lombok i. 27 8.30S116.20E
Lomé 50 6.10N 1.21E
Lomela r. 52 0.14S 20.45E
Lomié 52 3.09N 13.35E
Lomond, Loch 11 56.07N 4.36W
Łomża 17 53.11N 22.04E
London Canada 44 42.59N 81.14W
London U.K. 9 51.32N 0.06W
Londonderry 10 55.00N 7.21W
Londonderry d. 10 55.00N 7.00W
Londonderry, C. 32 13.58S126.55E
Londrina 48 23.30S 51.13W
Long Beach town Calif. 40 33.57N118.15W
Long Eaton 8 52.54N 1.16W
Longford 10 53.44N 7.48W
Longford d. 10 53.42N 7.45W
Long I. 44 40.46N 73.00W
Long L. 44 49.29N 86.44W
Longniddry 11 55.58N 2.53W
Longreach 34 23.26S144.15E
Longtown 8 55.01N 2.58W
Lonsdale, L. 36 37.05S142.15E
Looe 9 50.51N 4.26W
Lookout, C. 41 34.34N 76.34W
Loop Head 10 52.33N 9.56W
Lopari r. 52 1.20N 20.22E
Lopez, C. 52 0.36S 8.40E
Lop Nur l. 26 40.30N 90.30E
Lorain 44 41.28N 82.11W
Loralai 25 30.22N 68.36E
Lorca 13 37.40N 1.41W
Lordsburg 40 32.22N108.43W
Lorient 12 47.45N 3.21W
Lorne 36 38.34S144.01E
Los Angeles 40 34.00N118.17W
Los Blancos 13 37.37N 0.48W
Lossiemouth 11 57.43N 3.18W
Lot r. 12 44.17N 0.22E
Lothian d. 11 55.50N 3.00W
Lotoi r. 52 1.30S 18.30E
Lotsani r. 54 22.42S 28.11E
Louangphrabang 26 19.53N102.10E
Loubomo 52 4.09S 12.40E
Loudéac 12 48.11N 2.45W
Loudima 52 4.06S 13.05E
Loughborough 8 52.47N 1.11W
Loughrea 10 53.12N 8.35W
Loughros More B. 10 54.48N 8.32W
Louisburgh 10 53.46N 9.49W
Louisiana d. 41 31.00N 92.30W
Louis Trichardt 54 23.03S 29.54E
Louisville Ky. 44 38.13N 85.48W
Lourdes 12 43.06N 0.02W
Louth d. 10 53.55N 6.30W
Louth 8 53.23N 0.00
Lovat r. 20 58.06N 31.37E
Lovech 15 43.08N 24.44E
Lovoi r. 53 8.14S 26.40E
Lovua r. 52 6.08S 20.35E
Lowa r. Kivu 52 1.25S 25.55E
Lowell 44 42.39N 71.18W
Lower Hutt 29 41.13S174.55E
Lower Lough Erne 10 54.28N 7.48W
Lowestoft 9 52.29N 1.44E
Łowicz 17 52.06N 19.55E
Loxton 36 34.38S140.38E
Loyauté, Îles is. 30 21.00S167.00E
Luachimo r. 52 6.32S 20.57E
Luama r. 53 4.45S 26.55E
Luanda 52 8.50S 13.20E
Luanginga r. 52 15.11S 23.05E
Luangwa r. Central 53 15.32S 30.28E
Luanshya 53 13.09S 28.24E
Luapula r. 53 9.25S 28.36E
Luarca 13 43.33N 6.31W
Luau 52 10.41S 22.09E
Lubango 52 14.52S 13.30E
Lubao 52 5.19S 25.43E
Lubbock 40 33.35N101.53W
Lübeck 16 53.52N 10.40E
Lubefu r. 52 4.05S 23.00E
Lubilash r. 52 4.59S 23.25E
Lublin 17 51.18N 22.31E
Lubudi 52 9.57S 25.59E
Lubudi r. K.Occidental 52 4.00S 21.23E
Lubudi r. Shaba 52 9.13S 25.40E
Lubumbashi 53 11.44S 27.29E
Lubutu 52 0.48S 26.19E
Luce B. 11 54.45N 4.47W
Lucena 13 37.25N 4.29W
Lučenec 17 48.20N 19.40E
Lucero 42 30.50N106.30W
Luckenwalde 16 52.05N 13.11E
Lucknow 25 26.51N 80.55E
Lüda see Dalian 26
Lüderitz 54 26.37S 15.09E
Ludhiāna 25 30.55N 75.51E
Ludington 44 43.58N 86.27W
Ludlow 9 52.23N 2.42W
Ludvika 19 60.09N 15.11E
Ludwigshafen 16 49.29N 8.27E
Luebo 52 5.16S 21.27E
Luengue r. 52 16.58S 21.15E
Lufeng 26 23.01N115.35E
Lufira r. 52 8.15S 26.30E
Lufkin 41 31.21N 94.47W
Luga 20 58.42N 29.49E
Lugano 12 46.01N 8.57E
Lugansk 21 48.35N 39.20E
Lugenda r. 53 11.23S 38.30E
Lugnaquilla Mtn. 10 52.58N 6.28W
Lugo 13 43.00N 7.33W
Lugoj 17 45.42N 21.56E
Luiana r. 52 17.28S 23.02E
Luilaka r. 52 0.15S 19.00E
Luilu r. 52 6.22S 23.53E
Luiro r. 18 67.18N 27.28E
Luisa 52 7.15S 22.27E
Lukala 52 5.23S 13.02E
Lukanga Swamp f. 53 14.15S 27.30E
Lukenie r. 52 2.43S 18.12E
Lukuga r. 53 5.37S 26.58E
Lukula r. 52 4.15S 17.59E
Luleå 18 65.34N 22.10E
Lulonga r. 52 0.42N 18.26E
Lulua r. 52 5.03S 21.07E
Lumsden 29 45.44S168.26E
Lund 19 55.42N 13.11E
Lundazi 53 12.19S 33.11E
Lundi r. 54 21.20S 32.23E
Lundy i. 9 51.10N 4.41W
Lune r. 8 54.03N 2.49W
Lüneburg 16 53.15N 10.24E
Lunga r. 52 14.28S 26.27E
Lungwebungu r. 52 14.20S 23.15E
Luofo 53 0.12S 29.15E
Luoyang 26 34.48N112.25E
Lurgan 10 54.28N 6.21W
Lurio 53 13.30S 40.30E
Lurio r. 53 13.32S 40.31E
Lusaka 53 15.20S 28.14E
Lusambo 52 4.59S 23.26E
Lushoto 53 4.48S 38.20E
Lusk 40 42.47N104.26W
Luton 9 51.53N 0.25W
Lutsk 17 50.42N 25.15E
Lutterworth 9 52.28N 1.12W
Luuq 53 3.56N 42.32E
Luvua r. 53 6.45S 27.00E
Luwegu r. 53 8.30S 37.28E
Luwingu 53 10.13S 30.05E
Luxembourg 16 49.50N 6.15E
Luxembourg town 16 49.37N 6.08E
Luxor see Al Uqṣur 51
Luzern 16 47.03N 8.17E
Luzhou 26 28.48N105.23E
Luziânia 47 16.18S 47.57W
Luzon i. 27 17.50N121.00E
Lvov 17 49.50N 24.00E
Lybster 11 58.18N 3.18W
Lycksele 18 64.36N 18.40E
Lydenburg 54 25.06S 30.27E
Lyme B. 9 50.40N 2.55W
Lyme Regis 9 50.44N 2.57W
Lymington 9 50.46N 1.32W
Lyndhurst 36 30.19S138.24E
Lynn 44 42.28N 70.57W
Lynn Lake town 39 56.51N101.01W
Lynton 9 51.14N 3.50W
Lyon 12 45.46N 4.50E
Lyons r. 32 25.02S115.09E
Lysekil 19 58.16N 11.26E
Lytham St. Anne's 8 53.45N 3.01W
Lyubertsy 20 55.38N 37.58E

M

Maamakeogh mtn. 10 54.17N 9.29W
Maamturk Mts. 10 53.32N 9.42W
Ma'ān 24 30.11N 35.43E
Maas r. 16 51.44N 4.42E
Maastricht 16 50.51N 5.42E
Mablethorpe 8 53.21N 0.14E
Macalister r. 37 37.55S146.50E
Macapá 47 0.04N 51.04W
Macau 26 22.11N113.33E
Macclesfield 8 53.16N 2.09W
Macdonald, L. 32 23.30S129.00E
Macdonnell Ranges mts. 34 23.45S133.20E
Macduff 11 57.40N 2.29W
Macedon, Mt. 37 37.27S144.34E
Maceió 47 9.40S 35.44W
Macerata 14 43.18N 13.30E
Macfarlane, L. 36 31.55S136.42E
Macgillycuddy's Reeks mts. 10 52.00N 9.43W
Machattie, L. 34 24.50S139.48E
Macheke 54 18.08S 31.49E
Machrihanish 11 55.25N 5.44W
Machynlleth 9 52.35N 3.51W
Macintyre r. 37 28.50S150.50E
Mackay, L. 32 22.30S129.10E
Mackenzie r. Australia 34 22.48S149.15E
Mackenzie r. Canada 38 69.20N134.00W
Mackenzie Mts. 38 64.00N130.00W
Mackinnon Road town 53 3.50S 39.03E
Maclear 54 31.04S 28.21E
Macleay r. 37 30.52S153.01E
Macomer 14 40.16N 8.45E
Mâcon 12 46.18N 4.50E
Macon Ga. 41 32.47N 83.37W
Macquarie r. 37 30.07S147.24E
Macquarie Marshes 37 30.50S147.32E
Macroom 10 51.54N 8.58W
Macumba r. 35 27.55S137.15E
Madagascar 53 17.00S 46.00E
Madawaska 44 47.21N 68.20W
Madeira i. 50 32.45N 17.00W
Madeira r. 46 3.20S 59.00W
Madeira, Arquipélago da is. 50 32.40N 16.45W
Madeleine, Îles de la is. 39 47.30N 61.45W
Madhya Pradesh d. 25 23.30N 78.30E
Madison Wisc. 41 43.04N 89.22W
Mado Gashi 53 0.40N 39.11E
Madras 25 13.05N 80.18E
Madre del Sur, Sierra mts. 42 17.00N100.00W
Madrid 13 40.25N 3.43W
Madukani 53 3.57S 35.49E
Madura i. 27 7.02S113.22E
Madurai 25 9.55N 78.07E
Maestra, Sierra mts. 43 20.10N 76.30W
Mafeteng 54 29.51S 27.13E
Mafia I. 53 7.50S 39.50E
Mafikeng 54 25.52S 25.36E
Magadi 53 1.53S 36.18E
Magallanes, Estrecho de str. 49 53.00S 71.00W
Magalluf 13 39.30N 2.31E
Magangué 46 9.14N 74.46W
Magdalena r. 46 10.56N 74.58W
Magdeburg 16 52.08N 11.36E
Magellan's Str. see Magallanes, Estrecho de str. 49
Mageröya i. 18 71.03N 25.45E
Maggiore, Lago l. 14 46.00N 8.40E
Magherafelt 10 54.45N 6.38W
Magnetic I. 34 19.08S146.50E
Magnitogorsk 20 53.28N 59.06E
Magué 53 15.46S 31.42E
Mahadday Weyne 53 2.58N 45.32E
Mahagi 53 2.16N 30.59E
Mahalapye 54 23.04S 26.47E
Mahārāshtra d. 25 19.40N 76.00E
Mahdia 46 5.10N 59.12W
Mahia Pen. 29 39.10S177.50E
Mahón 13 39.55N 4.18E
Maidenhead 9 51.32N 0.44W
Maidstone 9 51.17N 0.32E
Maiduguri 50 11.53N 13.16E
Maiko r. 52 0.15N 25.35E
Main r. 16 50.00N 8.19E
Mai Ndombe l. 52 2.00S 18.20E
Maine d. 44 45.15N 69.15W
Mainland i. Orkney Is. 11 59.00N 3.10W
Mainz 16 50.00N 8.16E
Maípo mtn. 49 34.10S 69.50W
Maitland N.S.W. 37 32.33S151.33E
Majene 27 3.33S118.59E
Majorca i. see Mallorca i. 13
Majuba Hill 54 27.26S 29.48E
Makasar, Selat str. 27 3.00S118.00E
Makeyevka 21 48.01N 38.00E
Makgadikgadi Salt Pan f. 54 20.50S 25.45E
Makhachkala 21 42.59N 47.30E
Makkah 24 21.26N 39.49E
Makó 17 46.13N 20.30E
Makran f. 24 26.30N 61.20E
Makurdi 50 7.44N 8.35E
Malabo 52 3.45N 8.48E
Malacca, Str. of 27 3.00N100.30E
Málaga 13 36.43N 4.25W
Malakāl 51 9.31N 31.40E
Malakand 25 34.34N 71.56E
Malanje 52 9.36S 16.21E
Mälaren l. 19 59.30N 17.12E
Malatya 21 38.22N 38.18E
Malawi 53 12.00S 34.00E
Malawi, L. 53 12.00S 34.30E
Malaysia 27 5.00N110.00E
Malbork 17 54.02N 19.01E
Maldives 24 6.20N 73.00E
Maldon 9 51.43N 0.41E
Maldonado 45 34.57S 54.59W
Maléa, Ákra c. 15 36.27N 23.11E
Malebo Pool f. 52 4.15S 15.25E
Malema 53 14.55S 37.09E
Mali 50 16.00N 3.00W
Malindi 53 3.14S 40.08E
Malin Head 10 55.23N 7.24W
Malin More 10 54.42N 8.48W
Mallacoota Inlet b. 37 37.34S149.43E
Mallaig 11 57.00N 5.50W
Mallorca i. 13 39.35N 3.00E
Mallow 10 52.08N 8.39W
Malmesbury 54 33.28S 18.43E
Malmö 19 55.36N 13.00E
Malone 44 44.51N 74.17W
Malonga 52 10.26S 23.10E
Malpas 36 34.44S140.43E
Malta 14 35.55N 14.25E
Maltby 8 53.25N 1.12W
Malton 8 54.09N 0.48W
Mambasa 53 1.20N 29.05E
Mambilima Falls town 53 10.32S 28.45E
Mamore r. 48 12.00S 65.15W
Mamuju 27 2.21S118.55E
Man 50 7.31N 7.37W
Man, Isle of 8 54.15N 4.30W
Manacor 13 39.32N 3.12E
Manado 27 1.30N124.58E
Managua 43 12.06N 86.18W
Managua, Lago de l. 43 12.10N 86.30W
Manapouri, L. 29 45.30S167.00E
Manaus 46 3.06S 60.00W
Manchester 8 53.30N 2.15W
Manchurian Plain f. see Dongbei Pingyuan f. 26
Mandal 19 58.02N 7.27E
Mandalay 26 21.58N 96.04E
Mandalgovi 26 45.40N106.10E
Mandeb, Bāb el str. 24 13.00N 43.10E
Mandurah 33 32.31S115.41E
Manfredonia, Golfo di g. 14 41.35N 16.05E
Mangalia 17 43.50N 28.35E
Mangalore 25 12.54N 74.51E
Mangaweka 29 39.49S175.48E
Mangnai 26 37.52N 91.26E
Mango 50 10.23N 0.30E
Mangochi 53 14.29S 35.15E
Manhiça 54 25.24S 32.49E
Maniamba 53 12.30S 35.05E
Manica 54 19.00S 33.00E
Manila 27 14.36N120.59E
Manildra 37 33.12S148.41E
Manipur d. 25 25.00N 93.40E
Manisa 15 38.37N 27.28E
Manistee r. 44 44.14N 86.20W
Manitoba d. 39 54.00N 96.00W
Manitoba, L. 39 51.35N 99.00W
Manitoulin I. 44 45.45N 82.30W
Manizales 46 5.03N 75.32W
Manjimup 33 34.14S116.06E
Manly 37 33.47S151.17E
Mann r. 34 12.20S134.07E
Mannahill 36 32.26S139.59E
Mannar, G. of 25 8.20N 79.00E
Mannheim 16 49.30N 8.28E
Mannin B. 10 53.28N 10.06W
Mannum 36 34.50S139.20E
Manokwari 27 0.53S134.05E
Manono 53 7.18S 27.24E
Manorhamilton 10 54.18N 8.10W
Manresa 13 41.43N 1.50E
Mansa 53 11.10S 28.52E
Mansel I. 39 62.00N 80.00W
Mansfield 8 53.08N 1.12W
Mantova 14 45.09N 10.47E
Mänttä 19 62.02N 24.38E
Manukau Harbour est. 29 37.10S174.00E
Manus i. 30 2.05S147.00E
Manyara, L. 53 3.40S 35.50E
Manych r. 21 47.14N 40.20E
Manyinga r. 52 13.28S 24.25E
Manyoni 53 5.46S 34.50E
Manzanares 13 39.00N 3.23W
Manzanillo 43 20.21N 77.21W
Manzhouli 26 49.36N117.28E
Manzini 54 26.29S 31.24E
Maoke, Pegunungan mts. 27 4.00S137.30E
Maoming 26 21.50N110.58E
Mapai 54 22.51S 32.00E
Mapi 27 7.06S139.23E
Maputo 54 25.58S 32.35E
Maquela do Zombo 52 6.06S 15.12E
Mar, Serra do mts. 45 23.00S 44.40W
Mara r. 53 1.30S 33.52E
Maracaibo 46 10.44N 71.37W
Maracaju, Serra de mts. 45 21.38S 55.10W
Maracay 46 10.20N 67.28W
Maradi 50 13.29N 7.10E
Marahuaca, Cerro mtn. 46 3.37N 65.25W
Marajó, Ilha de i. 47 1.00S 49.40W
Maralal 53 1.15N 36.48E
Maramba 52 17.40S 25.50E
Maranoa r. 35 27.55S148.30E
Marão 54 24.21S 34.07E
Marathón 15 38.10N 23.59E
Marbella 13 36.31N 4.53W
Marble Bar 32 21.16S119.45E
Marburg 16 50.49N 8.36E
March 9 52.33N 0.05E
Mar Chiquita l. 48 30.42S 62.36W
Mardān 25 34.12N 72.02E
Mar del Plata 49 38.00S 57.32W
Marden 9 51.11N 0.30E
Mardie 32 21.14S115.57E
Mardin 21 37.19N 40.43E
Maree, Loch 11 57.41N 5.28W
Mareeba 34 17.00S145.26E
Marettimo i. 14 37.58N 12.05E
Margaret r. 36 29.26S137.00E
Margarita, Isla de i. 46 11.00N 64.00W
Margate 9 51.23N 1.24E
Maria I. 34 14.52S135.40E
Marianao 43 23.03N 82.29W
Marie-Galante i. 43 15.54N 61.11W
Mariental 54 24.38S 17.58E
Mariestad 19 58.43N 13.51E
Marília 45 22.13S 50.20W
Maringá 45 23.36S 52.02W
Maringa r. 52 1.13N 19.50E
Maringue 54 17.55S 34.24E
Marinha Grande 13 39.45N 8.55W
Mariscal Estigarribia 45 22.03S 60.35W
Maritsa r. 15 41.00N 26.15E
Mariupol' 21 47.05N 37.34E
Market Drayton 8 52.55N 2.30W
Market Harborough 9 52.29N 0.55W
Market Rasen 8 53.24N 0.20W
Market Weighton 8 53.52N 0.04W
Markha r. 23 63.37N119.00E
Marlborough 9 51.26N 1.44W
Marmara i. 15 40.38N 27.37E
Marmara, Sea of see Marmara Denizi sea 15
Marmara Denizi sea 15 40.45N 28.15E
Marmaris 15 36.50N 28.17E
Marne r. 12 48.50N 2.25E
Marnoo 36 36.40S142.55E
Maroua 50 10.35N 14.20E
Marquard 54 28.39S 27.25E
Marquesas Is. see Marquises, Îles is. 31
Marquises, Îles is. 31 9.00S139.30W
Marra r. 37 30.05S147.05E
Marrakech 50 31.49N 8.00W
Marree 36 29.40S138.04E
Marrupa 53 13.10S 37.30E
Marsabit 53 2.20N 37.59E
Marsala 14 37.48N 12.27E
Marsden 37 33.46S147.35E
Marseille 12 43.18N 5.22E
Marshall Tex. 41 32.33N 94.22W
Marshall Is. 30 10.00N172.00E
Martaban, G. of 27 15.10N 96.30E
Martés, Sierra mts. 13 39.10N 1.00W
Martha's Vineyard i. 44 41.25N 70.40W
Martigny 16 46.07N 7.05E
Martinique i. 43 14.40N 61.00W
Martin Pt. 38 70.10N143.50W
Marton 29 40.04S175.25E
Maryland d. 44 39.00N 76.45W
Maryport 8 54.43N 3.30W
Masai Steppe f. 53 4.30S 37.00E
Masaka 53 0.20S 31.46E
Masasi 53 10.43S 38.48E
Masbate i. 27 12.00N123.30E
Maseru 54 29.18S 27.28E
Mashhad 24 36.16N 59.34E
Mashonaland f. 54 18.20S 32.00E
Masi-Manimba 52 4.47S 17.54E
Masindi 53 1.41N 31.45E
Maṣīrah i. 24 20.30N 58.50E
Mask, Lough 10 53.38N 9.22W
Mason City 41 43.10N 93.10W
Masqaṭ 24 23.36N 58.37E
Massachusetts d. 44 42.15N 71.50W
Massangena 54 21.31S 33.03E
Massif Central mts. 12 45.00N 3.30E
Massinga 54 23.20S 35.25E
Masterton 29 40.57S175.39E
Masvingo 54 20.10S 30.49E
Matabeleland f. 54 19.50S 28.15E
Matadi 52 5.50S 13.36E
Matagorda B. 41 28.30N 96.20W
Matakana I. 29 37.35S176.15E
Matam 50 15.40N 13.15W
Matamata 29 37.49S175.46E
Matamoros Tamaulipas 42 25.50N 97.31W
Matandu r. 53 8.44S 39.22E
Matanzas 43 23.04N 81.35W
Mataura r. 29 46.34S168.45E
Matawai 29 38.21S177.32E
Matehuala 42 23.40N100.40W
Matlock 8 53.09N 1.32W
Mato Grosso town 48 15.05S 59.57W
Mato Grosso, Planalto do f. 48 16.00S 54.00W
Matope 53 15.20S 34.57E
Matopo Hills 54 20.45S 28.30E
Matsue 26 35.29N133.00E
Matsusaka 28 34.34N136.32E
Matsuyama 26 33.50N132.47E
Mattagami r. 44 50.43N 81.29W
Matterhorn mtn. 12 45.58N 7.38E
Maude 36 34.27S144.21E
Maui i. Hawaii 40 20.45N156.15W
Maumere 27 8.35S122.13E
Maun 54 19.52S 23.40E
Mauna Loa mtn. 31 19.29N155.36W
Mauritania 50 20.00N 10.00W
Mavinga 52 15.47S 20.21E
Mawlaik 26 23.50N 94.30E
Maya i. 27 1.09S109.45E
Maya 13 43.12N 1.29W
Mayaguana I. 43 22.30N 73.00W
Mayagüez 43 18.13N 67.09W
Maya Mts. 43 16.30N 89.00W
Maybole 11 55.21N 4.41W
Maydena 35 42.45S146.38E
Mayenne 12 48.18N 0.37W
Mayenne r. 12 47.30N 0.37W
Maykop 21 44.37N 40.48E
Mayo d. 10 53.47N 9.07W
Mayo, Plains of f. 10 53.46N 9.05W
Mayo Landing 38 63.45N135.45W
Mayor I. 29 37.15S176.15E
Mayotte, Île i. 53 12.50S 45.10E
Mayumba 52 3.23S 10.38E
Mazabuka 53 15.50S 27.47E
Mazatenango 42 14.31N 91.30W
Mazatlán 42 23.11N106.25W
Mažeikiai 19 56.19N 22.20E
Mazowe r. 54 16.32S 33.25E
Mazowe 54 17.30S 30.58E
Mbabane 54 26.19S 31.08E
M'Baiki 52 3.53N 18.01E
Mbala 53 8.50S 31.24E
Mbale 53 1.04N 34.12E
Mbanza Congo 52 6.18S 14.16E
Mbarara 53 0.36S 30.40E
Mbeya 53 8.54S 33.29E
Mbinda 52 2.11S 12.55E
M'bridge r. 52 7.12S 12.55E
Mbuji Mayi 52 6.08S 23.39E
Mbulamuti 53 0.50N 33.05E
McArthur r. 34 15.54S136.40E
McClintock Channel 39 71.20N102.00W
McClure Str. 38 74.30N116.00W
McConaughy, L. 40 41.20N102.00W
McCook 40 40.15N100.45W
McGrath 38 62.58N155.40W
Mchinja 53 9.44S 39.45E
Mchinji 53 13.48S 32.55E
McIlwraith Range mts. 34 14.00S143.10E
McKeesport 44 40.21N 79.52W
McKinley, Mt. 38 63.00N151.00W
McPherson Range mts. 37 28.15S153.00E
Meath d. 10 53.32N 6.40W
Meaux 12 48.58N 2.54E
Mecca see Makkah 24
Meconta 53 15.00S 39.50E
Medan 27 3.35N 98.39E
Mededsiz mtn. 21 37.33N 34.38E
Medellín 46 6.15N 75.36W
Médenine 50 33.24N 10.25E
Mederdra 50 16.55N 15.39W
Medford Oreg. 40 42.20N122.52W
Medicine Hat 38 50.03N110.41W
Medina see Al Madīnah 24
Medina del Campo 13 41.20N 4.55W
Medina de Rioseco 13 41.53N 5.03W
Mediterranean Sea 50 37.00N 15.00E
Medvedītsa r. 21 49.35N 42.45E
Medway r. 9 51.24N 0.31E
Meekatharra 32 26.35S118.30E
Meerut 25 28.59N 77.42E
Mégara 15 38.00N 23.21E
Meghalaya d. 25 25.30N 91.00E
Meiktila 26 20.53N 95.50E
Meiningen 16 50.34N 10.25E
Meissen 16 51.10N 13.28E
Meknès 50 33.53N 5.37W
Mekong r. 27 10.00N106.40E
Melanesia is. 30 5.00N165.00E
Melbourne 37 37.45S144.58E
Melfi 14 40.59N 15.39E
Melilla 13 35.17N 2.57W
Melitopol 21 46.51N 35.22E
Mellerud 19 58.42N 12.28E
Melmore Pt. 10 55.15N 7.49W
Melo 45 32.22S 54.10W
Melrose 11 55.36N 2.43W
Melton Mowbray 8 52.46N 0.53W
Melun 12 48.32N 2.40E
Melvich 11 58.33N 3.55W
Melville B. 34 12.10S136.32E
Melville I. 34 11.30S131.00E
Melville Pen. 39 68.00N 84.00W
Melvin, Lough 10 54.26N 8.12W
Memba 53 14.16S 40.30E
Memmingen 16 47.59N 10.11E
Memphis Tenn. 41 35.05N 90.00W
Menai Str. 8 53.17N 4.20W
Mendawai r. 27 3.17S113.20E
Mende 12 44.32N 3.30E
Mendip Hills 9 51.15N 2.40W
Mendocino, C. 40 40.26N124.24W
Mendoza 49 32.54S 68.50W
Menindee 36 32.23S142.30E
Menongue 52 14.40S 17.41E
Menorca i. 13 40.00N 4.00E
Mentawai, Kepulauan is. 27 2.50S 99.00E
Menton 12 43.47N 7.30E
Menzies 33 29.41S121.02E
Meppel 16 52.42N 6.12E
Meppen 16 52.41N 7.17E
Merano 14 46.41N 11.10E
Merauke 27 8.30S140.22E
Merbein 36 34.11S142.04E
Merced 40 37.17N120.29W
Mere 9 51.05N 2.16W
Meredith 36 37.50S144.05E
Mergui 27 12.26N 98.38E
Mergui Archipelago is. 27 11.15N 98.00E
Meribah 36 34.42S140.53E
Mérida 43 20.59N 89.39W
Meridian 41 32.21N 88.42W
Merino 36 37.45S141.35E
Merrick mtn. 11 55.08N 4.29W
Mersea I. 9 51.47N 0.58E
Merseburg 16 51.22N 12.00E
Mersey r. 8 53.22N 2.37W
Merseyside d. 8 53.28N 3.00W
Mersin 21 36.47N 34.37E
Mersing 27 2.25N103.50E
Merthyr Tydfil 9 51.45N 3.23W
Merton 9 51.25N 0.12W
Meru mtn. 53 3.15S 36.44E
Merzifon 21 40.52N 35.28E
Mesolóngion 15 38.23N 21.23E
Mesopotamia f. 24 33.30N 44.30E
Messalo r. 53 11.38S 40.27E
Messina 14 38.13N 15.34E
Messíni 15 37.03N 22.00E
Messiniakós, Kólpos g. 15 36.50N 22.05E
Mesta r. Bulgaria see Néstos r. 15
Meta r. 46 6.10N 67.30W
Metković 15 43.03N 17.38E
Metz 12 49.07N 6.11E
Meuse r. Belgium see Maas r. 16
Mexicali 42 32.26N115.30W
Mexico 42 20.00N100.00W
Mexico, G. of 42 25.00N 90.00W
Mexico City see Ciudad de México 42
Mezen r. 20 65.50N 44.18E
Miami Fla. 41 25.45N 80.10W
Mianyang Sichuan 26 31.26N104.45E
Miass 22 55.00N 60.00E
Michigan d. 44 44.00N 85.00W
Michigan, L. 44 44.00N 87.00W
Michigan City 44 41.43N 86.54W
Michurinsk 20 52.54N 40.30E
Micronesia is. 30 8.00N160.00E
Middle I. 33 34.07S123.12E
Middlesbrough 8 54.34N 1.13W
Middletown Ind. 44 39.31N 84.13W
Mid Glamorgan d. 9 51.38N 3.25W
Midland Mich. 44 43.38N 84.14W
Midleton 10 51.55N 8.10W
Midway Is. 30 28.15N177.25W
Midye 15 41.37N 28.07E
Mieres 13 43.15N 5.46W
Mijares r. 13 39.58N 0.01W
Mikhaylovka 21 50.05N 43.15E
Miki 28 34.48N134.59E
Mikindani 53 10.16S 40.05E
Mikkeli 20 61.44N 27.15E
Míkonos i. 15 37.29N 25.25E
Mikumi 53 7.22S 37.00E
Milan see Milano 14
Milange 53 16.09S 35.44E
Milano 14 45.28N 9.10E
Milâs 24 37.18N 27.48E
Mildenhall 9 52.20N 0.30E
Mildura 36 34.14S142.13E
Miles City 40 46.24N105.48W
Milford Haven town 9 51.43N 5.02W
Milford Sound town 29 44.41S167.56E
Miling 33 30.27S116.20E
Milk r. 40 47.55N106.15W
Millau 12 44.06N 3.05E
Miller r. 36 30.05S136.07E
Millerovo 21 48.55N 40.25E
Milleur Pt. 11 55.01N 5.07W
Millicent 36 37.36S140.22E
Millmerran 35 27.51S151.17E
Millom 8 54.13N 3.16W
Mílos i. 15 36.40N 24.26E
Milparinka 36 29.45S141.55E
Milton Keynes 9 52.03N 0.42W
Milwaukee 41 43.03N 87.56W
Minas 49 34.23S 55.14W
Minatitlán 42 17.59N 94.32W
Mindanao i. 27 7.30N125.00E
Mindarie 36 34.51S140.12E
Minden 16 52.18N 8.54E
Mindoro i. 27 13.00N121.00E
Mindra mtn. 17 45.20N 23.32E
Minehead 9 51.12N 3.29W
Minerva 34 24.00S148.05E
Mingary 36 32.09S140.46E
Mingela 34 19.53S146.40E
Mingenew 33 29.11S115.26E
Minigwal, L. 33 29.35S123.12E
Minneapolis 41 45.00N 93.15W
Minnesota d. 41 46.00N 95.00W
Minnipa 36 32.51S135.09E
Miño r. 13 41.50N 8.52W
Minorca i. see Menorca i. 13
Minsk 17 53.51N 27.30E
Miranda de Ebro 13 42.41N 2.57W
Miranda do Douro 13 41.30N 6.16W
Mirande 12 43.31N 0.25E
Mirandela 13 41.28N 7.10W
Mirecourt 12 48.18N 6.08E
Miriam Vale town 34 24.20S151.34E
Mirim, L. 45 33.10S 53.30W
Mīrpur Khās 25 25.33N 69.05E
Mirzāpur 25 25.09N 82.35E
Misool i. 27 1.50S130.10E
Mississippi d. 41 33.00N 90.00W
Mississippi r. 41 28.55N 89.05W
Missoula 40 46.52N114.00W
Missouri d. 41 39.00N 93.00W
Missouri r. 41 38.40N 90.20W
Mistassini, Lac l. 44 51.15N 73.10W
Mitchell r. Qld. 34 15.12S141.35E
Mitchell r. Vic. 37 37.53S147.41E
Mitchell, Mt. 41 35.57N 82.16W
Mitchelstown 10 52.16N 8.17W
Mittagong 37 34.27S150.25E
Mitumba, Monts mts. 53 3.00S 28.30E
Mitwaba 53 8.32S 27.20E
Mitzic 52 0.48N 11.30E
Miyakonojō 26 31.43N131.02E
Mizen Head 10 51.27N 9.50W
Mizoram d. 25 23.40N 92.40E
Mjölby 19 58.19N 15.08E
Mjösa l. 19 60.40N 11.00E
Mkushi 53 13.40S 29.26E
Mladá Boleslav 16 50.26N 14.55E
Mljet i. 15 42.45N 17.30E
Moamba 54 25.35S 32.13E
Moanda 52 1.25S 13.18E
Moatize 53 16.10S 33.40E
Moba 53 7.03S 29.42E
Mobile 41 30.40N 88.05W
Mobridge 40 45.31N100.25W
Moçambique town 53 15.00S 40.47E
Mocimboa da Praia 53 11.19S 40.19E
Mocuba 53 16.52S 37.02E
Modane 12 45.12N 6.40E
Modder r. 54 29.03S 23.56E
Modena 14 44.39N 10.55E
Modica 14 36.51N 14.51E
Moffat 11 55.20N 3.27W
Mogadishu see Muqdisho 53
Mogilev 17 53.54N 30.20E
Mogincual 53 15.33S 40.29E
Mogok 25 23.00N 96.30E
Mohoro 53 8.09S 39.10E
Mo-i-Rana 18 66.19N 14.10E
Moisie r. 39 50.13N 66.02W
Moissac 12 44.07N 1.05E
Mokp'o 26 34.50N126.25E
Mold 8 53.10N 3.08W
Molde 18 62.44N 7.08E
Molepolole 54 24.26S 25.34E
Molfetta 15 41.12N 16.36E
Molina de Aragón 13 40.50N 1.54W
Moline 41 41.31N 90.26W
Moliro 53 8.11S 30.29E
Mölndal 19 57.39N 12.01E
Molodechno 17 54.16N 26.50E
Molokai i. Hawaii 40 21.20N157.00W
Molopo r. 54 28.30S 20.22E
Molteno 54 31.23S 26.21E
Moluccas is. 27 4.00S128.00E
Moma 53 16.40S 39.10E
Mombasa 53 4.04S 39.40E
Mön i. 19 55.00N 12.20E
Mona i. 43 18.06N 67.54W
Monaco 12 43.40N 7.25E
Monadhliath Mts. 11 57.09N 4.08W
Monaghan 10 54.15N 6.58W
Monaghan d. 10 54.10N 7.00W
Monchegorsk 20 67.55N 33.01E
Mönchen-Gladbach 16 51.12N 6.25E
Monclova 42 26.55N101.20W
Moncton 39 46.06N 64.50W
Mondovì 14 44.24N 7.50E
Monforte 13 42.32N 7.30W
Monga 51 4.05N 22.56E
Mongala r. 52 1.58N 19.55E
Mongolia 26 46.30N104.00E
Mongu 52 15.10S 23.09E
Monifieth 11 56.29N 2.50W
Monkoto 52 1.39S 20.41E
Monmouth 9 51.48N 2.43W
Monroe La. 41 32.31N 92.06W
Monrovia 50 6.20N 10.46W
Mons 16 50.27N 3.57E
Montana d. 40 47.00N110.00W
Montargis 12 48.00N 2.44E
Montauban 12 44.01N 1.20E
Montbrison 12 45.37N 4.04E
Mont Cenis, Col du pass 12 45.15N 6.55E
Mont de Marsan town 12 43.54N 0.30W
Monte Azul town 45 15.53S 42.53W
Monte Carlo 12 43.44N 7.25E
Montecristo i. 14 42.20N 10.19E
Montego Bay town 43 18.27N 77.56W
Montélimar 12 44.33N 4.45E
Monterey B. 40 36.45N122.00W
Montería 46 8.45N 75.54W
Montero 48 17.20S 63.15W
Monterrey 42 25.40N100.20W
Monte Santu, Capo di c. 14 40.05N 9.44E
Montes Claros 45 16.45S 43.52W
Montevideo 49 34.53S 56.11W
Montgomery Ala. 41 32.22N 86.20W
Montijo 13 38.42N 8.59W
Montluçon 12 46.20N 2.36E
Montmagny 44 46.56N 70.28W
Montmédy 12 49.31N 5.21E
Montmorillon 12 46.26N 0.52E
Montoro 13 38.02N 4.23W
Montpellier 12 43.36N 3.53E
Montreal 44 45.30N 73.36W
Montreal r. 44 47.14N 84.39W
Montrejeau 12 43.05N 0.33E
Montreuil 12 50.28N 1.46E
Montreux 16 46.27N 6.55E
Montrose 11 56.43N 2.29W
Montserrat i. 43 16.45N 62.14W
Montserrat, Serra de mts. 13 41.20N 1.00E
Monywa 26 22.05N 95.15E
Monza 14 45.35N 9.16E
Monze 53 16.16S 27.28E
Monzón 13 41.52N 0.10E
Moora 33 30.40S116.01E
Moore, L. 33 29.30S117.30E
Moorfoot Hills 11 55.43N 3.03W
Moorhead 41 46.51N 96.44W
Moosehead L. 44 45.40N 69.40W
Moose Jaw 38 50.23N105.35W
Mootwingee 36 31.52S141.14E
Mopti 50 14.29N 4.10W
Morādābād 25 28.50N 78.47E
Moralana 36 31.42S138.12E
Morar, Loch 11 56.56N 5.40W
Moray Firth est. 11 57.35N 5.15W
Morecambe 8 54.03N 2.52W
Morelia 42 19.40N101.11W
Morella 13 40.37N 0.06W
Morena, Sierra mts. 13 38.10N 5.00W
Moreton I. 35 27.10S153.25E
Morez 12 46.31N 6.02E
Morgan 36 34.02S139.40E
Morgan City 41 29.41N 91.13W
Morlaix 12 48.35N 3.50W
Mornington I. 34 16.33S139.24E
Morocco 50 31.00N 5.00W
Morogoro 53 6.47S 37.40E
Moroni 53 11.40S 43.19E
Morotai i. 27 2.10N128.30E
Moroto 53 2.32N 34.41E
Morpeth 8 55.10N 1.40W
Morrinsville 29 37.39S175.32E
Mortagne 12 48.32N 0.33E
Mortlake town 36 38.05S142.48E
Morundah 37 34.56S146.18E
Morven 34 26.25S147.05E
Morvern f. 11 56.37N 5.45W
Moscow see Moskva 20
Mosel r. 16 50.23N 7.37E
Mosgiel 29 45.53S170.22E
Moshi 53 3.20S 37.21E
Mosjöen 18 65.50N 13.10E
Moskva 20 55.45N 37.42E
Moskva r. 20 55.08N 38.50E
Mosquitos, Costa de f. 43 13.00N 84.00W
Moss 19 59.26N 10.42E
Mossaka 52 1.20S 16.44E
Mossburn 29 45.41S168.15E
Mossgiel 37 33.18S144.05E
Mossman 34 16.28S145.22E
Mossoró 47 5.10S 37.18W
Most 16 50.31N 13.39E
Mostar 15 43.20N 17.50E
Motagua r. 43 15.56N 87.45W
Motala 19 58.33N 15.03E
Motherwell 11 55.48N 4.00W
Mouila 52 1.50S 11.02E
Moulamein 36 35.03S144.05E
Moulins 12 46.34N 3.20E
Moulmein 27 16.55N 97.49E
Moundou 50 8.34N 16.05E
Mountain Ash 9 51.42N 3.22W
Mount Barker town W.A. 33 34.36S117.37E
Mount Bellew town 10 53.28N 8.30W
Mount Darwin town 53 16.46S 31.36E
Mount Eba town 36 30.12S135.33E
Mount Fletcher town 54 30.41S 28.30E
Mount Gambier town 36 37.51S140.50E
Mount Isa town 34 20.50S139.29E
Mount Magnet town 33 28.06S117.50E
Mountmellick 10 53.08N 7.21W
Mount's B. 9 50.05N 5.25W
Mount Vernon town 32 24.09S118.10E
Mount Willoughby 36 27.58S134.08E
Mourne Mts. 10 54.10N 6.02W
Moussoro 50 13.39N 16.29E
Moxico 52 11.50S 20.05E
Moy r. 10 54.10N 9.09W
Moyale 53 3.31N 39.04E
Moyowosi r. 53 4.59S 30.58E
Mozambique 54 17.30S 35.45E
Mozdok 21 43.45N 44.43E
Mozyr 17 52.02N 29.10E
M'Pama r. 52 0.59S 15.40E
Mpanda 53 6.21S 31.01E
Mpika 53 11.52S 31.30E
Mporokoso 53 9.22S 30.06E
M'Pouya 52 2.38S 16.08E
Mpwapwa 53 6.23S 36.38E
Msta r. 20 58.28N 31.20E
Mtakuja 53 7.21S 30.37E
Mtsensk 20 53.18N 36.35E
Mtwara 53 10.17S 40.11E
Muang Chiang Rai 25 19.56N 99.51E
Muang Nakhon Sawan 27 17.22N104.45E
Mubende 53 0.30N 31.24E
Muchinga Mts. 53 12.15S 31.00E
Muck i. 11 56.50N 6.14W
Mucojo 53 12.05S 40.26E
Mudanjiang 26 44.36N129.42E
Mufulira 53 12.30S 28.12E
Mugia 13 43.06N 9.14W
Muğla 15 37.12N 28.22E
Mühlhausen 16 51.12N 10.27E
Muine Bheag town 10 52.42N 6.58W
Muir, L. 33 34.30S116.30E
Mukachevo 17 48.26N 22.45E

Mukah 27 2.56N112.02E
Mukawa 34 9.48S150.00E
Mukinbudin 33 30.52S118.08E
Mulanje Mts. 53 15.57S 35.33E
Mulchén 49 37.43S 72.14W
Mulhacén mtn. 13 37.04N 3.22W
Mulhouse 12 47.45N 7.21E
Mull i. 11 56.28N 5.56W
Mull, Sd. of str. 11 56.32N 5.55W
Mullaghareirk Mts. 10 52.19N 9.06W
Mullaghmore mtn. 10 54.51N 6.51W
Mullaley 37 31.06S149.55E
Mullet Pen. 10 54.12N 10.04W
Mullingar 10 53.31N 7.21W
Mull of Galloway c. 11 54.39N 4.52W
Mull of Kintyre c. 11 55.17N 5.45W
Mulobezi 54 16.49S 25.09E
Multān 25 30.11N 71.29E
Multyfarnham 10 53.37N 7.25W
Mumbwa 53 14.57S 27.01E
Muna i. 27 5.00S122.30E
München 16 48.08N 11.35E
Muncie 44 40.11N 85.23W
Mungari 54 17.12S 33.31E
Mungbere 53 2.40N 28.25E
Munich see München 16
Münster N.-Westfalen 16 51.58N 7.37E
Muonio 18 67.57N 23.42E
Muonio r. 18 67.10N 23.40E
Muqdisho 53 2.02N 45.21E
Mur r. Austria see Mura r. 16
Mura r. 16 46.18N 16.53E
Muranga 53 0.43S 37.10E
Murchison r. 32 27.30S114.10E
Murcia 13 37.59N 1.08W
Mureş r. 17 46.16N 20.10E
Muret 12 43.28N 1.19E
Murewa 54 17.40S 31.47E
Murmansk 20 68.59N 33.08E
Murom 20 55.04N 42.04E
Muroran 26 42.21N140.59E
Murray r.S.A. 36 35.23S139.20E
Murray r.W.A. 33 32.35S115.46E
Murray Bridge town 36 35.10S139.17E
Murrumbidgee r. 36 34.38S143.10E
Murrurundi 37 31.47S150.51E
Murtoa 36 36.40S142.31E
Murwāra 25 23.51N 80.24E
Muş 21 38.45N 41.30E
Muscat see Masqaţ 24
Musgrave Ranges mts. 32 26.10S131.50E
Mushie 52 2.59S 16.55E
Musi r. 27 2.20S104.57E
Muskegon 44 43.13N 86.15W
Muskogee 41 35.45N 95.21W
Musoma 53 1.31S 33.48E
Musselburgh 11 55.57N 3.04W
Mussende 52 10.33S 16.02E
Mustjala 19 58.28N 22.14E
Mut 21 36.38N 33.27E
Mutare 54 18.59S 32.40E
Muyinga 53 2.48S 30.21E
Muzaffarpur 25 26.07N 85.24E
Mvuma 54 19.16S 30.30E
Mwali i. 53 12.22S 43.45E
Mwanza 52 7.51S 26.43E
Mwaya Mbeya 53 9.33S 33.56E
Mweka 52 4.51S 21.34E
Mwene Ditu 52 7.04S 23.27E
Mwenezi r. 54 22.42S 31.45E
Mweru, L. 53 9.00S 28.40E
Mwinilunga 52 11.44S 24.24E
Myrdal 19 60.44N 7.08E
Mysore 25 12.18N 76.37E
Mytishchi 20 55.54N 37.47E
Mzimba 53 12.00S 33.39E

N

Naas 10 53.13N 6.41W
Naberezhnyye Chelny 22 55.42N 52.20E
Nacala 53 14.34S 40.41E
Nachingwea 53 10.21S 38.46E
Naestved 19 55.14N 11.46E
Nāgāland d. 25 26.10N 94.30E
Nagano d. 28 35.33N137.50E
Nagasaki 26 32.45N129.52E
Nāgercoil 25 8.11N 77.30E
Nagles Mts. 10 52.06N 8.26W
Nagoya 28 35.10N136.55E
Nāgpur 25 21.09N 79.06E
Nagykanizsa 17 46.27N 17.01E
Naha 26 26.10N127.40E
Nahr al Furāt r. 24 31.00N 47.27E
Nain 39 56.30N 61.45W
Nairn 11 57.35N 3.52W
Nairobi 53 1.17S 36.50E
Naivasha 53 0.44S 36.26E
Nakatsugawa 28 35.29N137.30E
Nakhodka 23 42.53N132.54E
Nakhon Ratchasima 27 14.58N102.06E
Nakskov 19 54.50N 11.09E
Nakuru 53 0.16S 36.04E
Nalchik 21 43.31N 43.38E
Nalón r. 13 43.35N 6.06W
Namacurra 53 17.35S 37.00E
Namanga 53 2.33S 36.48E
Namangan 22 40.59N 71.41E
Namapa 53 13.48S 39.44E
Namaponda 53 15.51S 39.52E
Namarroi 53 15.58S 36.55E
Nam Co l. 25 30.45N 90.30E
Nam Dinh 26 20.21N106.09E
Namecala 53 12.50S 39.38E
Nametil 53 15.41S 39.30E
Namib Desert 54 23.00S 15.20E
Namibe 52 15.10S 12.10E
Namibia 54 21.30S 16.45E
Namlea 27 3.15S127.07E
Nampula 53 15.09S 39.14E
Namsos 18 64.28N 11.30E
Namur 16 50.28N 4.52E
Namutoni 54 18.48S 16.58E
Namwala 52 15.44S 26.25E
Nanaimo 38 49.08N123.58W
Nanchang 26 28.37N115.57E
Nancy 12 48.42N 6.12E
Nānder 25 19.09N 77.20E
Nandewar Range mts. 37 30.20S150.45E
Nānga Parbat mtn. 25 35.10N 74.35E
Nanjing 26 32.02N118.52E
Nan Ling mts. 26 25.10N110.00E
Nanning 26 22.48N108.10E
Nantes 12 47.14N 1.35W
Nantucket I. 44 41.16N 70.03W
Nantwich 8 53.05N 2.31W
Nanyang 26 33.07N112.30E
Nanyuki 53 0.01N 37.03E
Napier 29 39.29S176.58E
Naples see Napoli 14
Napoli 14 40.50N 14.14E
Napoli, Golfo di g. 14 40.42N 14.15E
Nara 28 34.41N135.50E
Naracoorte 36 36.58S140.46E
Nārāyanganj 25 23.37N 90.30E
Narbonne 12 43.11N 3.00E
Narembeen 33 32.04S118.23E
Nares Str. 39 78.30N 75.00W
Narmada r. 25 21.40N 73.00E
Narodnaya mtn. 20 65.00N 61.00E
Narok 53 1.04S 35.54E
Narrabri 37 30.20S149.49E
Narrandera 37 34.36S146.34E
Narran L. 37 29.40S147.25E
Narrogin 33 32.58S117.10E
Narva 20 59.22N 28.17E
Narvik 18 68.26N 17.25E
Nasarawa 50 8.35N 7.44E
Nashua N.H. 44 42.46N 71.27W
Nashville 41 36.10N 86.50W
Näsijärvi l. 19 61.37N 23.42E
Nāsik 25 19.59N 73.48E
Nāşir, Buḩayrat l. 24 22.40N 32.00E
Nassau 43 25.03N 77.20W
Nasser, L. see Nāşir, Buḩayrat l. 51
Nässjö 19 57.39N 14.41E
Natal 47 5.46S 35.15W
Natchez 41 31.22N 91.24W
Natuna Besar i. 27 4.00N108.20E
Nauru 30 0.32S166.55E
Nava r. 53 1.45N 27.06E
Navalmoral de la Mata 13 39.54N 5.33W
Navan 10 53.39N 6.42W
Naver r. 11 58.32N 4.14W
Navlya 20 52.51N 34.30E
Navojoa 42 27.06N109.26W
Návpaktos 15 38.24N 21.49E
Návplion 15 37.33N 22.47E
Navrongo 50 10.51N 1.03W
Náxos i. 15 37.03N 25.30E
Nazas r. 42 25.34N103.25W
Nazilli 21 37.55N 28.20E
N'dalatando 52 9.12S 14.54E
N'Dendé 52 2.20S 11.23E
N'Djamena 50 12.10N 14.59E
Ndjolé 52 0.07S 10.45E
Ndola 53 12.58S 28.39E
Neagh, Lough 10 54.36N 6.25W
Neath 9 51.39N 3.49W
Nebit-Dag 21 39.31N 54.24E
Nebraska d. 40 41.30N100.00W
Neches r. 41 29.55N 93.50W
Neckar r. 16 49.32N 8.26E
Necochea 49 38.31S 58.46W
Necuto 52 4.55S 12.38E
Needles 40 34.51N114.36W
Nefyn 8 52.55N 4.31W
Negotin 17 44.14N 22.33E
Negrais, C. 25 16.00N 94.12E
Negro r. Argentina 49 40.50S 63.00W
Negro r. Brazil 46 3.00S 59.55W
Negro r. Uruguay 49 33.27S 58.20W
Negros i. 27 10.00N123.00E
Neijiang 26 29.29N105.03E
Nei Monggol d. 26 41.00N112.00E
Neisse r. 16 52.05N 14.42E
Neiva 46 2.58N 75.15W
Neksö 19 55.04N 15.09E
Nellore 25 14.29N 80.00E
Nelson r. 39 57.00N 93.20W
Nelson 8 53.50N 2.14W
Nelson, C. 36 38.27S141.35E
Nelson-Marlborough d. 29 41.40S173.40E
Nelspruit 54 25.27S 30.58E
Néma 50 16.32N 7.12W
Neman r. 19 55.18N 21.23E
Nemours 12 48.16N 2.41E
Nenagh 10 52.52N 8.13W
Nenana 38 64.35N149.20W
Nene r. 8 52.49N 0.12E
Nepal 25 28.00N 84.00E
Nephin Beg Range mts. 10 54.00N 9.37W
Nera r. 14 42.33N 12.43E
Neretva r. 15 43.02N 17.28E
Neriquinha 52 15.50S 21.40E
Ness, Loch 11 57.16N 4.30W
Netherlands 16 52.00N 5.30E
Netherlands Antilles 43 12.30N 69.00W
Neto r. 15 39.12N 17.08E
Neubrandenburg 16 53.33N 13.16E
Neuchâtel 16 47.00N 6.56E
Neuchâtel, Lac de l. 16 46.55N 6.55E
Neufchâtel 12 49.44N 1.26E
Neuquén r. 49 39.02S 68.07W
Neuse r. 41 35.04N 77.04W
Neustrelitz 16 53.22N 13.05E
Neuwied 16 50.26N 7.28E
Nevada d. 40 39.00N117.00W
Nevada, Sierra mts. Spain 13 37.04N 3.20W
Nevada, Sierra mts. U.S.A. 40 37.30N119.00W
Nevel 20 56.00N 29.59E
Nevers 12 47.00N 3.09E
Nevertire 37 31.52S147.47E
Nevşehir 21 38.38N 34.43E
New Amsterdam 47 6.18N 57.30W
Newark N.J. 44 40.44N 74.11W
Newark-on-Trent 8 53.06N 0.48W
New Bedford 44 41.38N 70.56W
New Bern 41 35.05N 77.04W
Newbiggin-by-the-Sea 8 55.11N 1.30W
New Brunswick d. 44 46.30N 66.15W
New Brunswick 44 40.29N 74.27W
Newburgh 44 41.30N 74.00W
Newbury 9 51.24N 1.19W
New Caledonia is. see Nouvelle Calédonie is. 30
Newcastle Australia 37 32.55S151.46E
Newcastle U.K. 10 54.13N 5.53W
Newcastle Emlyn 9 52.02N 4.29W
Newcastle-under-Lyme 8 53.02N 2.15W
Newcastle upon Tyne 8 54.58N 1.36W
Newcastle West 10 52.26N 9.04W
New Delhi 25 28.36N 77.12E
New England Range mts. 37 30.30S151.50E
Newent 9 51.56N 2.24W
New Forest f. 9 50.50N 1.35W
Newfoundland d. 39 55.00N 60.00W
Newfoundland i. 39 48.30N 56.00W
New Galloway 11 55.05N 4.09W
New Guinea i. 27 5.00S140.00E
New Hampshire d. 44 43.35N 71.40W
Newhaven 9 50.47N 0.04E
New Haven 44 41.18N 72.55W
New Jersey d. 44 40.15N 74.30W
New London Conn. 44 41.21N 72.06W
Newman 32 23.22S119.43E
Newmarket 9 52.15N 0.23E
Newmarket on Fergus 10 52.46N 8.55W
New Mexico d. 40 34.00N106.00W
New Norfolk 35 42.46S147.02E
New Orleans 41 30.00N 90.03W
New Plymouth 29 39.03S174.04E
Newport Mayo 10 53.53N 9.34W
Newport Tipperary 10 52.42N 8.25W
Newport Dyfed 9 52.01N 4.51W
Newport Essex 9 51.58N 0.13E
Newport Gwent 9 51.34N 2.59W
Newport Hants. 9 50.43N 1.18W
Newport R.I. 44 41.13N 71.18W
Newquay 9 50.24N 5.06W
New Quay 9 52.13N 4.22W
New Radnor 9 52.15N 3.10W
New Romney 9 50.59N 0.58E
New Ross 10 52.24N 6.57W
Newry 10 54.11N 6.21W
New Scone 11 56.25N 3.25W
New South Wales d. 37 32.40S147.40E
Newton Abbot 9 50.32N 3.37W
Newton Aycliffe 8 54.36N 1.34W
Newtonmore 11 57.04N 4.08W
Newton Stewart 11 54.57N 4.29W
Newtown 9 52.31N 3.19W
Newtownabbey 10 54.39N 5.57W
Newtownards 10 54.35N 5.41W
Newtown Butler 10 54.12N 7.22W
Newtown St. Boswells 11 55.35N 2.40W
Newtownstewart 10 54.43N 7.25W
New York 44 40.40N 73.50W
New York d. 44 43.00N 75.00W
New Zealand 29 41.00S175.00E
Nezhin 17 51.03N 31.54E
Ngami, L. 54 20.32S 22.38E
Ngamiland f. 54 20.00S 22.30E
N'Gao 52 2.28S 15.40E
Ngaoundéré 50 7.20N 13.35E
Ngaruawahia 29 37.40S175.09E
Ngaruroro r. 29 39.34S176.54E
N'Giva 52 17.03S 15.47E
Ngong 53 1.22S 36.40E
Ngonye Falls f. 52 16.35S 23.39E
Ngozi 53 2.52S 29.50E
Nguigmi 50 14.00N 13.06E
Nha Trang 27 12.15N109.10E
Nhill 36 36.20S141.40E
Nhulunbuy 34 12.11S136.46E
Niagara Falls town 44 43.06N 79.02W
Niamey 50 13.32N 2.05E
Niangara 53 3.47N 27.54E
Niassa d. 53 13.00S 36.30E
Nicaragua 43 13.00N 85.00W
Nicaragua, Lago de l. 43 11.30N 85.30W
Nicastro 14 38.58N 16.16E
Nice 12 43.42N 7.16E
Nicobar Islands 25 8.00N 93.30E
Nicosia see Levkosía 24
Nicoya, Golfo de g. 43 9.30N 85.00W
Nid r. 19 58.24N 8.48E
Niğde 21 37.58N 34.42E
Niger 50 17.00N 9.30E
Niger r. 50 4.15N 6.05E
Nigeria 50 9.00N 7.30E
Niigata 26 37.58N139.02E
Niiza 28 35.48N139.34E
Nijmegen 16 51.50N 5.52E
Nikel 18 69.20N 30.00E
Nikiniki 27 9.49S124.29E
Nikki 50 9.55N 3.18E
Nikolayev 21 46.57N 32.00E
Nikolayevsk-na-Amure 23 53.20N140.44E
Nikopol 21 47.34N 34.25E
Niksar 21 40.35N 36.59E
Nil, An r. 51 31.30N 30.25E
Nile r. see Nil, An r. 51
Niles Mich. 44 41.51N 86.15W
Nilgiri Hills 25 11.30N 77.30E
Nîmes 12 43.50N 4.21E
Ningbo 26 29.56N121.32E
Niobrara r. 40 42.45N 98.10W
Nioro 50 15.12N 9.35W
Niort 12 46.19N 0.27W
Nipigon, L. 44 49.50N 88.30W
Nipissing, L. 44 46.17N 80.00W
Niš 15 43.20N 21.54E
Niterói 45 22.54S 43.06W
Nith r. 11 55.00N 3.35W
Niue i. 30 19.02S169.52W
Nizāmābād 25 18.40N 78.05E
Nizhneudinsk 23 54.55N 99.00E
Nizhnevartovsk 22 60.57N 76.40E
Nizhniy Tagil 20 58.00N 60.00E
Njazidja i. 53 11.35S 43.20E
Njombe r. 53 7.02S 35.55E
Njoro 53 5.16S 36.30E
Nkhata Bay town 53 11.37S 34.20E
Nkhotakota 53 12.55S 34.19E
Nkungwe Mt. 53 6.15S 29.54E
Noatak 38 67.34N162.59W
Nogales 42 31.20N111.00W
Nogent-le-Rotrou 12 48.19N 0.50E
Noguera Ribagorçana r. 13 41.27N 0.25E
Noirmoutier, Île de i. 12 47.00N 2.15W
Nokia 19 61.28N 23.30E
Nola 52 3.28N 16.08E
Noma Omuramba r. 54 19.14S 22.15E
Nome 38 64.30N165.30W
Noonthorangee Range mts. 36 31.00S142.20E
Noorvik 38 66.50N161.14W
Nordenham 16 53.30N 8.29E
Nordfriesische Inseln is. 16 54.30N 8.00E
Nordvik 23 73.40N110.50E
Nore r. 10 52.25N 6.58W
Norfolk d. 9 52.39N 1.00E
Norfolk Va. 41 36.54N 76.18W
Norfolk Broads f. 8 52.43N 1.35E
Norilsk 23 69.21N 88.02E
Normanton 34 17.40S141.05E
Norman Wells 38 65.19N126.46W
Nörresundby 19 57.04N 9.56E
Norris L. 41 36.20N 83.55W
Norristown 44 40.07N 75.20W
Norrköping 19 58.36N 16.11E
Norrtälje 19 59.46N 18.42E
Norseman 33 32.15S121.47E
Norte, C. 47 1.40N 49.55W
Northallerton 8 54.20N 1.26W
Northam 33 31.41S116.40E
Northampton 9 52.14N 0.54W
Northamptonshire d. 9 52.18N 0.55W
North Battleford 38 52.47N108.19W
North Bay town 44 46.19N 79.28W
North Bend Oreg. 40 43.26N124.14W
North Berwick 11 56.04N 2.43W
North C. 29 34.28S173.00E
North Canadian r. 41 35.30N 95.45W
North Carolina d. 41 35.30N 79.00W
North Channel 10 55.15N 5.52W
North China Plain f. see Huabei Pingyuan f. 26
North Dakota d. 40 47.00N100.00W
North Downs hills 9 51.18N 0.40E
Northern Ireland d. 10 54.40N 6.45W
Northern Marianas is. 30 16.00N145.30E
Northern Territory d. 34 20.00S133.00E
North Esk r. 11 56.45N 2.25W
North Foreland c. 9 51.23N 1.26E
North Frisian Is. see Nordfriesische Inseln is. 16
North I. 29 39.00S175.00E
Northiam 9 50.59N 0.39E
North Korea 26 40.00N128.00E
Northland d. 29 35.25S174.00E
North Platte r. 40 41.09N100.55W
North Ronaldsay i. 11 59.23N 2.26W
North Sea 7 56.00N 5.00E
North Sporades see Voríai Sporádhes is. 15
North Taranaki Bight b. 29 38.45S174.15E
North Tawton 9 50.48N 3.55W
North Uist i. 11 57.35N 7.20W
Northumberland d. 8 55.12N 2.00W
North Walsham 8 52.49N 1.22E
Northway 38 62.58N142.00W
North West Highlands 11 57.30N 5.15W
North West River town 39 53.30N 60.10W
Northwest Territories d. 39 66.00N 95.00W
Northwich 8 53.16N 2.30W
North York Moors hills 8 54.21N 0.50W
North Yorkshire d. 8 54.14N 1.14W
Norton Sound b. 38 63.50N164.00W
Norwalk Conn. 44 41.07N 73.25W
Norway 18 65.00N 13.00E
Norway House town 39 53.59N 97.50W
Norwich 9 52.38N 1.17E
Noss Head 11 58.28N 3.03W
Noteć r. 16 52.44N 15.26E
Nottingham 8 52.57N 1.10W
Nottinghamshire d. 8 53.10N 1.00W
Nouadhibou 50 20.54N 17.01W
Nouakchott 50 18.09N 15.58W
Nouméa 30 22.16S166.27E
Nouvelle Anvers 52 1.38N 19.10E
Nouvelle Calédonie is. 30 21.30S165.30E
Nova Iguaçu 45 22.45S 43.27W
Novara 14 45.27N 8.37E
Nova Scotia d. 39 45.00N 64.00W
Nova Sofala 54 20.09S 34.24E
Novaya Ladoga 20 60.09N 32.15E
Novelda 13 38.24N 0.45W
Novgorod 20 58.30N 31.20E
Novi Pazar 15 43.08N 20.28E
Novi Sad 17 45.16N 19.52E
Novocherkassk 21 47.25N 40.05E
Novograd Volynskiy 17 50.34N 27.32E
Novogrudok 17 53.35N 25.50E
Novo Hamburgo 45 29.37S 51.07W
Novokazalinsk 22 45.48N 62.06E
Novokuznetsk 22 53.45N 87.12E
Novomoskovsk R.S.F.S.R. 20 54.06N 38.15E
Novorossiysk 21 44.44N 37.46E
Novoshakhtinsk 21 47.46N 39.55E
Novosibirsk 22 55.04N 82.55E
Novouzensk 21 50.29N 48.08E
Novyy Port 22 67.38N 72.33E
Nowa Ruda 16 50.34N 16.30E
Nowa Sól 16 51.49N 15.41E
Nowra 37 35.54S150.36E
Nowy Sącz 17 49.39N 20.40E
Noyon 12 49.35N 3.00E
Nsanje 53 16.55S 35.12E
Nubian Desert 51 21.00N 34.00E
Nueces r. 41 27.55N 97.30W
Nueva Gerona 43 21.53N 82.49W
Nuevitas 43 21.34N 77.18W
Nuevo Laredo 42 27.30N 99.30W
Nu Jiang r. see Salween r. 26
Nuku'alofa 31 21.07S175.12W
Nullarbor Plain f. 33 31.30S128.00E
Numazu 28 35.06N138.52E
Nuneaton 9 52.32N 1.29W
Nungo 53 13.25S 37.45E
Nunivak I. 38 60.00N166.30W
Nürnberg 16 49.27N 11.05E
Nusaybin 21 37.05N 41.11E
Nuweveldberge mts. 54 32.15S 21.50E
Nyahururu Falls town 53 0.04N 36.22E
Nyakanazi 53 3.05S 31.16E
Nyala 51 12.01N 24.50E
Nyamandhlovu 54 19.50S 28.15E
Nyanga r. 52 3.00S 10.17E
Nyanza 53 2.20S 29.42E
Nyborg 19 55.19N 10.48E
Nybro 19 56.45N 15.54E
Nyeri 53 0.22S 36.56E
Nyika Plateau f. 53 10.25S 33.50E
Nyköping 19 58.45N 17.00E
Nylstroom 54 24.42S 28.24E
Nynäshamn 19 58.54N 17.57E
Nyong r. 52 3.15N 9.55E
Nyons 12 44.22N 5.08E
Nyunzu 53 5.55S 28.00E
Nzega 53 4.13S 33.09E
N'zeto 52 7.13S 12.56E
Nzwani i. 53 12.12S 44.28E

O

Oahe Resr. 40 45.45N100.20W
Oakland Calif. 40 37.50N122.15W
Oakville 44 43.27N 79.41W
Oamaru 29 45.07S170.58E
Oaxaca 42 17.05N 96.41W
Ob r. 20 66.50N 69.00E
Oba 44 49.04N 84.07W
Oban 11 56.26N 5.28W
Oberá 48 27.30S 55.07W
Obi i. 27 1.45S127.30E
Ocaña 46 8.16N 73.21W
Ocean I. see Banaba i. 30 0.52S169.35E
Ochil Hills 11 56.16N 3.25W
Ocotal 43 13.37N 86.31W
Ocotlán 42 20.21N102.42W
Ocua 53 13.40S 39.46E
Oda 50 5.55N 0.56W
Odawara 28 35.15N139.10E
Odda 19 60.04N 6.33E
Ödemiş 15 38.12N 28.00E
Odense 19 55.24N 10.23E
Odenwald mts. 16 49.40N 9.20E
Oder r. Germany see Odra r. 16
Odessa 24 46.30N 30.46E
Odorhei 17 46.18N 25.18E
Odra r. 16 53.30N 14.36E
Ofanto r. 14 41.22N 16.12E
Offaly d. 10 53.15N 7.30W
Offenbach 16 50.06N 8.46E
Offenburg 16 48.29N 7.57E
Ōgaki 28 35.21N136.37E
Ogbomosho 50 8.05N 4.11E
Ogden Utah 40 41.14N111.59W
Ogeechee r. 41 32.54N 81.05W
Ognon r. 12 47.20N 5.37E
Ogoja 50 6.40N 8.45E
Ogooué r. 52 1.00S 9.05E
Ogosta r. 15 43.44N 23.51E
Ogulin 16 45.17N 15.14E
Ohio d. 44 40.15N 82.45W
Ohio r. 44 36.59N 89.08W
Ohře r. 16 50.32N 14.08E
Ohrid 15 41.06N 20.48E
Oise r. 12 49.00N 2.10E
Ojocaliente 42 22.35N102.18W
Ojo de Agua 48 29.30S 63.44W
Oka r. 20 56.09N 43.00E
Okahandja 54 21.58S 16.44E
Okanogan r. 40 47.45N120.05W
Okavango r. 54 18.30S 22.04E
Okavango Basin f. 54 19.30S 22.30E
Okazaki 28 34.57N137.10E
Okeechobee, L. 41 27.00N 80.45W
Okefenokee Swamp f. 41 30.40N 82.40W
Okehampton 9 50.44N 4.01W
Okere r. 53 1.37N 33.53E
Okha 23 53.35N142.50E
Okhotsk 23 59.20N143.15E
Okhotsk, Sea of 23 55.00N150.00E
Okinawa jima i. 26 26.30N128.00E
Okipoko r. 54 18.40S 16.03E
Oklahoma d. 41 35.00N 97.00W
Oklahoma City 41 35.28N 97.33W
Öland i. 19 56.45N 16.38E
Olary 36 32.18S140.19E
Olavarría 49 36.57S 60.20W
Oldenburg Nschn. 16 53.08N 8.13E
Oldham 8 53.33N 2.08W
Old Head of Kinsale c. 10 51.37N 8.33W
Olenëk r. 23 73.00N120.00E
Oléron, Île d' i. 12 45.55N 1.16W
Olga 23 43.46N135.14E
Olhão 13 37.01N 7.50W
Olifants r. C.P. 54 31.42S 18.10E
Olifants r. Trans. 54 24.08S 32.39E
Ólimbos 15 35.44N 27.11E
Ólimbos mtn. 15 40.04N 22.20E
Oliva 48 32.05S 63.35W
Olivares 13 39.45N 2.21W
Olney 9 52.09N 0.42W
Olomouc 17 49.36N 17.16E
Oloron 12 43.12N 0.35W
Olot 13 42.11N 2.30E
Olsztynek 17 53.36N 20.17E
Olteţ r. 17 44.13N 24.28E
Olympus mtn. see Ólimbos mtn. 15
Omagh 10 54.36N 7.20W
Omaha 41 41.15N 96.00W
Oman 24 22.30N 57.30E
Oman, G. of 24 25.00N 58.00E
Omaruru 54 21.25S 15.57E
Omdurman see Umm Durmān 51
Omolon r. 23 68.50N158.30E
Omsk 22 55.00N 73.22E
Omulew r. 17 53.05N 21.32E
Oña 13 42.44N 3.25W
Onega r. 20 63.59N 38.11E
Onitsha 50 6.10N 6.47E
Onslow 32 21.41S115.12E
Ontario d. 39 52.00N 86.00W
Ontario Oreg. 40 44.02N116.58W
Ontario, L. 44 43.45N 78.00W
Oostende 16 51.13N 2.55E
Opole 17 50.40N 17.56E
Oporto see Porto 13
Opotiki 29 38.00S177.18E
Oradea 17 47.03N 21.55E
Oran 50 35.45N 0.38W
Orange 12 44.08N 4.48E
Orange r. 54 28.38S 16.38E
Orangeburg 41 33.28N 80.53W
Oranjemund 54 28.35S 16.26E
Orbost 37 37.42S148.30E
Orchila i. 43 11.52N 66.10W
Ord r. 32 15.30S128.30E
Ordu 21 41.00N 37.52E
Orduña 13 43.00N 3.00W
Örebro 19 59.17N 15.13E
Oregon d. 40 44.00N120.00W
Öregrund 19 60.20N 18.26E
Orekhovo-Zuyevo 20 55.47N 39.00E
Orel 20 52.58N 36.04E
Orenburg 20 51.50N 55.00E
Orense 13 42.20N 7.52W
Orihuela 13 38.05N 0.56W
Orinoco r. 46 9.00N 61.30W
Orissa d. 25 20.20N 84.00E
Oristano 14 39.53N 8.36E
Orizaba 42 18.51N 97.08W
Orkney Is. d. 11 59.00N 3.00W
Orlando 41 28.33N 81.21W
Orléans 12 47.54N 1.54E
Ormond 29 38.35S177.58E
Ormskirk 8 53.35N 2.53W
Orne r. 12 49.17N 0.10W
Örnsköldsvik 18 63.17N 18.50E
Oromocto 44 45.50N 66.28W
Orosei 14 40.23N 9.40E
Oroville Wash. 40 48.57N119.27W
Orsha 20 54.30N 30.23E
Orsk 20 51.13N 58.35E
Orşova 17 44.42N 22.22E
Orthez 12 43.29N 0.46W
Oryakhovo 15 43.42N 23.58E
Ōsaka 28 34.40N135.30E
Osh 22 40.37N 72.49E
Oshawa 44 43.54N 78.51W
Ō shima i. Tosan 28 34.43N139.24E
Oshogbo 50 7.50N 4.35E
Oshwe 52 3.27S 19.32E
Osijek 15 45.35N 18.43E
Oskarshamn 19 57.16N 16.26E
Oskol r. 21 49.08N 37.10E
Oslo 19 59.56N 10.45E
Osmancik 21 40.58N 34.50E
Osmaniye 21 37.04N 36.15E
Osnabrück 16 52.17N 8.03E
Osorno 49 40.35S 73.14W
Ossa, Mt. 35 41.52S146.04E
Ostashkov 20 57.09N 33.10E
Ostend see Oostende 16
Österdal r. 19 61.03N 14.30E
Österö i. 18 62.10N 7.00W
Östersund 18 63.10N 14.40E
Ostrava 17 49.50N 18.15E
Ostrov 20 57.22N 28.22E
Ostrów Mazowiecka 17 52.50N 21.51E
Osuna 13 37.14N 5.06W
Oswestry 8 52.52N 3.03W
Otago d. 29 45.10S169.20E
Otago Pen. 29 45.48S170.45E
Otavi 54 19.37S 17.21E
Otju 54 18.15S 13.18E
Otra r. 19 58.09N 8.00E
Otranto 15 40.09N 18.30E
Otranto, Str. of 15 40.10N 19.00E
Otta 19 61.46N 9.32E
Ottawa 44 45.25N 75.43W
Ottawa r. 44 45.20N 73.58W
Ottawa Is. 39 59.50N 80.00W
Otter r. 9 50.38N 3.19W
Otterburn 8 55.14N 2.10W
Ottumwa 41 41.02N 92.26W
Otway, C. 36 38.51S143.34E
Ouachita r. 41 33.10N 92.10W
Ouachita Mts. 41 34.40N 94.30W
Ouagadougou 50 12.20N 1.40W
Ouahigouya 50 13.31N 2.21W
Ouargla 50 32.00N 5.16E
Oudtshoorn 54 33.35S 22.11E
Ouessant, Île d' i. 12 48.28N 5.05W
Ouesso 52 1.38N 16.03E
Oughter, Lough 10 54.01N 7.28W
Oujda 50 34.41N 1.45W
Oulu 18 65.01N 25.28E
Oulu r. 18 65.01N 25.25E
Oulujärvi l. 18 64.20N 27.15E
Oundle 9 52.28N 0.28W
Ourinhos 45 23.00S 49.54W
Ouse r. Humber. 8 53.41N 0.42W
Outer Hebrides is. 11 57.40N 7.35W
Outjo 54 20.07S 16.10E
Ouyen 36 35.06S142.22E
Ovamboland f. 54 17.45S 16.00E
Oviedo 13 43.21N 5.50W
Owando 52 0.30S 15.48E
Owen Falls Dam 53 0.30N 33.07E
Owen Stanley Range mts. 34 9.30S148.00E
Oxelösund 19 58.40N 17.06E
Oxford 9 51.45N 1.15W
Oxfordshire d. 9 51.46N 1.10W
Oxley 36 34.11S144.10E
Oykel r. 11 57.53N 4.21W
Oymyakon 23 63.30N142.44E
Ozark Plateau 41 36.00N 93.35W

P

Paarl 54 33.44S 18.58E
Pachuca 42 20.10N 98.44W
Pacific Ocean 31
Padang 27 0.55S100.21E
Paderborn 16 51.43N 8.44E
Padova 14 45.27N 11.52E
Padre I. 41 27.00N 97.20W
Padstow 9 50.33N 4.57W
Padua see Padova 16
Paeroa 29 37.23S175.41E
Paible 11 57.35N 7.27W
Paihia 29 35.16S174.05E
Päijänne l. 19 61.35N 25.30E
Paisley 11 55.50N 4.26W
Pakistan 25 31.00N 70.00E
Pakwach 53 2.27N 31.18E
Palana 23 59.05N159.59E
Palapye 54 22.33S 27.07E
Palawan i. 27 9.30N118.30E
Paldiski 19 59.20N 24.06E
Palembang 27 2.59S104.50E
Palencia 13 42.01N 4.34W
Palermo 14 38.09N 13.22E
Palliser, C. 29 41.35S175.15E
Palma 13 39.36N 2.39E
Palma, Bahía de b. 13 39.30N 2.40E
Palma del Río 13 37.43N 5.17W
Palmas, Golfo di g. 14 39.00N 8.30E
Palmerston North 29 40.20S175.39E
Palmi 14 38.22N 15.50E
Palmira 46 3.33N 76.17W
Palm Springs town 40 33.49N116.34W
Palmyras Pt. 25 20.46N 87.02E
Pamiers 12 43.07N 1.36E
Pamir mts. 22 38.00N 73.30E
Pampa 40 35.32N100.58W
Pampas f. 49 34.00S 64.00W
Pamplona 13 42.49N 1.39W
Panama 43 9.00N 80.00W
Panamá town 43 8.57N 79.30W
Panamá, Golfo de g. 43 8.30N 79.00W
Panama City 41 30.10N 85.41W
Panay i. 27 11.10N122.30E
Panevežys 19 55.44N 24.21E
Pangi 52 3.10S 26.38E
Pangnirtung 39 66.05N 65.45W
Pannawonica 32 21.42S116.22E
Pantano del Esla l. 13 41.40N 5.50W
Pantelleria i. 14 36.48N 12.00E
Paola 14 39.21N 16.03E
Papeete 31 17.32S149.34W
Papenburg 16 53.03N 7.23E
Paracatu r. 45 16.30S 45.10W
Paraguaçu r. 47 12.35S 38.59W
Paraguarí 45 25.36S 57.06W
Paraguay r. 45 27.30S 58.50W
Paraguay 45 23.00S 57.00W
Paraíba r. 45 21.45S 41.10W
Parakou 50 9.23N 2.40E
Paramaribo 47 5.52N 55.14W
Paraná 49 31.45S 60.30W
Paraná r. 49 34.00S 58.30W
Paranã r. 47 12.30S 48.10W
Paranaguá 45 25.32S 48.36W
Paranaíba r. 45 20.00S 51.00W
Paranapanema r. 45 22.30S 53.03W
Paranapiacaba, Serra mts. 45 24.30S 49.15W
Paranavaí 45 23.02S 52.36W
Paraparaumu 29 40.55S175.00E
Pardo r. Bahia 45 15.40S 39.38W
Pardo r. Mato Grosso 45 21.56S 52.07W
Pardo r. São Paulo 45 20.10S 48.36W
Pardubice 16 50.03N 15.45E
Paris 12 48.52N 2.20E
Parkano 19 62.01N 23.01E
Parker Dam 40 34.25N114.05W
Parkersburg 44 39.17N 81.33W
Parkes 37 33.10S148.13E
Parma 14 44.48N 10.18E
Parnaíba r. 47 2.58S 41.47W
Parnassós mtn. 15 38.33N 22.35E
Pärnu r. 19 58.23N 24.29E
Paroo r. 36 31.30S143.24E
Páros i. 15 37.04N 25.11E
Parral 49 36.09S 71.50W
Parramatta 37 33.50S150.57E
Parry Is. 39 76.00N102.00W
Parsęta r. 16 54.12N 15.33E
Parthenay 12 46.39N 0.14W
Partry Mts. 10 53.40N 9.30W
Parys 54 26.54S 27.26E
Pasadena Calif. 40 34.10N118.09W
Pascua, Isla de i. 31 27.08S109.23W
Passau 16 48.35N 13.28E
Passo Fundo 45 28.16S 52.20W
Passos 45 20.45S 46.38W
Patagonia f. 49 42.20S 67.00W
Pate I. 53 2.08S 41.02E
Paterson 44 40.55N 74.10W
Pathfinder Resr. 40 42.25N106.55W
Patía r. 46 1.54N 78.30W
Patkai Hills 25 26.30N 95.30E
Pátmos i. 15 37.20N 26.33E
Patna 25 25.36N 85.07E
Patos de Minas 45 18.35S 46.32W
Pátrai 15 38.15N 21.45E
Patraïkós Kólpos g. 15 38.15N 21.35E
Patrickswell 10 52.36N 8.43W
Patuca r. 43 15.50N 84.18W
Pau 12 43.18N 0.22W
Pauillac 12 45.12N 0.44W
Pavia 14 45.10N 9.10E
Pavlodar 22 52.21N 76.59E
Paysandú 49 32.19S 58.05W
Peace r. 38 59.00N111.26W
Peace River town 38 56.15N117.18W
Peak Hill town N.S.W. 37 32.47S148.13E
Pearl r. 41 30.15N 89.25W
Pebane 53 17.14S 38.10E
Peć 15 42.40N 20.17E
Pechenga 18 69.28N 31.04E
Pechora r. 20 68.10N 54.00E
Pechorskoye More sea 20 69.00N 55.00E
Pecos r. 40 29.45N101.25W
Pécs 17 46.05N 18.14E
Pedro Juan Caballero 45 22.30S 55.44W
Peebinga 36 34.55S140.57E
Peebles 11 55.39N 3.12W
Peel r. 38 68.13N135.00W
Peel 8 54.14N 4.42W
Peene r. 16 53.53N 13.49E
Pegasus B. 29 43.15S173.00E
Pegu 27 17.20N 96.36E
Pehuajó 49 35.50S 61.50W
Pekanbaru 27 0.33N101.20E
Peking see Beijing 26
Peleng i. 27 1.30S123.10E
Pelly r. 38 62.50N137.35W
Pelotas 45 31.45S 52.20W
Pematangsiantar 27 2.59N 99.01E
Pemba I. 53 5.10S 39.45E
Pembroke 9 51.41N 4.57W
Peñaranda de Bracamonte 13 40.54N 5.13W
Penarth 9 51.26N 3.11W
Peñas, Cabo de c. 13 43.42N 5.52W
Pendine 9 51.44N 4.33W
Penge 52 5.31S 24.37E
Penicuik 11 55.49N 3.13W
Pennsylvania d. 44 40.45N 77.30W
Penny Highland mtn. 39 67.10N 66.50W
Penola 36 37.23S140.21E
Penonomé 43 8.30N 80.20W
Penrith 8 54.40N 2.45W
Penryn 9 50.10N 5.07W
Pensacola 41 30.30N 87.12W
Penticton 38 49.29N119.38W
Pentland Firth str. 11 58.40N 3.00W
Pentland Hills 11 55.50N 3.20W
Penzance 9 50.07N 5.32W
Pereira 46 4.47N 75.46W
Pergamino 49 33.53S 60.35W
Péribonca r. 44 48.45N 72.05W
Périgueux 12 45.12N 0.44E
Perm 20 58.01N 56.10E
Péronne 12 49.56N 2.57E
Perpendicular, Pt. 37 35.03S150.50E
Perpignan 12 42.42N 2.54E
Perranporth 9 50.21N 5.09W
Perth Australia 33 31.58S115.49E
Perth U.K. 11 56.24N 3.28W
Peru 46 10.00S 75.00W
Perugia 14 43.06N 12.24E
Pervouralsk 20 56.59N 59.58E
Pesaro 14 43.54N 12.54E
Pescara 14 42.27N 14.13E
Pescara r. 14 42.28N 14.13E
Peshāwar 25 34.01N 71.33E
Petatlán 42 17.31N101.16W
Petauke 53 14.16S 31.21E
Peterborough 9 52.35N 0.14W
Peterhead 11 57.30N 1.46W
Peterlee 8 54.45N 1.18W
Petersfield 9 51.00N 0.56W
Petropavlovsk 22 54.53N 69.13E
Petropavlovsk Kamchatskiy 23 53.03N158.43E
Petrópolis 45 22.30S 43.06W
Petrovsk 20 52.20N 45.24E
Petrovsk Zabaykal'skiy 23 51.20N108.55E
Petrozavodsk 20 61.46N 34.19E
Pforzheim 16 48.53N 8.41E
Phangnga 27 8.29N 98.31E
Philadelphia Penn. 44 39.57N 75.07W
Philippines 27 13.00N123.00E
Philippine Sea 30 18.00N135.00E
Philipstown 54 30.25S 24.26E
Phnom Penh 27 11.35N104.55E
Phoenix Ariz. 40 33.30N111.55W
Phoenix Is. 30 4.00S172.00W
Phuket 27 7.55N 98.23E

Piacenza 14 45.03N 9.42E
Piangil 35 35.04S143.20E
Pianosa i. 14 42.35N 10.05E
Piave r. 14 45.33N 12.45E
Pic r. 44 48.36N 86.28W
Picardie d. 12 49.42N 2.40E
Pickering 8 54.15N 0.46W
Pickwick L. resr. 41 35.00N 88.10W
Picton Australia 37 34.12S150.35E
Picton New Zealand 29
41.17S174.02E
Piedras Negras 42 28.40N100.32W
Pierre 40 44.23N100.20W
Pietermaritzburg 54 29.36S 30.23E
Pietersburg 54 23.54S 29.27E
Piet Retief 54 27.00S 30.49E
Pikes Peak mtn. 40 38.50N105.03W
Piketberg 54 32.54S 18.43E
Piła 16 53.09N 16.44E
Pilcomayo r. 48 25.15S 57.43W
Pílos 15 36.55N 21.40E
Pinang, Pulau i. 27 5.30N100.10E
Pinarbaşi 21 38.43N 36.23E
Píndhos Óros mts. 15 39.40N 21.00E
Pine Bluff town 41 34.13N 92.00W
Ping r. 27 15.47N100.05E
Pingliang 26 35.21N107.12E
Piniós r. 15 39.51N 22.37E
Pinnaroo 36 35.18S140.54E
Pinsk 17 52.08N 26.01E
Pinto 48 29.09S 62.38W
Piombino 14 42.56N 10.30E
Piracicaba 45 22.45S 47.40W
Piraeus see Piraiévs 15
Piraiévs 15 37.56N 23.38E
Pirna 16 50.58N 13.58E
Pirot 15 43.10N 22.32E
Pisa 14 43.43N 10.24E
Pisciotta 14 40.08N 15.12E
Písek 16 49.19N 14.10E
Pita 50 11.05N 12.15W
Pitcairn I. 31 25.04S130.06W
Piteå 18 65.20N 21.30E
Piteşti 17 44.52N 24.51E
Pitlochry 11 56.43N 3.45W
Pittsburgh 44 40.26N 80.00W
Pittsfield 44 42.27N 73.15W
Piura 46 5.15S 80.38W
Plasencia 13 40.02N 6.05W
Platani r. 14 37.24N 13.15E
Plate, R. est. see La Plata, Río de 49
Platinum 38 59.00N161.50W
Platte r. 41 41.05N 96.50W
Plauen 16 50.29N 12.08E
Pleiku 27 13.57N108.01E
Plenty, B. of 29 37.40S176.50E
Pleven 15 43.25N 24.39E
Ploieşti 17 44.57N 26.02E
Plombières 12 47.58N 6.28E
Plovdiv 15 42.09N 24.45E
Plumtree 54 20.30S 27.50E
Plymouth 9 50.23N 4.09W
Plzeň 16 49.45N 13.22E
Po r. 14 44.51N 12.30E
Pobla de Segur 13 42.15N 0.58E
Pocatello 40 42.53N112.26W
Pocklington 8 53.56N 0.48W
Poços de Caldas 45 21.48S 46.33W
Podolsk 20 55.23N 37.32E
Podor 50 16.40N 14.57W
Pofadder 54 29.08S 19.22E
Poh 27 1.00S122.50E
Pointe-à-Pitre 43 16.14N 61.32W
Pointe Noire town 52 4.46S 11.53E
Poitiers 12 46.35N 0.20E
Pokhara 25 28.12N 83.59E
Poko 52 3.08N 26.51E
Poland 17 52.30N 19.00E
Polatli 21 39.34N 32.08E
Poligny 12 46.50N 5.42E
Pollino mtn. 14 39.53N 16.11E
Polperro 9 50.19N 4.31W
Poltava 21 49.35N 34.35E
Polynesia is. 30 4.00S165.00W
Pombal 47 6.45S 37.45W
Ponce 43 18.00N 66.40W
Ponferrada 13 42.32N 6.31W
Pongola r. 54 26.13S 32.38E
Ponta Grossa 45 25.00S 50.09W
Ponta Porã 45 22.27S 55.39W
Pontefract 8 53.42N 1.19W
Pontevedra 13 42.25N 8.39W
Pontiac Mich. 44 42.39N 83.18W
Pontianak 27 0.05S109.16E
Pontoise 12 49.03N 2.05E
Pontrilas 9 51.56N 2.53W
Pontypool 9 51.42N 3.01W
Pontypridd 9 51.36N 3.21W
Poole 9 50.42N 2.02W
Poplar Bluff town 41 36.40N 90.25W
Popocatépetl mtn. 42 19.02N 98.38W
Popokabaka 52 5.41S 16.40E
Popondetta 34 8.45S148.15E
Porbandar 25 21.38N 69.36E
Porcupine r. 38 66.25N145.20W
Pori 19 61.29N 21.47E
Porirua 29 41.08S174.50E
Porkkala 19 59.59N 24.26E
Pornic 12 47.07N 2.05W
Poronaysk 23 49.13N142.55E
Porsgrunn 19 59.09N 9.40E
Portadown 10 54.25N 6.27W
Portaferry 10 54.23N 5.33W
Portage la Prairie town 39 49.58N
98.20W
Portalegre 13 39.17N 7.25W
Port Alfred 54 33.36S 26.52E
Port Angeles 40 48.06N123.26W
Port Antonio 43 18.10N 76.27W
Port Arthur 35 43.08S147.50E
Port Augusta 36 32.30S137.46E
Port-au-Prince 43 18.33N 72.20W
Portbou 13 42.25N 3.09E
Port Chalmers 29 45.49S170.37E
Port Elizabeth 54 33.57S 25.34E
Port Ellen 11 55.38N 6.12W
Port Erin 8 54.05N 4.45W
Port Gentil 52 0.40S 8.46E
Portglenone 10 54.52N 6.30W
Port Harcourt 50 4.43N 7.05E
Porthcawl 9 51.28N 3.42W
Port Hedland 32 20.24S118.36E
Porthmadog 8 52.55N 4.08W
Port Huron 44 42.59N 82.28W
Portimão 13 37.08N 8.32W
Port Kembla 37 34.28S150.54E
Portland Maine 44 43.39N 70.17W
Portland Oreg. 40 45.32N122.40W
Port Laoise 10 53.03N 7.20W
Port Lincoln 36 34.43S135.49E
Port Macquarie 37 31.28S152.25E
Portmarnock 10 53.25N 6.09W
Port Moresby 34 9.30S147.07E
Portnaguiran 11 58.15N 6.10W
Port-Nouveau Québec 39 58.35N
65.59W
Porto 13 41.09N 8.37W
Pôrto Alegre 45 30.03S 51.10W
Porto Amboim 52 10.45S 13.43E
Porto Esperança 45 19.36S 57.24W
Port of Spain 43 10.38N 61.31W
Pörtom 18 62.42N 21.37E
Porton 9 51.08N 1.44W
Porto-Novo 50 6.30N 2.47E
Porto Torres 14 40.49N 8.24E
Porto Vecchio 12 41.35N 9.16E
Pôrto Velho 46 8.45S 63.54W
Portpatrick 11 54.51N 5.07W
Port Phillip B. 37 38.05S144.50E
Port Pirie 36 33.11S138.01E
Portree 11 57.24N 6.12W
Portrush 10 55.12N 6.40W
Port St. Louis 12 43.25N 4.40E
Portsmouth 9 50.48N 1.06W
Portsoy 11 57.41N 2.41W
Portstewart 10 55.11N 6.43W
Port Sudan see Būr Sūdān 51
Port Talbot 9 51.35N 3.48W
Portugal 13 39.30N 8.05W
Port Vendres 12 42.31N 3.06E
Posadas 48 27.25S 55.48W
Posse 45 14.05S 46.22W
Postmasburg 54 28.19S 23.03E
Potchefstroom 54 26.42S 27.05E
Potenza 14 40.40N 15.47E
Potgietersrus 54 24.11S 29.00E
Poti r. 47 5.01S 42.48W
Potiskum 50 11.40N 11.03E
Potosí 48 19.35S 65.45W
Potsdam 16 52.24N 13.04E
Pottstown 44 40.15N 75.38W
Povorino 21 51.12N 42.15E
Powder r. 40 46.40N105.15W
Powell, L. 40 37.30N110.45W
Powys d. 9 52.26N 3.26W
Požarevac 17 44.38N 21.12E
Poznań 16 52.25N 16.53E
Pozoblanco 13 38.23N 4.51W
Prachuap Kiri Khan 27 11.50N 99.49E
Prades 12 42.38N 2.25E
Prague see Praha 16
Praha 16 50.05N 14.25E
Prato 14 43.52N 11.06E
Preesall 8 53.55N 2.58W
Prescott Ariz. 40 34.34N112.28W
Presidencia Roque Sáenz Peña 48
26.50S 60.30W
Presidente Epitácio 45 21.56S
52.07W
Presidente Prudente 45 22.09S
51.24W
Prespa, L. 15 40.53N 21.02E
Presteigne 9 52.17N 3.00W
Preston 8 53.46N 2.42W
Preston Idaho 40 42.06N111.53W
Prestonpans 11 55.57N 3.00W
Prestwick 11 55.30N 4.36W
Pretoria 54 25.43S 28.11E
Préveza 15 38.58N 20.43E
Příbram 16 49.42N 14.00E
Prieska 54 29.40S 22.43E
Prilep 15 41.20N 21.32E
Primorsk R.S.F.S.R. 20 60.18N
28.35E
Prince Albert 54 33.14S 22.02E
Prince Albert Sd. 38 70.25N115.00W
Prince Charles I. 39 67.50N 76.00W
Prince Edward Island d. 39 46.15N
63.10W
Prince of Wales, C. 38
66.00N168.30W
Prince of Wales I. 39 73.00N 99.00W
Prince Patrick I. 38 77.00N120.00W
Prince Rupert 38 54.09N130.20W
Princeton Ind. 44 38.21N 87.33W
Príncipe i. 50 1.37N 7.27E
Prinzapolca 43 13.19N 83.35W
Priština 15 42.39N 21.10E
Prizren 15 42.13N 20.42E
Prokopyevsk 22 53.55N 86.45E
Prome 26 18.50N 95.14E
Providence 44 41.50N 71.25W
Provins 12 48.34N 3.18E
Provo 40 40.15N111.40W
Prudhoe Bay town 38 70.20N148.25W
Prüm 16 50.12N 6.25E
Prut r. 17 45.29N 28.14E
Przemyśl 17 49.48N 22.48E
Przhevalsk 22 42.31N 78.22E
Psel r. 21 49.00N 33.30E
Pskov 20 57.48N 28.00E
Puebla 42 19.03N 98.10W
Pueblo 40 38.17N104.38W
Puente-Genil 13 37.24N 4.46W
Puerto Barrios 43 15.41N 88.32W
Puerto Cabezas 43 14.02N 83.24W
Puerto de Santa Maria 13 36.36N
6.14W
Puerto Juárez 43 21.26N 86.51W
Puertollano 13 38.41N 4.07W
Puerto Natales 49 51.44S 72.31W
Puerto Peñasco 42 31.20N113.35W
Puerto Pinasco 45 22.36S 57.53W
Puerto Plata 43 19.48N 70.41W
Puerto Princessa 27 9.46N118.45E
Puerto Quepos 43 9.28N 84.10W
Puerto Rico 43 18.20N 66.30W
Puerto Sastre 45 22.02S 58.00W
Pukaki, L. 29 44.00S170.10E
Pukekohe 29 37.12S174.56E
Pula 16 44.52N 13.53E
Puncak Jaya mtn. 27 4.00S137.15E
Pune 25 18.34N 73.58E
Punjab d. 25 30.45N 75.30E
Puno 46 15.53S 70.03W
Punta Alta town 49 38.50S 62.00W
Punta Arenas town 49 53.10S 70.56W
Punta Gorda town 43 16.10N 88.45W
Puntarenas 43 10.00N 84.50W
Pur r. 22 67.30N 75.30E
Purus r. 46 3.58S 61.25W
Pusan 26 35.05N129.02E
Pushkin 20 59.43N 30.22E
Pustoshka 20 56.20N 29.20E
Putao 26 27.22N 97.27E
Putaruru 29 38.03S175.47E
Putumayo r. 46 3.05S 68.10W
Puy de Dôme mtn. 12 45.46N 2.56E
Puysegur Pt. 29 46.10S166.35E
Pweto 53 8.27S 28.52E
Pwllheli 8 52.53N 4.25W
Pyasina r. 23 73.10N 84.55E
Pyatigorsk 21 44.04N 43.06E
Pyhä r. 18 64.28N 24.13E
Pyhäjoki 18 64.28N 24.14E
Pyinmana 26 19.45N 96.12E
Pyŏngyang 26 39.00N125.47E
Pyramid L. 40 40.00N119.35W
Pyrénées mts. 12 42.40N 0.30E

Q

Qamdo 26 31.11N 97.18E
Qarqan He r. 25 40.56N 86.27E
Qatar 24 25.20N 51.10E
Qattara Depression see Qaţţārah, Munkhafaḑ al f. 51
Qaţţārah, Munkhafaḑ al f. 51 29.40N
27.30E
Qāyen 24 33.44N 59.07E
Qiemo 25 38.08N 85.33E
Qilian Shan mts. 26 38.30N 99.20E
Qingdao 26 36.02N120.25E
Qingjiang 26 33.35N119.02E
Qiqihar 26 47.23N124.00E
Qishn 24 15.25N 51.40E
Quanzhou 26 24.57N118.36E
Queanbeyan 37 35.24S149.17E
Québec 44 46.50N 71.15W
Québec d. 39 51.00N 70.00W
Quedlinburg 16 51.48N 11.09E
Queen Charlotte Is. 38
53.00N132.30W
Queen Charlotte Str. 38
51.00N129.00W
Queen Elizabeth Is. 39 78.30N
99.00W
Queen Maud G. 39 68.30N 99.00W
Queensland d. 34 23.30S144.00E
Quelimane 53 17.53S 36.57E
Querétaro 42 20.38N100.23W
Quesnel 38 53.03N122.31W
Quetta 25 30.12N 67.00E
Quezaltenango 42 14.50N 91.30W
Quezon City 27 14.39N121.01E
Quibala 52 10.48S 14.56E
Quibaxi 52 8.34S 14.37E
Quiberon 12 47.29N 3.07W
Quilengues 52 14.09S 14.04E
Quimbele 52 6.29S 16.25E
Quimper 12 48.00N 4.06W
Quimperlé 12 47.52N 3.33W
Quincy Ill. 41 39.55N 91.22W
Qui Nhon 27 13.47N109.11E
Quinto 13 41.25N 0.30W
Quirindi 37 31.30S150.42E
Quissanga 53 12.24S 40.33E
Quissico 54 24.42S 34.44E
Quito 46 0.14S 78.30W
Quorn 36 32.20S138.02E
Qurlurtuuq 38 67.49N115.12W

R

Raasay i. 11 57.25N 6.05W
Raba 27 8.27S118.45E
Rabat 50 34.02N 6.51W
Rach Gia 27 10.02N105.05E
Racine 41 42.42N 87.50W
Radebeul 16 51.06N 13.41E
Radom 17 51.26N 21.10E
Radomir 15 42.32N 22.56E
Radstock 9 51.17N 2.25W
Rafaela 48 31.16S 61.44W
Rafsanjān 24 30.24N 56.00E
Ragusa 14 36.56N 14.44E
Rainier, Mt. 40 46.52N121.45W
Raipur 25 21.14N 81.38E
Rājasthān d. 25 26.15N 74.00E
Rājkot 25 22.18N 70.47E
Rakaia r. 29 43.52S172.13E
Rakvere 20 59.22N 26.28E
Raleigh 41 35.46N 78.39W
Rama 43 12.09N 84.15W
Ramelton 10 55.02N 7.40W
Ramos Arizpe 42 25.35N100.59W
Ramsey England 9 52.27N 0.06W
Ramsey I.o.M. 8 54.19N 4.23W
Ramsgate 9 51.20N 1.25E
Rancagua 49 34.10S 70.45W
Rānchi 25 23.21N 85.20E
Randalstown 10 54.45N 6.20W
Randers 19 56.28N 10.03E
Rangiora 29 43.18S172.38E
Rangitaiki r. 29 37.55S176.50E
Rangoon 27 16.47N 96.10E
Rannoch, Loch 11 56.41N 4.20W
Rann of Kachchh f. 25 23.50N 69.50E
Rapallo 14 44.20N 9.14E
Rapid City 40 44.06N103.14W
Rarotonga i. 30 21.14S159.46W
Rasht 24 37.18N 49.38E
Rathcormack 10 52.05N 8.18W
Rathdrum 10 52.56N 6.15W
Rathenow 16 52.37N 12.21E
Rathlin I. 10 55.17N 6.15W
Rath Luirc 10 52.21N 8.41W
Rathmullen 10 55.06N 7.32W
Raton 40 36.54N104.27W
Rattray Head 11 57.37N 1.50W
Rättvik 19 60.53N 15.06E
Rauma r. 18 62.32N 7.43E
Ravena 44 42.29N 73.49W
Ravenna 14 44.25N 12.12E
Ravensburg 16 47.47N 9.37E
Rāwalpindi 25 33.36N 73.04E
Rawlinna 33 31.00S125.21E
Rawlins 40 41.46N107.16W
Razgrad 17 43.32N 26.30E
Ré, Île de i. 12 46.10N 1.26W
Reading 9 51.27N 0.57W
Recife 47 8.06S 34.53W
Reconquista 48 29.08S 59.38W
Red r. Canada 39 50.30N 96.50W
Red r. U.S.A. 41 31.10N 92.00W
Red Basin f. see Sichuan Pendi f. 26
Red Bluff 40 40.11N122.16W
Redcar 8 54.37N 1.04W
Redding 40 40.35N122.24W
Redditch 9 52.18N 1.57W
Red Lake town 39 50.59N 93.40W
Redruth 9 50.14N 5.14W
Red Sea 24 20.00N 39.00E
Ree, Lough 10 53.31N 7.58W
Regensburg 16 49.01N 12.07E
Reggane 50 26.30N 0.30E
Reggio Calabria 14 38.07N 15.38E
Reggio Emilia-Romagna 14 44.40N
10.37E
Regina 38 50.30N104.38W
Reigate 9 51.14N 0.13W
Reims 12 49.15N 4.02E
Reindeer L. 38 57.00N102.20W
Rendsburg 16 54.19N 9.39E
Rengat 27 0.26S102.35E
Reni 17 45.28N 28.17E
Renmark 36 34.10S140.45E
Rennes 12 48.06N 1.40W
Reno r. 14 44.36N 12.17E
Reno 40 39.32N119.49W
Republican r. 41 39.05N 94.50W
Republic of Ireland 10 53.00N 8.00W
Republic of South Africa 54 28.30S
24.50E
Requena 46 5.05S 73.52W
Resistencia 48 27.28S 59.00W
Resolute 39 74.40N 95.00W
Rethel 12 49.30N 4.20E
Réthimnon 15 35.22N 24.29E
Reus 13 41.10N 1.06E
Reutlingen 16 48.30N 9.13E
Revelstoke 38 51.02N118.12W
Revue r. 54 19.58S 34.40E
Reykjavík 18 64.09N 21.58W
Rēzekne 20 56.30N 27.22E
Rhayader 9 52.19N 3.30W
Rhein r. 16 51.53N 6.03E
Rheine 16 52.17N 7.26E
Rhine see Rhein r. 16
Rhinelander 41 45.39N 89.23W
Rhino Camp town 53 2.58N 31.20E
Rhode Island d. 44 41.40N 71.30W
Rhodes i. see Ródhos i. 15
Rhondda 9 51.39N 3.30W
Rhône r. 12 43.25N 4.45E
Rhum i. 11 57.00N 6.20W
Rhyl 8 53.19N 3.29W
Ribadeo 13 43.32N 7.04W
Ribauè 53 14.57S 38.27E
Ribble r. 8 53.45N 2.44W
Ribeirão Prêto 45 21.09S 47.48W
Ribérac 12 45.14N 0.22E
Richland 40 46.20N119.17W
Richmond U.K. 8 54.24N 1.43W
Richmond Va. 41 37.34N 77.27W
Riesa 16 51.18N 13.18E
Rieti 14 42.24N 12.53E
Riga 19 56.53N 24.08E
Riga, G. of see Rīgas Jūras Līcis g. 19
Rīgas Jūras Līcis g. 19 57.30N
23.35E
Riihimäki 19 60.45N 24.46E
Rimah, Wādi ar r. 24 26.10N 44.00E
Rimini 14 44.01N 12.34E
Ringkøbing 19 56.05N 8.15E
Riobamba 46 1.44S 78.40W
Rio Branco 46 9.59S 67.49W
Río Claro 45 22.19S 47.35W
Rio de Janeiro 45 22.53S 43.17W
Río Gallegos 49 51.37S 69.10W
Rio Grande town 45 32.03S 52.08W
Río Grande r. 42 25.55N 97.08W
Río Grande r. 43 12.48N 83.30W
Rio Verde town 48 17.50S 50.55W
Ripley N.Y. 44 42.16N 79.43W
Ripon 8 54.08N 1.31W
Rirapora 45 17.20S 45.02W
Risör 19 58.43N 9.14E
Riverina f. 37 34.30S145.20E
Riversdale 54 34.05S 21.15E
Riyadh see Ar Riyāḑ 24
Rize 21 41.03N 40.31E
Rjukan 19 59.52N 8.34E
Roag, Loch 11 58.14N 6.50W
Roanne 12 46.02N 4.05E
Roanoke r. 41 36.00N 76.35W
Robin Hood's Bay town 8 54.26N
0.31W
Robinvale 36 34.37S142.50E
Roboré 48 18.20S 59.45W
Robson, Mt. 38 53.00N119.09W
Roccella 15 38.19N 16.24E
Rocha 45 34.30S 54.22W
Rochdale 8 53.36N 2.10W
Rochechouart 12 45.49N 0.50E
Rochefort 12 45.57N 0.58W
Rochester Kent 9 51.22N 0.30E
Rochester N.Y. 44 43.12N 77.37W
Rockford 41 42.16N 89.06W
Rockhampton 34 23.22S150.32E
Rockland Mich. 44 46.44N 89.12W
Rocklands Resr. 36 37.13S141.52E
Rock Springs Wyo. 40
41.35N109.13W
Rockville 44 39.05N 77.09W
Rodel 11 57.44N 6.58W
Ródhos i. 15 36.12N 28.00E
Rolla Mo. 41 37.56N 91.55W
Roma 14 41.54N 12.29E
Romaine r. 39 50.20N 63.45W
Romania 17 46.30N 24.00E
Romano, C. 41 25.50N 81.42W
Romans 12 45.03N 5.03E
Rome see Roma 14
Romilly 12 48.31N 3.44E
Romney Marsh f. 9 51.03N 0.55E
Rona i. 11 57.33N 5.58W
Ronda 13 36.45N 5.10W
Rondonópolis 47 16.29S 54.37W
Rönne 19 55.06N 14.42E
Roof Butte mtn. 40 36.29N109.05W
Roosendaal 16 51.32N 4.28E
Roosevelt r. 46 7.35S 60.20W
Ropcha 20 62.50N 51.55E
Roper r. 34 14.40S135.30E
Roraima, Mt. 46 5.14N 60.44W
Röros 18 62.35N 11.23E
Rosa, Monte mtn. 16 45.56N 7.51E
Rosario 49 32.57S 60.40W
Roscoff 12 48.44N 4.00W
Roscommon 10 53.38N 8.13W
Roscommon d. 10 53.38N 8.11W
Roscrea 10 52.57N 7.49W
Roseau 43 15.18N 61.23W
Roseburg 40 43.13N123.21W
Rosenheim 16 47.51N 12.09E
Rosetown 38 51.34N107.59W
Roskilde 19 55.39N 12.05E
Roslags-Näsby 19 59.26N 18.04E
Roslavl 20 53.55N 32.53E
Rosslare 10 52.17N 6.23W
Ross-on-Wye 9 51.55N 2.36W
Rostock 16 54.06N 12.09E
Rostov R.S.F.S.R. 21 47.15N 39.45E
Rothbury 8 55.19N 1.54W
Rotherham 8 53.26N 1.21W
Rothes 11 57.31N 3.13W
Rothesay 11 55.50N 5.03W
Roti i. 27 10.30S123.10E
Roto 37 33.04S145.27E
Rotorua 29 38.07S176.17E
Rotorua, L. 29 38.00S176.00E
Rotterdam 16 51.55N 4.29E
Roubaix 12 50.42N 3.10E
Rouen 12 49.26N 1.05E
Round Mt. 37 30.26S152.15E
Roundup 40 46.27N108.34W
Rouyn 44 48.14N 79.01W
Rovaniemi 18 66.30N 25.40E
Rovinj 16 45.06N 13.39E
Rovno 17 50.39N 26.10E
Roxburgh 29 45.33S169.19E
Royale, Isle i. 44 48.00N 89.00W
Royal Leamington Spa 9 52.18N
1.32W
Royal Tunbridge Wells 9 51.07N
0.16E
Royston 9 52.03N 0.01W
Rtishchevo 20 52.16N 43.45E
Ruahine Range mts. 29
40.00S176.00E
Ruapehu mtn. 29 39.20S175.30E
Ruapuke I. 29 46.45S168.30E
Rubi r. 52 2.50N 24.06E
Rudolstadt 16 50.44N 11.20E
Ruffec 12 46.02N 0.12E
Rufino 49 34.16S 62.45W
Rugby 9 52.23N 1.16W
Ruhr r. 16 51.27N 6.41E
Rukwa, L. 53 8.00S 32.20E
Ruma 17 44.59N 19.51E
Rum Cay i. 43 23.41N 74.53W
Runcorn 8 53.20N 2.44W
Rungwa r. 53 7.38S 31.55E
Rungwe Mt. 53 9.10S 33.40E
Ruo Shui r. 26 42.15N101.03E
Rusape 54 18.30S 32.08E
Ruse 15 43.50N 25.59E
Rushden 9 52.17N 0.37W
Rustavi 21 41.34N 45.03E
Rustenburg 54 25.39S 27.13E
Rutana 53 3.58S 30.00E
Ruteng 27 8.35S120.28E
Ruthin 8 53.07N 3.18W
Rutland 44 43.36N 72.59W
Rutshuru 53 1.10S 29.26E
Ruvu Coast 53 6.50S 38.42E
Ruvuma r. 53 10.30S 40.30E
Ruwenzori Range mts. 53 0.30N
30.00E
Ruyigi 53 3.26S 30.14E
Ruzayevka 20 54.04N 44.55E
Rwanda 53 2.00S 30.00E
Ryan, Loch 11 54.56N 5.02W
Ryazan 20 54.37N 39.43E
Ryazhsk 20 53.40N 40.07E
Rye 9 50.57N 0.46E
Rye r. 8 54.10N 0.44W
Rzeszów 17 50.04N 22.00E
Rzhev 20 56.15N 34.18E

S

Saale r. 16 51.58N 11.53E
Saarbrücken 16 49.15N 6.58E
Saarijärvi 18 62.43N 25.16E
Saba i. 43 17.42N 63.26W
Šabac 17 44.45N 19.41E
Sabadell 13 41.33N 2.07E
Sabi r. 54 21.16S 32.20E
Sabinas 42 26.33N101.10W
Sabinas Hidalgo 42 26.33N100.10W
Sabine r. 41 29.40N 93.50W
Sable I. 39 44.00N 60.00W
Sacedón 13 40.29N 2.44W
Sacramento 40 38.32N121.30W
Sacramento r. 40 38.05N122.00W
Sádaba 13 42.19N 1.10W
Sadani 53 6.00S 38.40E
Sadiya 25 27.49N 95.38E
Säffle 19 59.08N 12.56E
Saffron Walden 9 52.02N 0.15E
Safi 50 32.20N 9.17W
Sagamihara 28 35.32N139.23E
Saginaw 44 43.25N 83.54W
Sagua la Grande 43 22.55N 80.05W
Saguenay r. 44 48.10N 69.45W
Sagunto 13 39.40N 0.17W
Sahagún 13 42.23N 5.02W
Sahara des. 50 18.00N 12.00E
Sa'īdābād 24 29.28N 55.43E
Saidpur 25 25.47N 88.54E
Saigon see Ho Chi Minh 27
Saimbeyli 21 38.07N 36.08E
St. Abb's Head 11 55.54N 2.07W
St. Albans 9 51.46N 0.21W
St. Amand-Mont-Rond town 12
46.43N 2.29E
St. Andrews 11 56.20N 2.48W
St. Ann's Bay town 43 18.26N 77.12W
St. Anthony 39 51.24N 55.37W
St. Arnaud 36 36.40S143.20E
St. Augustine 41 29.54N 81.19W
St. Austell 9 50.20N 4.48W
St. Bees Head 8 54.31N 3.39W
St. Boniface 39 49.54N 97.07W
St. Brides B. 9 51.48N 5.03W
St. Brieuc 12 48.31N 2.45W
St. Catharines 44 43.10N 79.15W
St. Catherine's Pt. 9 50.34N 1.18W
St. Céré 12 44.52N 1.53E
St. Cloud 41 45.34N 94.10W
St. David's 9 51.54N 5.16W
St. David's Head 9 51.55N 5.19W
St. Denis 12 48.56N 2.21E
St. Dié 12 48.17N 6.57E
St. Dizier 12 48.38N 4.58E
St. Elias, Mt. 38 60.20N139.00W
Saintes 12 45.44N 0.38W
St. Étienne 12 45.26N 4.26E
Saintfield 10 54.28N 5.50W
St. Flour 12 45.02N 3.05E
St. Gallen 16 47.25N 9.23E
St. Gaudens 12 43.07N 0.44E
St. George 35 28.03S148.30E
St. George's 43 12.04N 61.44W
St. George's Channel 10 51.30N
6.20W
St. Germain 12 48.53N 2.04E
St. Girons 12 42.59N 1.08E
St. Gotthard Pass 12 46.30N 8.55E
St. Govan's Head 9 51.36N 4.55W
St. Helena B. 54 32.35S 18.05E
St. Helens 8 53.28N 2.43W
St. Helier 9 49.12N 2.07W
St. Hyacinthe 44 45.38N 72.57W
St. Ives 9 50.13N 5.29W
St. Jean Pied-de-Port 12 43.10N
1.14W
St. John 44 45.16N 66.03W
St. John r. 44 45.15N 66.04W
St. John's Antigua 43 17.07N 61.51W
St. John's Canada 39 47.34N 52.41W
St. John's Pt. 10 54.14N 5.39W
St. Joseph Mo. 41 39.45N 94.51W
St. Kitts-Nevis 43 17.20N 62.45W
St. Lawrence r. 44 48.45N 68.30W
St. Lawrence, G. of 39 48.00N
62.00W
St. Lawrence I. 38 63.00N170.00W
St. Lô 12 49.07N 1.05W
St. Louis 41 38.40N 90.15W
St. Lucia 43 14.05N 61.00W
St. Malo 12 48.39N 2.00W
St.-Marc 43 19.08N 72.41W
St. Margaret's Hope 11 58.49N
2.57W
St. Martin 9 49.27N 2.34W
St. Martin's i. 9 49.57N 6.16W
St. Mary 9 49.14N 2.10W
St. Marys 35 41.33S148.12E
St. Mary's i. 9 49.55N 6.16W
St. Maurice r. 44 46.21N 72.31W
St. Moritz 16 46.30N 9.51E
St. Nazaire 12 47.17N 2.12W
St. Neots 9 52.14N 0.16W
St. Omer 12 50.45N 2.15E
St. Paul Minn. 41 45.00N 93.10W
St. Peter Port 9 49.27N 2.32W
St. Petersburg 41 27.45N 82.40W
St. Pierre and Miquelon is. 39 47.00N
56.15W
St. Pölten 16 48.13N 15.37E
St. Quentin 12 49.51N 3.17E
St. Thomas 44 42.47N 81.12W
St. Tropez 12 43.16N 6.39E
St. Vallier 12 45.11N 4.49E
St. Vincent, G. 36 35.00S138.05E
St. Vincent and the Grenadines 43
13.00N 61.15W
St. Vith 16 50.15N 6.08E
St. Yrieix 12 45.31N 1.12E
Sakai 28 34.35N135.28E
Sakania 53 12.44S 28.34E
Sakarya r. 21 41.08N 30.36E
Sakhalin i. 23 50.00N143.00E
Sakrivier 54 30.53S 20.24E
Sal r. 21 47.33N 40.40E
Sala 19 59.55N 16.36E
Salado r. Buenos Aires 49 35.44S
57.22W
Salado r. Santa Fé 49 31.40S 60.41W
Salado r. La Pampa 49 36.15S
66.55W
Salālah 24 17.00N 54.04E
Salamanca 13 40.58N 5.40W
Salbris 12 47.26N 2.03E
Salcombe 9 50.14N 3.47W
Sale 37 38.06S147.06E
Salem 25 11.38N 78.08E
Salerno 14 40.41N 14.45E
Salerno, Golfo di g. 14 40.30N
14.45E
Salford 8 53.30N 2.17W
Salima 53 13.45S 34.29E
Salina Cruz 42 16.11N 95.12W
Salins 12 46.56N 5.53E
Salisbury 9 51.04N 1.48W
Salisbury Plain f. 9 51.15N 1.55W
Salluit 39 62.10N 75.40W
Salmon r. 40 45.50N116.50W
Salmon River Mts. 40
44.30N114.30W
Salo 19 60.23N 23.08E
Salobreña 13 36.45N 3.35W
Salon 12 43.38N 5.06E
Salonga r. 52 0.09S 19.52E
Salsk 21 46.30N 41.33E
Salso r. 14 37.07N 13.57E
Salt r. 40 33.23N112.18W
Salta 48 24.47S 65.24W
Saltee Is. 10 52.08N 6.36W
Saltfleet 8 53.25N 0.11E
Saltillo 42 25.30N101.00W
Salt Lake City 40 40.45N111.55W
Salto 49 31.23S 57.58W
Salto da Divisa 47 16.04S 40.00W
Salvador 47 12.58S 38.29W
Salween r. 27 16.32N 97.35E
Salyany 21 39.36N 48.59E
Salzburg 16 47.54N 13.03E
Samaná 43 19.14N 69.20W
Samar i. 27 11.45N125.15E
Samarinda 27 0.30S117.09E
Samarkand 22 39.40N 66.57E
Sambalpur 25 21.27N 83.58E
Sambre r. 12 50.29N 4.52E
Same 53 4.10S 37.43E
Samoa is. 30 14.20S170.00W
Samoa Is. 30 14.00S171.00W
Sámos i. 15 37.44N 26.45E
Samothráki i. 15 40.26N 25.35E
Sampit 27 2.34S112.59E
Samsun 21 41.17N 36.22E
Şan'ā' 24 15.23N 44.14E
Sana r. 16 45.03N 16.23E
Sanaga r. 50 3.35N 9.40E
San Antonio Tex. 40 29.25N 98.30W
San Antonio Oeste 49 40.44S
64.57W
San Bernardino 40 34.07N117.18W
San Blas, C. 41 29.40N 85.25W
San Carlos de Bariloche 49 41.08S
71.15W
San Cristóbal 46 7.46N 72.15W
Sancti Spíritus 43 21.55N 79.28W
Sanda i. 11 55.17N 5.34W
Sandakan 27 5.52N118.04E
Sanday i. 11 59.15N 2.33W
Sandgate 37 27.18S153.00E
San Diego 40 32.45N117.10W
Sandnes 19 58.51N 5.44E
Sandness 11 60.18N 1.38W
Sandoa 52 9.41S 22.56E
Sandoway 26 18.28N 94.20E
Sandown 9 50.39N 1.09W
Sandpoint town 40 48.17N116.34W
Sandringham 8 52.50N 0.30E
Sandusky Ohio 44 41.27N 82.42W
Sandviken 19 60.37N 16.46E
San Fernando de Apure 46 7.35N
67.15W
San Francisco 40 37.45N122.27W
San Francisco, C. 46 0.50N 80.05W
San Francisco de Macorís 43 19.19N
70.15W
Sangha r. 52 1.10S 16.47E
Sangonera r. 13 37.58N 1.04W
San Gottardo, Passo del pass 16
46.30N 8.55E
San José 43 9.59N 84.04W
San Jose 40 37.20N121.55W
San José de Chiquitos 48 17.53S
60.45W
San José de Mayo 49 34.20S 56.42W
San Juan 43 18.29N 66.08W
San Juan r. 40 37.20N110.05W
San Juan del Norte 43 10.58N
83.40W
San Juan Mts. 40 37.30N107.00W
Sankuru r. 52 4.20S 20.27E
San Leonardo 13 41.49N 3.04W
Sanlúcar de Barrameda 13 36.46N
6.21W
San Luis Obispo 40 35.16N120.40W
San Luis Potosí 42 22.10N101.00W
San Marino 14 43.55N 12.27E
San Matías, Golfo g. 49 41.30S
64.00W
San Miguel 43 13.28N 88.10W
San Miguel de Tucumán 48 26.49S
65.13W
San Miguelito 43 9.02N 79.30W
San Nicolas 49 33.20S 60.13W
San Pedro Sula 43 15.26N 88.01W
San Pietro i. 14 39.09N 8.16E
Sanquhar 11 55.22N 3.56W
San Remo 14 43.48N 7.46E
San Salvador i. 43 24.00N 74.32W
San Salvador 43 13.40N 89.10W
San Sebastián 13 43.19N 1.59W
San Severo 14 41.40N 15.24E
Santa Ana 40 33.44N117.54W
Santa Bárbara 42 26.48N105.49W
Santa Barbara 40 34.25N119.41W
Santa Clara 43 22.25N 79.58W
Santa Cruz Bolivia 48 17.45S 63.14W
Santa Cruz Canary Is. 50 28.27N
16.14W
Santa Cruz r. 49 50.03S 68.35W
Santa Cruz Is. 30 10.30S166.00E
Santa Elena, C. 43 10.54N 85.56W
Santa Fé 49 31.40S 60.40W
Santa Fe 40 35.41N105.57W
Santa Maria 40 34.56N120.25W
Santana do Livramento 49 30.53S
55.31W
Santander 13 43.28N 3.48W
Santañy 13 39.20N 3.07E
Santarém 47 2.26S 54.41W
Santa Rosa Calif. 40 38.26N122.43W
Santa Rosalía 42 27.20N112.20W
Santiago 49 33.27S 70.40W
Santiago r. 46 4.30S 77.48W
Santiago de Compostela 13 42.52N
8.33W
Santiago de Cuba 43 20.00N 75.49W
Santiago del Estero 48 27.50S
64.15W
Santo André 45 23.39S 46.29W
Santo Angelo 45 28.18S 54.16W
Santo Domingo 43 18.30N 69.57W
Santos 45 23.56S 46.22W
Santo Tomé 48 28.31S 56.03W
San Vicente 43 13.38N 88.42W
Sanza Pombo 52 7.20S 16.12E
São Borja 45 28.35S 56.01W
São Carlos 45 22.01S 47.54W
São Francisco r. 47 10.20S 36.20W
São Francisco do Sul 45 26.17S
48.39W
São João del Rei 45 21.08S 44.15W
São José do Rio Prêto 45 20.50S
49.20W
São José dos Campos 45 23.07S
45.52W
São Leopoldo 45 29.46S 51.09W
São Luís 47 2.34S 44.16W
São Miguel d'Oeste 45 26.45S
53.34W
Saône r. 16 45.46N 4.52E
São Paulo 45 23.33S 46.39W
São Paulo de Olivença 46 3.34S
68.55W
São Tomé i. 50 0.19N 6.43E
São Tomé & Príncipe 50 1.00N 7.00E
São Vicente 45 23.57S 46.23W
Sapporo 26 43.05N141.21E
Sapri 14 40.04N 15.38E
Sara Buri 27 14.30N100.59E
Sarajevo 17 43.52N 18.26E
Saransk 20 54.12N 45.10E
Saratov 21 51.30N 45.55E
Sarbāz 24 26.39N 61.20E
Sardegna i. 14 40.00N 9.00E
Sardinia i. see Sardegna i. 14
Sargodha 25 32.01N 72.40E
Sarh 50 9.08N 18.22E
Sark i. 9 49.26N 2.22W
Sarmi 27 1.51S138.45E
Sarmiento 49 45.35S 69.05W
Särna 19 61.41N 13.08E
Sarnia 44 42.58N 82.23W
Sarpsborg 19 59.17N 11.07E
Sarrebourg 12 48.43N 7.03E
Sarria 13 42.47N 7.25W
Sarthe r. 12 47.29N 0.30W
Saskatchewan d. 38 55.00N105.00W
Saskatchewan r. 39 53.25N100.15W
Saskatoon 38 52.10N106.40W
Sasovo 20 54.21N 41.58E
Sassandra 50 4.58N 6.08W
Sassari 14 40.43N 8.33E
Sassnitz 16 54.32N 13.40E
Satu Mare 17 47.48N 22.52E
Sauda 19 59.39N 6.20E
Saudi Arabia 24 26.00N 44.00E
Saulieu 12 47.17N 4.14E
Sault Sainte Marie Canada 44 46.31N
84.20W
Sault Sainte Marie U.S.A. 44 46.29N
84.22W
Saumlaki 34 7.59S131.22E
Saumur 12 47.16N 0.05W
Saurimo 52 9.38S 20.20E
Sava r. 17 44.50N 20.26E
Savannah r. 41 32.10N 81.00W
Savannah Ga. 41 32.09N 81.01W
Savé 50 8.04N 2.37E
Save r. 54 20.59S 35.02E
Savona 16 44.18N 8.28E
Savonlinna 20 61.52N 28.51E
Sawston 9 52.07N 0.11E
Sawtell 37 30.21S153.05E
Saxmundham 9 52.13N 1.29E
Saynshand 26 44.58N110.12E
Sayula 42 19.52N103.36W
Sázava r. 16 49.53N 14.21E
Scafell Pike mtn. 8 54.27N 3.12W
Scalloway 11 60.08N 1.17W
Scammon Bay town 38
61.50N165.35W
Scapa Flow str. 11 58.53N 3.05W
Scarborough 8 54.17N 0.24W
Schaffhausen 16 47.42N 8.38E
Schelde r. 16 51.13N 4.25E
Schenectady 44 42.47N 73.53W
Schleswig 16 54.32N 9.34E
Schouten, Kepulauan is. 27
0.45S135.50E
Schwandorf 16 49.20N 12.08E
Schwaner, Pegunungan mts. 27
0.45S113.20E
Schweinfurt 16 50.03N 10.16E
Schwerin 16 53.38N 11.25E
Sciacca 14 37.31N 13.05E
Scilly, Isles of 9 49.55N 6.20W
Scone 37 32.01S150.53E
Scotland 11 55.30N 4.00W
Scottsbluff 40 41.52N103.40W

Scottsdale 35 41.09S147.31E
Scranton 44 41.24N 75.40W
Scunthorpe 8 53.35N 0.38W
Seahouses 8 55.35N 1.38W
Seal *r.* **39** 59.00N 95.00W
Seascale 8 54.24N 3.29W
Seaton 9 50.43N 3.05W
Seattle 40 47.35N122.20W
Sebinkarahisar 21 40.19N 38.25E
Sêda *r.* **13** 38.55N 7.30W
Sédhiou 50 12.44N 15.33W
Ségou 50 13.28N 6.18W
Segovia 13 40.57N 4.07W
Segre *r.* **13** 41.25N 0.21E
Segura *r.* **13** 38.07N 0.14W
Segura, Sierra de *mts.* **13** 38.00N 2.50W
Seiland *i.* **18** 70.25N 23.10E
Seinäjoki 18 62.47N 22.50E
Seine *r.* **12** 49.28N 0.25E
Selaru *i.* **34** 8.09S131.00E
Selayar *i.* **27** 6.07S120.28E
Selby 8 53.47N 1.05W
Sele *r.* **14** 40.30N 14.50E
Sélestat 16 48.16N 7.28E
Selkirk 11 55.33N 2.51W
Selkirk Mts. 38 49.00N116.00W
Selsey Bill *c.* **9** 50.44N 0.47W
Selvas *f.* **46** 6.00S 65.00W
Selwyn Mts. 38 63.00N130.00W
Selwyn Range *mts.* **34** 21.35S140.35E
Seman *r.* **15** 40.53N 19.25E
Semarang 27 6.58S110.29E
Seminoe Resr. 40 42.05N106.50W
Semliki *r.* **53** 1.12N 30.27E
Semmering Pass 16 47.40N 16.00E
Semu *r.* **53** 3.57S 34.20E
Senanga 52 15.52S 23.19E
Sendai 26 38.16N140.52E
Senegal 50 14.15N 14.15W
Sénégal *r.* **50** 16.00N 16.28W
Senekal 54 28.18S 27.37E
Senigallia 16 43.42N 13.14E
Senlis 12 49.12N 2.35E
Sennen 9 50.04N 5.42W
Sens 16 48.12N 3.18E
Sept Îles *town* **44** 50.13N 66.22W
Serengeti Nat. Park 53 2.30S 35.00E
Serenje 53 13.12S 30.50E
Sergach 20 55.32N 45.27E
Serov 20 59.42N 60.32E
Serowe 54 22.22S 26.42E
Serpa 13 37.56N 7.36W
Serpukhov 20 54.53N 37.25E
Sérrai 15 41.04N 23.32E
Serui 27 1.53S136.15E
Sesheke 52 17.14S 24.22E
Sesimbra 13 38.26N 9.06W
Sète 12 43.25N 3.43E
Sete Lagoas 45 19.29S 44.15W
Sétif 50 36.09N 5.26E
Settat 50 33.04N 7.37W
Setté Cama 52 2.32S 9.46E
Settle 8 54.05N 2.18W
Setúbal 13 38.31N 8.54W
Sevastopol' 21 44.36N 33.31E
Sevenoaks 9 51.16N 0.12E
Sévérac 12 44.20N 3.05E
Severn *r.* **9** 51.50N 2.21W
Severnaya Zemlya *is.* **23** 80.00N 96.00E
Severodvinsk 20 64.35N 39.50E
Sevilla 13 37.24N 5.59W
Sèvre Niortaise *r.* **12** 46.35N 1.05W
Seward Pen. 38 65.00N164.10W
Seydhisfjördhur *town* **18** 65.16N 14.02W
Seylac 51 11.21N 43.30E
Seymour 37 37.01S145.10E
Sézanne 12 48.44N 3.44E
Sfax 50 34.45N 10.43E
'sGravenhage 16 52.05N 4.16E
Shabeelle *r.* **53** 0.30N 43.10E
Shabunda 53 2.42S 27.20E
Shaftesbury 9 51.00N 2.12W
Shāhjahānpur 25 27.53N 79.55E
Shakhty 21 47.43N 40.16E
Shamva 53 17.20S 31.38E
Shanghai 26 31.18N121.50E
Shannon *r.* **10** 52.39N 8.43W
Shantou 26 23.22N116.39E
Shaoguan 26 24.53N113.31E
Shaoxing 26 30.01N120.40E
Shaoyang 26 27.10N111.14E
Shap 8 54.32N 2.40W
Shapinsay *i.* **11** 59.03N 2.51W
Shaqrā' 24 13.21N 45.42E
Shashi *r.* **54** 22.10S 29.15E
Shashi 26 30.18N112.20E
Shasta, Mt. 40 41.35N122.12W
Shawinigan 44 46.33N 72.45W
Sheboygan 41 43.46N 87.44W
Sheeffry Hills 10 53.41N 9.42W
Sheelin, Lough 10 53.48N 7.20W
Sheffield 8 53.23N 1.28W
Shellharbour 37 34.35S150.52E
Shenandoah Va. **44** 38.29N 78.37W
Shenyang 26 41.48N123.27E
Shepparton 37 36.25S145.26E
Sheppey, Isle of 9 51.24N 0.50E
Sherborne 9 50.56N 2.31W
Sherbrooke 44 45.24N 71.54W
Sheridan 40 44.48N107.05W
Sheringham 8 52.56N 1.11E
Sherkin I. 10 51.28N 9.25W
Sherman Tex. **41** 33.39N 96.35W
Sherridon 39 57.07N101.05W
'sHertogenbosch 16 51.42N 5.19E
Shetland Is. *d.* **11** 60.20N 1.15W
Shevchenko 21 43.37N 51.11E
Shiel, Loch 11 56.48N 5.33W
Shikoku *i.* **26** 33.30N133.30E
Shilka *r.* **23** 53.20N121.10E
Shillong 25 25.34N 91.53E
Shimizu 28 35.01N138.29E
Shin, Loch 11 58.06N 4.32W
Shinyanga 53 3.40S 33.20E
Shipka Pass 15 42.45N 25.25E
Shipston on Stour 9 52.04N 1.38W
Shīrāz 24 29.36N 52.33E
Shire *r.* **53** 17.46S 35.20E
Shizuoka 28 34.58N138.23E
Shkodër 15 42.03N 19.30E
Shkumbin *r.* **15** 41.01N 19.26E
Sholāpur 25 17.43N 75.56E
Shostka 20 51.53N 33.30E
Shreveport 41 32.30N 93.46W
Shrewsbury 9 52.42N 2.45W
Shropshire *d.* **9** 52.35N 2.40W
Shuangyashan 26 46.37N131.22E
Shumagin Is. 38 55.00N160.00W
Shurugwi 54 19.40S 30.00E
Shuya 20 56.49N 41.23E
Siālkot 25 32.30N 74.31E
Siauliai 19 55.56N 23.19E
Šibenik 14 43.45N 15.55E
Sibi 25 29.33N 67.53E
Sibiti 52 3.40S 13.24E
Sibiti *r.* **53** 3.47S 34.45E
Sibolga 27 1.42N 98.48E
Sicasica 48 17.22S 67.45W
Sichuan Pendi *f.* **26** 31.00N105.62E
Sicilia *i.* **14** 37.30N 14.00E
Sicily *i. see* Sicilia *i.* **14**
Sidlaw Hills 11 56.31N 3.10W
Sidmouth 9 50.40N 3.13W
Siedlce 17 52.10N 22.18E
Sieg *r.* **16** 50.49N 7.11E
Siegen 16 50.52N 8.02E
Siena 14 43.19N 11.20E
Sierra Leone 50 8.30N 12.00W
Sigüenza 13 41.04N 2.38W
Siguiri 50 11.28N 9.07W
Siirt 21 37.56N 41.56E
Sikasso 50 11.18N 5.38W
Sikhote Alin *mts.* **23** 44.00N135.00E
Sikkim *d.* **25** 27.30N 88.30E
Sil *r.* **13** 42.24N 7.15W
Silifke 21 36.22N 33.57E
Silistra 15 44.07N 27.17E
Silkeborg 19 56.10N 9.34E
Silloth 8 54.53N 3.25W
Silver City 40 32.47N108.16W
Silverstone 9 52.05N 1.03W
Silverton 36 31.53S141.13E
Simav *r.* **15** 40.24N 28.31E
Simcoe, L. 44 44.20N 79.20W
Simferopol' 21 44.57N 34.05E
Simiyu *r.* **53** 2.32S 33.25E
Simo *r.* **18** 65.37N 25.03E
Simon's Town 54 34.12S 18.26E
Simplon Pass 12 46.15N 8.03E
Simpson Desert 34 25.00S136.50E
Simrishamn 19 55.33N 14.20E
Sīnā', Shibh Jazīrat *pen.* **51** 29.00N 34.00E
Sinan 26 27.51N108.24E
Sindara 52 1.07S 10.41E
Sines 13 37.58N 8.52W
Singapore 27 1.20N103.45E
Singapore *town* **27** 1.20N103.45E
Singaraja 27 8.06S115.07E
Singida 53 4.45S 34.42E
Singkep *i.* **27** 0.30S104.20E
Sinj 15 43.42N 16.38E
Sinop 21 42.02N 35.09E
Sintang 27 0.03N111.31E
Sioux City 41 42.30N 96.28W
Sioux Falls *town* **41** 43.34N 96.42W
Sioux Lookout *town* **39** 50.07N 91.54W
Siping 26 43.10N124.24E
Sira *r.* **19** 58.17N 6.24E
Siracusa 14 37.05N 15.17E
Siret *r.* **15** 45.28N 27.56E
Síros *i.* **15** 37.26N 24.56E
Sisak 14 45.30N 16.21E
Sishen 54 27.46S 22.59E
Sisteron 12 44.16N 5.56E
Sitka 38 57.05N135.20W
Sittang *r.* **27** 17.25N 96.50E
Sivas 21 39.44N 37.01E
Sivrihisar 21 39.29N 31.32E
Sīwah 51 29.12N 25.31E
Sixmilecross 10 54.34N 7.08W
Skagen 19 57.44N 10.36E
Skagerrak *str.* **19** 57.45N 8.55E
Skagway 38 59.23N135.20W
Skaill 11 58.56N 2.43W
Skara 19 58.22N 13.25E
Skeena *r.* **38** 54.10N129.08W
Skegness 8 53.09N 0.20E
Skellefte *r.* **18** 64.42N 21.06E
Skelmersdale 8 53.34N 2.49W
Skene 19 57.29N 12.38E
Skerries 10 53.35N 6.07W
Skhíza *i.* **15** 36.42N 21.45E
Skiddaw *mtn.* **8** 54.40N 3.09W
Skien 19 59.12N 9.36E
Skipness 11 56.45N 5.22W
Skipton 8 53.57N 2.01W
Skíros *i.* **15** 38.50N 24.33E
Skjálfanda Fljót *r.* **18** 65.55N 17.30W
Skopje 15 41.58N 21.27E
Skövde 19 58.24N 13.50E
Skovorodino 23 54.00N123.53E
Skreia 19 60.39N 10.56E
Skull 10 51.32N 9.33W
Skye *i.* **11** 57.20N 6.15W
Slagelse 19 55.24N 11.22E
Slaney *r.* **10** 52.21N 6.30W
Slantsy 20 59.09N 28.09E
Slatina 15 44.26N 24.23E
Slave *r.* **38** 61.10N113.30W
Slavyansk 21 48.51N 37.36E
Sleaford 8 53.00N 0.22W
Sleat, Sd. of *str.* **11** 57.05N 5.48W
Sledmere 8 54.04N 0.35W
Sleetmute 38 61.40N157.11W
Slieve Aughty Mts. 10 53.05N 8.31W
Slieve Bloom Mts. 10 53.03N 7.35W
Slieve Callan *mtn.* **10** 52.51N 9.18W
Slieve Donard *mtn.* **10** 54.11N 5.56W
Slieve Gamph *mts.* **10** 54.06N 8.52W
Slieve Mish *mts.* **10** 52.48N 9.48W
Slieve Miskish *mts.* **10** 51.41N 9.56W
Slievenamon *mtn.* **10** 52.25N 7.34W
Slieve Snaght *mtn.* Donegal **10** 55.12N 7.20W
Sligo 10 54.17N 8.28W
Sligo *d.* **10** 54.10N 8.35W
Sligo B. 10 54.18N 8.40W
Sliven 15 42.41N 26.19E
Slobodskoy 20 58.42N 50.10E
Slough 9 51.30N 0.35W
Sluch *r.* **17** 52.08N 27.31E
Slyne Head 10 53.25N 10.12W
Smithfield 54 30.11S 26.31E
Smolensk 20 54.49N 32.04E
Smólikas *mtn.* **15** 40.06N 20.55E
Smolyan 15 41.34N 24.45E
Snaefell *mtn.* **8** 54.16N 4.28W
Snake *r.* Idaho **40** 43.50N117.05W
Snake *r.* Wash. **40** 46.15N119.00W
Sneek 16 53.03N 5.40E
Sneem 10 51.50N 9.54W
Sneeuwberg *mtn.* **54** 32.30S 19.09E
Snizort, Loch 11 57.35N 6.30W
Snowdon *mtn.* **8** 53.05N 4.05W
Snowy Mts. 37 36.30S148.20E
Sobral 47 3.45S 40.20W
Sochi 21 43.35N 39.46E
Société, Îles de la *is.* **31** 17.00S150.00W
Socorro, Isla *i.* **42** 18.45N110.58W
Socotra *i. see* Suquṭrá *i.* **24**
Sodankylä 18 67.29N 26.32E
Söderhamn 19 61.18N 17.03E
Södertälje 19 59.12N 17.37E
Sofia *see* Sofiya **15**
Sofiya 15 42.41N 23.19E
Sögüt 21 40.02N 30.10E
Soissons 12 49.23N 3.20E
Söke 15 37.46N 27.26E
Sokodé 50 8.59N 1.08E
Sokol 20 59.28N 40.04E
Sokolo 50 14.53N 6.11W
Sokoto 50 13.02N 5.15E
Solikamsk 20 59.40N 56.45E
Solingen 16 51.10N 7.05E
Solomon Is. 30 8.00S160.00E
Solway Firth *est.* **8** 54.50N 3.30W
Solwezi 52 12.11S 26.23E
Soma 15 39.11N 27.36E
Somabhula 54 19.40S 29.38E
Somali Republic 51 5.30N 47.00E
Sombor 15 45.48N 19.08E
Somerset *d.* **9** 51.09N 3.00W
Somerset East 54 32.43S 25.33E
Somerset I. 39 73.00N 93.30W
Somes *r.* **17** 48.40N 22.30E
Somme *r.* **12** 50.01N 1.40E
Son *r.* **25** 25.42N 84.52E
Sönderborg 19 54.55N 9.47E
Songea 53 10.42S 35.39E
Songkhla 27 7.12N100.35E
Songololo 52 5.40S 14.05E
Son La 25 21.20N103.55E
Sonneberg 16 50.22N 11.10E
Sonora *r.* **42** 28.45N111.55W
Soria 13 41.46N 2.28W
Sorocaba 45 23.29S 47.27W
Soroti 53 1.40N 33.37E
Söröya *i.* **18** 70.35N 22.30E
Sorraia *r.* **13** 39.00N 8.51W
Sorrento 14 40.37N 14.22E
Sortavala 20 61.40N 30.40E
Sotik 53 0.40S 35.08E
Sotra *i.* **19** 60.15N 5.10E
Sŏul 26 37.30N127.00E
Soure 13 40.04N 8.38W
Souris *r.* **40** 49.38N 99.35W
Sousse 50 35.48N 10.38E
Soustons 12 43.45N 1.19W
Southampton 9 50.54N 1.23W
Southampton I. 39 64.30N 84.00W
South Australia *d.* **36** 30.00S137.00E
South Bend Ind. **44** 41.40N 86.15W
South Carolina *d.* **41** 34.00N 81.00W
South Cerney 9 51.40N 1.55W
South China Sea 27 12.30N115.00E
South Dakota *d.* **40** 44.30N100.00W
South Dorset Downs *hills* **9** 50.40N 2.25W
South Downs *hills* **9** 50.04N 0.34W
South East C. 35 43.38S146.48E
Southend-on-Sea 9 51.32N 0.43E
Southern Alps *mts.* **29** 43.20S170.45E
Southern Cross 33 31.14S119.16E
Southern Lueti *r.* **52** 16.15S 23.12E
Southern Uplands *hills* **11** 55.30N 3.30W
South Esk *r.* **11** 56.43N 2.32W
South Glamorgan *d.* **9** 51.27N 3.22W
South Horr 53 2.10N 36.45E
South I. 29 43.00S171.00E
South Korea 26 36.00N128.00E
Southland *d.* **29** 45.40S168.00E
South Molton 9 51.01N 3.50W
Southport 8 53.38N 3.01W
South Ronaldsay *i.* **11** 58.47N 2.56W
South Shields 8 55.00N 1.24W
South Tyne *r.* **11** 54.59N 2.08W
South Uist *i.* **11** 57.15N 7.20W
Southwest C. 29 47.15S167.30E
Southwold 9 52.19N 1.41E
South Yorkshire *d.* **8** 53.28N 1.25W
Soutpansberg *mts.* **54** 22.58S 29.50E
Soweto 54 26.16S 27.51E
Soyo 52 6.12S 12.25E
Spain 13 40.00N 4.00W
Spalding 8 52.47N 0.09W
Spandau 16 52.32N 13.13E
Spárti 15 37.04N 22.28E
Speke G. 53 2.20S 33.30E
Spence Bay *town* **39** 69.30N 93.20W
Spencer G. 36 34.00S137.00E
Sperrin Mts. 10 54.49N 7.06W
Spétsai *i.* **15** 37.15N 23.10E
Spey *r.* **11** 57.40N 3.06W
Speyer 16 49.18N 8.26E
Spilsby 8 53.10N 0.06E
Spokane 40 47.40N117.25W
Spree *r.* **16** 52.32N 13.15E
Springbok 54 29.40S 17.50E
Springfontein 54 30.15S 25.41E
Springs *town* **54** 26.16S 28.27E
Spurn Head 8 53.35N 0.08E
Sri Lanka 25 7.30N 80.50E
Srīnagar 25 34.05N 74.49E
Staffa *i.* **11** 56.26N 6.21W
Stafford 8 52.49N 2.09W
Staffordshire *d.* **8** 52.40N 1.57W
Staines 9 51.26N 0.31W
Stainforth 8 53.37N 1.01W
Stakhanov 21 48.34N 38.40E
Stamford N.Y. **44** 42.25N 74.37W
Standerton 54 26.57S 29.14E
Stanley 49 51.42W 57.51W
Stanovoy Khrebet *mts.* **23** 56.00N125.40E
Stara Zagora 15 42.26N 25.37E
Starogard Gdański 17 53.59N 18.33E
Staryy Oskol 21 51.20N 37.50E
Stavanger 19 58.58N 5.45E
Stavropol' 21 45.03N 41.59E
Stawell 36 37.06S142.52E
Steelpoort 54 24.44S 30.13E
Stellenbosch 54 33.56S 18.51E
Stendal 16 52.36N 11.52E
Sterling Colo. **40** 40.37N103.13W
Steubenville 44 40.22N 80.39W
Stevenage 9 51.54N 0.11W
Stevenston 11 55.39N 4.45W
Stewart 38 55.56N130.01W
Stewart I. 29 47.00S168.00E
Steyr 16 48.04N 14.25E
Stikine Mts. 38 59.00N129.00W
Stilton 9 52.29N 0.17W
Stinchar *r.* **11** 55.06N 5.00W
Stirling 11 56.07N 3.57W
Stockbridge 9 51.07N 1.30W
Stockholm 19 59.20N 18.03E
Stockport 8 53.25N 2.11W
Stocksbridge 8 53.30N 1.36W
Stockton Calif. **40** 37.59N121.20W
Stockton-on-Tees 8 54.34N 1.20W
Stoke-on-Trent 8 53.01N 2.11W
Stone 8 52.55N 2.10W
Stonehaven 11 56.58N 2.13W
Store Baelt *str.* **19** 55.30N 11.00E
Stören 18 63.03N 10.18E
Stornoway 11 58.12N 6.23W
Storsjön *l.* **18** 63.10N 14.20E
Storuman 18 65.06N 17.06E
Stour *r.* Dorset **9** 50.43N 1.47W
Stour *r.* Kent **9** 51.19N 1.22E
Stour *r.* Suffolk **9** 51.56N 1.03E
Stowmarket 9 52.11N 1.00E
Stow on the Wold 9 51.55N 1.42W
Strabane 10 54.50N 7.30W
Stradbally Laois **10** 53.01N 7.09W
Strahan 35 42.08S145.21E
Stralsund 16 54.18N 13.06E
Strangford Lough 10 54.28N 5.35W
Stranraer 11 54.54N 5.02W
Strasbourg 12 48.35N 7.45E
Stratford Australia **37** 37.57S147.05E
Stratford New Zealand **29** 39.20S174.18E
Stratford-upon-Avon 9 52.12N 1.42W
Strathclyde *d.* **11** 55.45N 4.45W
Strathmore *f.* Tayside **11** 56.44N 2.45W
Strathspey *f.* **11** 57.25N 3.25W
Straubing 16 48.53N 12.35E
Street 9 51.07N 2.43W
Strimon *r.* **15** 40.47N 23.51E
Stromboli *i.* **14** 38.48N 15.14E
Stromeferry 11 57.21N 5.34W
Stromness 11 58.57N 3.18W
Strömö *i.* **18** 62.08N 7.00W
Strömstad 19 58.56N 11.10E
Stronsay *i.* **11** 59.07N 2.36W
Stroud 9 51.44N 2.12W
Strumica 15 41.26N 22.39E
Stryy 17 49.16N 23.51E
Sturminster Newton 9 50.56N 2.18W
Sturt Desert 36 28.30S141.12E
Stuttgart 16 48.47N 9.12E
Styr *r.* **17** 52.07N 26.35E
Suck *r.* **10** 53.16N 8.04W
Sucre 48 19.02S 65.17W
Sudan 51 14.00N 30.00E
Sudbury 44 46.30N 81.00W
Suez *see* As Suways **51**
Suffolk *d.* **9** 52.16N 1.00E
Suhl 16 50.37N 10.43E
Suide 26 37.35N110.08E
Suir *r.* **10** 52.17N 7.00W
Sukhona *r.* **20** 61.30N 46.28E
Sukhumi 21 43.01N 41.01E
Sukkertoppen 39 65.40N 53.00W
Sukkur 25 27.42N 68.52E
Sulawesi *i.* **27** 2.00S120.30E
Sulina 15 45.08N 29.40E
Sullana 46 4.52S 80.39W
Sulmona 14 42.04N 13.57E
Sulu Archipelago 27 5.30N121.00E
Sulu Sea 27 8.00N120.00E
Sumatera *i.* **27** 2.00S102.00E
Sumba *i.* **27** 9.30S119.55E
Sumbawa *i.* **27** 8.45S117.50E
Sumbawanga 53 7.58S 31.36E
Sumburgh Head 11 59.51N 1.16W
Sumy 21 50.55N 34.49E
Sunart, Loch 11 56.43N 5.45W
Sundarbans *f.* **25** 21.45N 89.00E
Sundays *r.* **54** 33.43S 25.50E
Sunderland 8 54.55N 1.22W
Sundsvall 19 62.23N 17.18E
Sunyani 50 7.22N 2.18W
Superior Wisc. **41** 46.42N 92.05W
Superior, L. 44 48.00N 88.00W
Süphan Dagi *mtn.* **21** 38.55N 42.55E
Suquṭrá *i.* **24** 12.30N 54.00E
Şūr 24 22.23N 59.32E
Sura 20 53.52N 45.45E
Surabaya 27 7.14S112.45E
Surakarta 27 7.32S110.50E
Surat 25 21.12N 72.50E
Surat Thani 27 9.09N 99.23E
Surgut 22 61.13N 73.20E
Surinam 47 4.00N 56.00W
Surrey *d.* **9** 51.16N 0.30W
Surtsey *i.* **18** 63.18N 20.30W
Susquehanna *r.* **44** 39.33N 76.05W
Sutherland 54 32.23S 20.38E
Sutlej *r.* **25** 29.23N 71.02E
Sutton England **9** 51.22N 0.12W
Sutton in Ashfield 8 53.08N 1.16W
Suways, Qanāt as *canal* **51** 30.40N 32.20E
Suzhou 26 31.22N120.45E
Svartisen *mtn.* **18** 66.40N 13.56E
Sveg 19 62.02N 14.21E
Svendborg 19 55.03N 10.37E
Svetogorsk 20 61.07N 28.50E
Svishtov 15 43.36N 25.23E
Svobodnyy 23 51.24N127.50E
Svolvaer 18 68.15N 14.40E
Swaffham 9 52.38N 0.42E
Swakop *r.* **54** 22.38S 14.32E
Swakopmund 54 22.40S 14.34E
Swale *r.* **8** 54.05N 1.20W
Swan *r.* **33** 32.03S115.45E
Swanage 9 50.36N 1.59W
Swansea 9 51.37N 3.57W
Swaziland 54 26.30S 32.00E
Sweden 18 63.00N 16.00E
Swidnica 16 50.51N 16.29E
Swilly, Lough 10 55.10N 7.32W
Swindon 9 51.33N 1.47W
Switzerland 12 47.00N 8.00E
Sydney 37 33.55S151.10E
Syktyvkar 20 61.42N 50.45E
Sylt *i.* **16** 54.50N 8.20E
Syracuse N.Y. **44** 43.03N 76.09W
Syr Darya *r.* **22** 46.00N 61.12E
Syria 24 35.00N 38.00E
Syrian Desert *see* Bādiyat ash Shām *des.* **24**
Syzran 20 53.10N 48.29E
Szczecin 16 53.25N 14.32E
Szeged 15 46.16N 20.08E

T

Ţabas Khorās-a **24** 33.36N 56.55E
Tabasco *d.* **42** 18.30N 93.00W
Tábor 16 49.25N 14.41E
Tabora 53 5.02S 32.50E
Tabou 50 4.28N 7.20W
Tabrīz 24 38.05N 46.18E
Tabūk 24 28.23N 36.36E
Tacoma 40 47.16N122.30W
Tacuarembó 49 31.44S 55.59W
Tademaït, Plateau du *f.* **50** 28.45N 2.10E
Tadoussac 44 48.09N 69.43W
Taegu 26 35.52N128.36E
Taganrog 21 47.14N 38.55E
Tagus *r.* Portugal/Spain *see* Tejo *r.* **13**
Tahiti *i.* **31** 17.37S149.27W
Taihape 29 39.40S175.48E
Tain 11 57.48N 4.04W
Taipei 26 25.05N121.30E
Taivalkoski 18 65.34N 28.15E
Taiwan 26 24.00N121.00E
Taiwan Str. 26 24.30N119.30E
Taiyuan 26 37.48N112.33E
Ta'izz 24 13.35N 44.02E
Tajo *r.* Spain *see* Tejo *r.* **13**
Tajuna *r.* **13** 40.10N 3.35W
Talaud, Kepulauan *is.* **27** 4.20N126.50E
Talca 49 35.26S 71.40W
Taldom 20 56.49N 37.30E
Tallahassee 41 30.28N 84.19W
Talsi 19 57.15N 22.36E
Tamale 50 9.26N 0.49W
Tamanrasset 50 22.50N 5.31E
Tamar *r.* **9** 50.28N 4.13W
Tambov 20 52.44N 41.28E
Tambre *r.* **13** 42.50N 8.55W
Tâmega *r.* **13** 41.04N 8.17W
Tamil Nadu *d.* **25** 11.15N 79.00E
Tampa 41 27.58N 82.38W
Tampere 19 61.30N 23.45E
Tampico 42 22.18N 97.52W
Tamworth 9 52.38N 1.42W
Tana 18 70.26N 28.14E
Tanacross 38 63.12N143.30W
T'ana Hāyk' *l.* **51** 12.00N 37.20E
Tandil 49 37.18S 59.10W
Tanga 53 5.07S 39.05E
Tanganyika, L. 53 6.00S 29.30E
Tanger 50 35.48N 5.45W
Tangier *see* Tanger **50**
Tangshan 26 39.32N118.08E
Tanimbar, Kepulauan *is.* **27** 7.50S131.30E
Tannu Ola *mts.* **23** 51.00N 93.30E
Ţanţā 51 30.48N 31.00E
Tanzania 53 5.00S 35.00E
Taoudenni 50 22.45N 4.00W
Tapajós *r.* **47** 2.25S 54.40W
Taquari *r.* **45** 19.00S 57.27W
Tara *r.* **15** 43.23N 18.47E
Ţarābulus 50 32.58N 13.12E
Tarakan 27 3.20N117.38E
Tarancón 13 40.01N 3.01W
Taranto 15 40.28N 17.14E
Tarbat Ness *c.* **11** 57.52N 3.46W
Tarbert Strath. **11** 55.51N 5.25W
Tarbert W. Isles **11** 57.54N 6.49W
Tarbes 12 43.14N 0.05E
Taree 37 31.54S152.26E
Tarifa 13 36.01N 5.36W
Tarija 48 21.31S 64.45W
Tarim He *r.* **25** 41.00N 83.30E
Tarn *r.* **12** 44.15N 1.15E
Tarnów 17 50.01N 20.59E
Tarragona 13 41.07N 1.15E
Tarsus 21 36.52N 34.52E
Tartu 20 58.20N 26.44E
Tashkent 22 41.16N 69.13E
Tasman B. 29 41.00S173.15E
Tasmania *d.* **35** 42.00S147.00E
Tasman Mts. 29 41.00S172.40E
Tasman Pen. 35 43.08S147.51E
Tasman Sea 30 38.00S162.00E
Tatarsk 22 55.14N 76.00E
Tatvan 21 38.31N 42.15E
Taubaté 45 23.00S 45.36W
Taumarunui 29 38.53S175.16E
Taung 54 27.32S 24.46E
Taunton 9 51.01N 3.07W
Taunus *mts.* **16** 50.07N 7.48E
Taupo 29 38.42S176.06E
Taupo, L. 29 38.45S175.30E
Tauranga 29 37.42S176.11E
Taurus Mts. *see* Toros Dağlari *mts.* **51**
Taveta 53 3.23S 37.42E
Tavira 13 37.07N 7.39W
Tavistock 9 50.33N 4.09W
Taw *r.* **9** 51.05N 4.05W
Tawau 27 4.16N117.54E
Tay *r.* **11** 56.21N 3.18W
Tay, Loch 11 56.32N 4.08W
Taylor, Mt. 40 35.14N107.36W
Taymyr, Ozero *l.* **23** 74.20N101.00E
Tayport 11 56.27N 2.53W
Tayshet 23 55.56N 98.01E
Tayside *d.* **11** 56.35N 3.28W
Taytay 27 10.47N119.32E
Taz *r.* **22** 67.30N 78.50E
Tbilisi 21 41.43N 44.48E
Tchad, Lac *see* Chad, L. **50**
Tchibanga 52 2.52S 11.07E
Te Anau, L. 29 45.10S167.15E
Tecuci 17 45.49N 27.27E
Tees *r.* **8** 54.35N 1.11W
Tegucigalpa 43 14.05N 87.14W
Tehrān 24 35.40N 51.26E
Tehuacán 42 18.30N 97.26W
Tehuantepec 42 16.21N 95.13W
Teifi *r.* **9** 52.05N 4.41W
Teignmouth 9 50.33N 3.30W
Tejo *r.* **13** 39.00N 8.57W
Tekapo, L. 29 43.35S170.30E
Tekirdağ 15 40.59N 27.30E
Te Kuiti 29 38.20S175.10E
Tela 43 15.56N 87.25W
Telavi 21 41.56N 45.30E
Tel Aviv-Yafo 24 32.05N 34.46E
Tele *r.* **52** 2.48N 24.00E
Telford 9 52.42N 2.30W
Tell Atlas *mts.* **50** 36.10N 4.00E
Telukbetung 27 5.28S105.06E
Tembo Aluma 52 7.42S 17.15E
Teme *r.* **9** 52.10N 2.13W
Temirtau 26 50.05N 72.55E
Temora 37 34.27S147.35E
Tempio 14 40.54N 9.06E
Temple 41 31.06N 97.22W
Templemore 10 52.48N 7.51W
Temuco 49 38.44S 72.36W
Tenby 9 51.40N 4.42W
Tenerife *i.* **50** 28.10N 16.30W
Tengiz, Ozero *l.* **22** 50.30N 69.00E
Tenke 52 10.34S 26.07E
Tennant Creek *town* **34** 19.31S134.15E
Tennessee *d.* **41** 36.00N 86.00W
Tennessee *r.* **41** 37.10N 88.25W
Tenterfield 37 29.01S152.04E
Teófilo Otoni 45 17.52S 41.31W
Tepic 42 21.30N104.51W
Teplice 16 50.40N 13.50E
Ter *r.* **13** 42.02N 3.10E
Tera *r.* **13** 38.55N 8.01W
Teramo 14 42.40N 13.43E
Teresina 47 5.09S 42.46W
Termez 22 37.15N 67.15E
Termini 14 37.59N 13.42E
Términos, Laguna de *b.* **42** 18.30N 91.30W
Termoli 14 41.58N 14.59E
Terni 14 42.34N 12.44E
Ternopol 17 49.35N 25.39E
Terschelling *i.* **16** 53.25N 5.25E
Teruel 13 40.21N 1.06W
Teslin *r.* **38** 62.00N135.00W
Test *r.* **9** 50.55N 1.29W
Têt *r.* **12** 42.43N 3.00E
Tete 53 16.10S 33.30E
Tétouan 50 35.34N 5.22W
Tevere *r.* **14** 41.45N 12.16E
Teviot *r.* **11** 55.36N 2.27W
Teviotdale *f.* **8** 55.26N 2.46W
Teviothead 11 55.20N 2.56W
Tewkesbury 9 51.59N 2.09W
Texarkana Ark. **41** 33.28N 94.02W
Texas *d.* **40** 32.00N100.00W
Texel *i.* **16** 53.05N 4.47E
Texoma, L. 41 34.00N 96.40W
Thabana Ntlenyana *mtn.* **54** 29.28S 29.17E
Thabazimbi 54 24.36S 27.23E
Thailand 27 17.00N101.30E
Thailand, G. of 27 11.00N101.00E
Thale Luang *l.* **27** 7.40N100.20E
Thallon 37 28.39S148.49E
Thames *r.* Canada **44** 42.19N 82.28W
Thames *r.* U.K. **9** 51.30N 0.05E
Thāna 25 19.12N 72.58E
Thar Desert 25 28.00N 72.00E
Thargomindah 35 27.59S143.45E
Tharrawaddy 25 17.37N 95.48E
Thásos *i.* **15** 40.40N 24.39E
The Cheviot *mtn.* **8** 55.29N 2.10W
The Cheviot Hills 8 55.22N 2.24W
The Coorong *g.* **36** 36.00S139.30E
The Everglades *f.* **41** 26.00N 80.30W
The Fens *f.* **9** 55.10N 4.13W
The Gulf 24 27.00N 50.00E
The Hague *see* 'sGravenhage **16**
The Little Minch *str.* **11** 57.40N 6.45W
Thelon *r.* **39** 64.23N 96.15W
The Machers *f.* **11** 54.45N 4.28W
The Minch *str.* **11** 58.10N 5.50W
The Needles *c.* **9** 50.39N 1.35W
Theodore Roosevelt L. 40 33.30N111.10W
The Pas 39 53.50N101.15W
The Pennines *hills* **8** 55.40N 2.20W
The Rhinns *f.* **11** 54.50N 5.02W
Thermopylae, Pass of 15 38.47N 22.34E
The Solent *str.* **9** 50.45N 1.20W
Thessaloníki 15 40.38N 22.56E
Thetford 9 52.25N 0.44E
The Wash *b.* **8** 52.55N 0.15E
The Weald *f.* **9** 51.05N 0.20E
Thiers 12 45.51N 3.33E
Thimbu 25 27.28N 89.39E
Thionville 12 49.22N 6.11E
Thíra *i.* **15** 36.24N 25.27E
Thirsk 8 54.15N 1.20W
Thisted 19 56.57N 8.42E
Thjórsá *r.* **18** 63.53N 20.38W
Thomasville Fla. **41** 30.50N 83.59W
Thonburi 25 13.43N100.27E
Thorshavn 18 62.02N 6.47W
Thouars 12 46.59N 0.13W
Thrapston 9 52.24N 0.32W
Thule 39 77.30N 69.29W
Thun 16 46.46N 7.38E
Thunder Bay *town* **44** 48.25N 89.14W
Thüringer Wald *mts.* **16** 50.40N 10.50E
Thurles 10 52.41N 7.50W
Thurso 11 58.35N 3.32W
Tianjin 26 39.07N117.08E
Tian Shan *mts.* **25** 42.00N 80.30E
Tianshui 26 34.25N105.58E
Tibati 50 6.25N 12.33E
Tiber *r. see* Tevere *r.* **14**
Tibesti *mts.* **50** 21.00N 17.30E
Tibetan Plateau *see* Qing Zang Gaoyuan *f.* **25**
Tibooburra 36 29.28S142.04E
Tiburón, Isla *i.* **42** 29.00N112.25W
Ticino *r.* **14** 45.09N 9.12E
Tierra Blanca 42 18.28N 96.12W
Tierra del Fuego *i.* **49** 54.00S 69.00W
Tietar *r.* **13** 39.50N 6.00W
Tigris *r. see* Dijlah *r.* **24**
Tihāmah *f.* **24** 19.00N 41.00E
Tijuana 42 32.29N117.10W
Tikhoretsk 21 45.52N 40.07E
Tikhvin 20 59.35N 33.29E
Tiksi 23 71.40N128.45E
Tilburg 16 51.34N 5.05E
Tilbury 9 51.28N 0.23E
Till *r.* Northum. **8** 55.41N 2.12W
Timaru 29 44.23S171.41E
Timbuktu *see* Tombouctou **50**
Timişoara 17 45.47N 21.15E
Timişul *r.* **15** 44.49N 20.28E
Timmins 44 48.30N 81.20W
Timok *r.* **15** 44.13N 22.40E
Timor *i.* **27** 9.30S125.00E
Timor Sea 32 11.00S127.00E
Tinahely 10 52.48N 6.19W
Tingsryd 19 56.32N 14.59E
Tinne *r.* **7** 59.05N 9.43E
Tínos *i.* **15** 37.36N 25.08E
Tipperary 10 52.29N 8.10W
Tipperary *d.* **10** 52.37N 7.55W
Tiranë 15 41.20N 19.48E
Tirano 14 46.12N 10.10E
Tiraspol 17 46.50N 29.38E
Tirebolu 21 41.02N 38.49E
Tiree *i.* **11** 56.30N 6.50W
Tîrgu-Jiu 17 45.03N 23.17E
Tîrgu Mureş 17 46.33N 24.34E
Tirso *r.* **14** 39.52N 8.33E
Tiruchchirāppalli 25 10.50N 78.43E
Tisa *r.* **17** 45.09N 20.16E
Tisza *r.* Hungary *see* Tisa *r.* **17**
Titicaca, L. 48 16.00S 69.00W
Titograd 15 42.30N 19.16E
Titovo Užice 17 43.52N 19.51E
Titov Veles 15 41.43N 21.49E
Tiverton 9 50.54N 3.30W
Tizimín 43 21.10N 88.09W
Tizi Ouzou 50 36.44N 4.05E
Tlemcen 50 34.53N 1.21W
Toba, Danau *l.* **27** 2.45N 98.50E
Tobelo 27 1.45N127.59E
Tobermory 11 56.37N 6.04W
Tobol *r.* **22** 58.15N 68.12E
Tobolsk 22 58.15N 68.12E
Tocantins *r.* **47** 1.50S 49.15W
Tocorpuri *mtn.* **48** 22.26S 67.53W
Tocumwal 37 35.51S145.34E
Togo 50 8.30N 1.00E
Tokaj 17 48.08N 21.27E
Tokat 21 40.20N 36.35E
Tokoroa 29 38.13S175.53E
Tōkyō 28 35.42N139.46E
Toledo 44 41.40N 83.35W
Toledo, Montes de *mts.* **13** 39.35N 4.30W
Tolosa 13 43.09N 2.04W
Toluca 42 19.20N 99.40W
Tol'yatti 20 53.32N 49.24E
Tombigbee *r.* **41** 31.05N 87.55W
Tombouctou 50 16.49N 2.59W
Tombua 52 15.55S 11.51E
Tomelloso 13 39.09N 3.01W
Tomini, Teluk *g.* **27** 0.30S120.45E
Tomintoul 11 57.15N 3.24W
Tom Price 32 22.49S117.51E
Tomsk 22 56.30N 85.05E
Tonalá 42 16.08N 93.41W
Tonbridge 9 51.12N 0.16E
Tönder 19 54.56N 8.54E
Tonga 31 20.00S175.00W
Tongking, G. of 27 20.00N108.00E
Tongue 11 58.28N 4.25W
Tônlé Sap *l.* **27** 12.50N104.15E
Tonnerre 12 47.51N 3.59E
Tönsberg 19 59.17N 10.25E
Toowoomba 35 27.35S151.54E
Topeka 41 39.03N 95.41W
Topko *mtn.* **23** 57.20N138.10E
Tordesillas 13 41.30N 5.00W
Töre 18 65.54N 22.39E
Torino 14 45.04N 7.40E
Tormes *r.* **13** 41.18N 6.29W
Torne *r.* Sweden *see* Tornio *r.* **18**
Torneträsk *l.* **18** 68.20N 19.10E
Tornio *r.* **18** 65.53N 24.07E
Toro 13 41.31N 5.24W
Toronto 44 43.39N 79.23W
Tororo 53 0.42N 34.13E
Toros Dağlari *mts.* **21** 37.15N 34.15E
Torquay 9 50.27N 3.31W
Torre de Moncorvo 13 41.10N 7.03W
Torrelavega 13 43.21N 4.00W
Torremolinos 13 36.38N 4.30W
Torrens, L. 36 31.00S137.50E
Torreón 42 25.34N103.25W
Torres Str. 34 10.00S142.20E
Torres Vedras 13 39.05N 9.15W
Torrevieja 13 37.59N 0.40W
Torridge *r.* **9** 51.01N 4.12W
Torridon 11 57.23N 5.31W
Torridon, Loch 11 57.35N 5.45W
Tortola *i.* **43** 18.28N 64.40W
Tortosa 13 40.49N 0.31E
Tortue, Île de la *i.* **43** 20.05N 72.57W
Toruń 17 53.01N 18.35E
Tory I. 10 55.16N 8.13W
Tory Sd. 10 55.14N 8.15W
Torzhok 20 57.02N 34.51E
Tosno 20 59.38N 30.46E
Tostado 48 29.15S 61.45W
Totana 13 37.46N 1.30W
Totma 20 59.59N 42.44E
Tottenham 37 32.14S147.24E
Toubkal *mtn.* **50** 31.03N 7.57W
Touggourt 50 33.08N 6.04E
Toul 12 48.41N 5.54E
Toulon 12 43.07N 5.53E
Toulouse 12 43.33N 1.24E
Tournai 16 50.36N 3.23E
Tournus 12 46.33N 4.55E
Tours 12 47.23N 0.42E
Towcester 9 52.07N 0.56W
Townsend, Mt. 37 36.24S148.15E
Townsville 34 19.13S146.48E
Towyn 9 52.37N 4.08W
Toyohashi 28 34.46N137.23E
Trabzon 21 41.00N 39.43E
Trafalgar, Cabo *c.* **13** 36.11N 6.02W
Trail 38 49.04N117.39W
Tralee 10 52.16N 9.42W
Tralee B. 10 52.18N 9.55W
Tranås 19 58.03N 14.59E
Trangie 37 32.03S148.01E
Transkei *f.* **54** 32.12S 28.20E
Transylvanian Alps *see* Carpaţii Meridionalimts. *mts.* **15**
Trapani 14 38.02N 12.30E
Traralgon 37 38.12S146.32E
Trasimeno, Lago *l.* **14** 43.09N 12.07E
Travers, Mt. 29 42.05S172.45E
Travnik 15 44.14N 17.40E
Třeboň 16 49.01N 14.50E
Tredegar 9 51.47N 3.16W
Tregaron 9 52.14N 3.56W
Treinta-y-Tres 45 33.16S 54.17W
Trelew 49 43.15S 65.20W
Trelleborg 19 55.22N 13.10E
Tremadog B. 8 52.52N 4.14W
Trenque Lauquen 49 35.56S 62.43W
Trent *r.* **8** 53.41N 0.41W
Trento 14 46.04N 11.08E
Trenton N.J. **44** 40.15N 74.43W
Tres Arroyos 49 38.26S 60.17W
Treuchtlingen 16 48.57N 10.55E
Treviso 14 45.40N 12.14E
Trier 16 49.45N 6.39E
Trieste 14 45.40N 13.47E
Triglav *mtn.* **14** 46.21N 13.50E
Tríkala 15 39.34N 21.46E
Trinidad & Tobago 43 10.30N 61.20W
Trinity *r.* **41** 29.55N 94.45W
Tripoli *see* Ţarābulus **50**
Tripura *d.* **25** 23.50N 92.00E
Trois-Rivières *town* **44** 46.21N 72.33W
Troitsko-Pechorsk 20 62.40N 56.08E
Trollhättan 19 58.16N 12.18E
Tromsö 18 69.42N 19.00E
Trondheim 18 63.36N 10.23E
Troon 11 55.33N 4.40W
Trostan *mtn.* **10** 55.03N 6.10W
Trowbridge 9 51.18N 2.12W
Troy N.Y. **44** 42.43N 73.40W
Troyes 12 48.18N 4.05E
Trujillo 46 8.06S 79.00W
Truk Is. 30 7.23N151.46E
Truro 9 50.17N 5.02W
Trysil *r.* **19** 61.03N 12.30E
Tselinograd 22 51.10N 71.28E
Tshane 54 24.02S 21.54E
Tshela 52 4.57S 12.57E
Tshikapa 52 6.28S 20.48E
Tshofa 52 5.13S 25.20E
Tshopo *r.* **52** 0.30N 25.07E
Tshuapa *r.* **52** 0.14S 20.45E
Tskhinvali 21 42.14N 43.58E
Tsu 28 34.43N136.31E

Tsuchiura 28 36.05N140.12E
Tsumeb 54 19.12S 17.43E
Tsushima 28 35.10N136.43E
Tuam 10 53.32N 8.52W
Tuamotu, Îles *is.* 31 17.00S142.00W
Tuapse 21 44.06N 39.05E
Tubarão 45 28.30S 49.01W
Tubbercurry 10 54.03N 8.45W
Tübingen 16 48.32N 9.04E
Tubruq 51 32.06N 23.58E
Tucson 40 32.15N110.57W
Tucumcari 40 35.11N103.44W
Tudela 13 42.04N 1.37W
Tukums 19 57.00N 23.10E
Tukuyu 53 9.20S 33.37E
Tula 20 54.11N 37.38E
Tulcea 15 45.10N 28.50E
Tuli 54 21.50S 29.15E
Tuli *r.* 54 21.49S 29.00E
Tullamore 10 53.17N 7.31W
Tulle 12 45.16N 1.46E
Tullins 12 45.18N 5.29E
Tullow 10 52.49N 6.45W
Tully 34 17.55S145.59E
Tuloma *r.* 18 68.56N 33.00E
Tulun 23 54.32N100.35E
Tulsa 41 36.07N 95.58W
Tumaco 46 1.51N 78.46W
Tumba, L. 52 0.45S 18.00E
Tummel, Loch 11 56.43N 3.55W
Tump 24 26.07N 62.22E
Tunceli 21 39.07N 39.34E
Tunduru 53 11.08S 37.21E
Tundzha *r.* 15 41.40N 26.34E
Tunis 50 36.47N 10.10E
Tunja 45 5.33N 73.23W
Tura 23 64.05N100.00E
Turangi 38 38.59S175.48E
Turgutlu 15 38.30N 27.43E
Türi 19 58.48N 25.26E
Turia *r.* 13 39.27N 0.19W
Turin *see* Torino 14
Turkana, L. 53 4.00N 36.00E
Turkestan *f.* 25 40.00N 79.00E
Turkestan 25 43.17N 68.16E
Turkey 24 39.00N 35.00E
Turks Is. 43 21.30N 71.10W
Turku 19 60.27N 22.17E
Turneffe Is. 43 17.30N 87.45W
Turnu Măgurele 15 43.43N 24.53E
Turnu-Severin 15 44.37N 22.39E
Turpan Pendi *f.* 26 43.40N 89.00E
Turquino, Mt. 43 20.05N 76.50W
Turriff 11 57.32N 2.28W
Tuscaloosa 41 33.12N 87.33W
Tuticorin 25 8.48N 78.10E
Tuttlingen 16 47.59N 8.49E
Tutubu 53 5.28S 32.43E
Tuvalu 30 8.00S178.00E
Tuxpan 42 21.00N 97.23W
Tuxtla Gutiérrez 42 16.45N 93.09W
Tuz Gölü 21 38.45N 33.24E
Tuzla 15 44.33N 18.40E
Tver 20 56.47N 35.57E
Tweed *r.* 11 55.46N 2.00W
Twyford 9 51.01N 1.19W
Tyler Tex. 41 32.22N 95.18W
Tyne *r.* 8 55.01N 1.25W
Tyne and Wear *d.* 8 54.57N 1.35W
Tynemouth 8 55.01N 1.24W
Tyrone *d.* 10 54.35N 7.15W
Tyrrell, L. 36 35.22S142.50E
Tyrrhenian Sea 14 40.00N 12.00E
Tyumen 22 57.11N 65.29E
Tywi *r.* 9 51.46N 4.22W
Tzaneen 54 23.49S 30.10E

U

Ubangi *r.* 52 0.25S 17.40E
Ubeda 13 38.01N 3.22W
Uberaba 45 19.47S 47.57W
Uberlândia 45 18.57S 48.17W
Ubombo 54 27.35S 32.05E
Ubundu 52 0.24S 25.28E
Ucayali *r.* 46 4.40S 73.20W
Udaipur 25 24.35N 73.41E
Uddevalla 19 58.21N 11.55E
Uddjaur *l.* 18 65.55N 17.49E
Udine 14 46.03N 13.15E
Udon Thani 27 17.26N102.45E
Uelzen 16 52.58N 10.34E
Ufa 20 54.45N 55.58E
Ugab *r.* 54 21.12S 13.37E
Ugalla *r.* 53 5.43S 31.10E
Uganda 53 2.00N 33.00E
Uglegorsk 23 49.01N142.04E
Ugra *r.* 20 54.30N 36.10E
Uig 11 57.35N 6.22W
Uige 52 7.40S 15.09E
Uinta Mts. 40 40.45N110.30W
Uitenhage 54 33.46S 25.23E
Ujiji 53 4.55S 29.39E
Ujjain 25 23.11N 75.46E
Ujpest 17 47.33N 19.05E
Ujung Pandang 27 5.09S119.28E
Uka 23 57.50N162.02E
Ukerewe I. 53 2.00S 33.00E
Ukiah 40 39.09N123.12W
Uku 52 11.24S 14.15E
Ulaanbaatar 26 47.54N106.52E
Ulaangom 26 49.59N 92.00E
Ulan Bator *see* Ulaanbaatar 26
Ulan-Ude 23 51.55N107.40E
Uliastay 26 47.42N 96.52E
Ulindi *r.* 52 1.38S 25.55E
Ulla *r.* 13 42.38N 8.45W
Ulladulla 37 35.21S150.25E
Ullapool 11 57.54N 5.10W
Ullswater *l.* 8 54.34N 2.52W
Ulm 16 48.24N 10.00E
Ulongwe 53 14.34S 34.21E
Ulsberg 18 62.45N 9.59E
Ulúa *r.* 43 15.50N 87.38W
Uluguru Mts. 53 7.05S 37.40E
Uluru 34 25.20S131.01E

Ulverston 8 54.13N 3.07W
Ul'yanovsk 20 54.19N 48.22E
Uman 17 48.45N 30.10E
Umeå 18 63.50N 20.15E
Umfuli *r.* 54 17.32S 29.23E
Umiat 38 69.22N152.20W
Umm Durmān 51 15.37N 32.59E
Umm Lajj 24 25.03N 37.17E
Umtata 54 31.35S 28.47E
Una *r.* 15 45.16N 16.55E
Uncompahgre Peak 40 38.04N107.28W
Underberg 54 29.46S 29.26E
Ungarie 37 33.38S147.00E
Ungava B. 39 59.00N 67.30W
União da Vitória 45 26.13S 51.05W
Uniondale 54 33.38S 23.07E
Union of Soviet Socialist Republics 17 50.00N 20.00E
United Arab Emirates 24 24.00N 54.00E
United Kingdom 7 54.00N 2.00W
United States of America 40 39.00N100.00W
Unst *i.* 11 60.45N 0.55W
Ünye 21 41.09N 37.15E
Upemba, L 52 8.35S 26.28E
Upernavik 39 72.50N 56.00W
Upington 54 28.26S 21.12E
Upper Hutt 29 41.07S175.04E
Upper Tean 8 52.57N 1.59W
Uppsala 19 59.52N 17.38E
Ural *r.* 21 47.00N 52.00E
Ural Mts. *see* Ural'skiye Gory *mts.* 20
Ural'sk 21 51.19N 51.20E
Ural'skiye Gory *mts.* 20 60.00N 59.00E
Urana, L. 37 35.21S146.19E
Uranium City 39 59.32N108.43W
Urapunga 34 14.41S134.34E
Urbino 14 43.43N 12.38E
Urda 21 48.44N 47.30E
Urdzhar 22 47.06N 81.33E
Ure *r.* 8 54.05N 1.20W
Uren 20 57.30N 45.50E
Urfa 21 37.08N 38.45E
Ürgüp 21 38.39N 34.55E
Urlingford 10 52.44N 7.35W
Uruaçu 47 14.30S 49.10W
Uruapan 42 19.26N102.04W
Uruguaiana 49 29.45S 57.05W
Uruguay *r.* 49 34.00S 58.30W
Uruguay 45 33.15S 56.00W
Ürümqi 26 43.43N 87.38E
Urunga 37 30.30S152.28E
Usa *r.* 20 66.00N 56.35E
Uşak 21 38.42N 29.25E
Usambara Mts. 53 4.45S 38.25E
Ushant *i. see* Ouessant, Île d' *i.* 12
Usk *r.* 9 51.34N 2.59W
Üsküdar 15 41.00N 29.03E
Ussuriysk 23 43.48N131.59E
Ustica *i.* 14 38.42N 13.11E
Ústí nad Labem 16 50.41N 14.00E
Ust'-kamchatsk 23 56.14N162.28E
Ust-Kamenogorsk 22 50.00N 82.40E
Ust'Maya 23 60.25N134.28E
Ust Olenëk 23 72.59N120.00E
Ust'Tsilma 20 65.28N 52.09E
U.S. Virgin Is. 43 18.30N 65.00W
Utah *d.* 40 39.00N112.00W
Utembo *r.* 52 17.03S 22.00E
Utete 53 8.00S 38.49E
Utiariti 46 13.02S 58.17W
Utica N.Y. 44 43.05N 75.14W
Utiel 13 39.33N 1.13W
Utrecht 16 52.04N 5.07E
Utrera 13 37.10N 5.47W
Uttaradit 27 17.38N100.05E
Uttar Pradesh *d.* 25 26.30N 81.30E
Uusikaupunki 19 60.48N 21.25E
Uvinza 53 5.08S 30.23E
Uvira 53 3.22S 29.06E
Uyuni 48 20.28S 66.50W
Uzhgorod 17 48.38N 22.15E

V

Vaagö *i.* 18 62.03N 7.14W
Vaal *r.* 54 29.04S 23.37E
Vaal Dam 54 26.51S 28.08E
Vaasa 18 63.06N 21.36E
Vadodara 25 22.19N 73.14E
Vaduz 16 47.08N 9.32E
Váh *r.* 17 48.00N 17.50E
Valday 20 57.59N 33.10E
Valdemarsvik 19 58.12N 16.36E
Valdepeñas 13 38.46N 3.24W
Valdez 38 61.07N146.17W
Valdivia 49 39.46S 73.15W
Valencia 13 39.29N 0.24W
Valencia *d.* 13 39.30N 0.40W
Valenciennes 12 50.22N 3.32E
Vale of Evesham *f.* 9 52.05N 1.55W
Vale of Pewsey *f.* 9 51.21N 1.45W
Vale of York *f.* 8 54.12N 1.25W
Valga 20 57.44N 26.00E
Valjevo 17 44.16N 19.56E
Valkeakoski 19 61.16N 24.02E
Valladolid 13 41.39N 4.45W
Valledupar 46 10.31N 73.16W
Valletta 14 35.53N 14.31E
Valleyfield 44 45.15N 74.08W
Valmiera 20 57.32N 25.29E
Valnera *mtn.* 13 43.10N 3.40W
Valognes 12 49.31N 1.28W
Valparaíso 49 33.02S 71.38W
Vals, Tanjung *c.* 27 8.30S137.30E
Valverde 43 19.37N 71.04W
Valverde del Camino 13 37.35N 6.45W
Van 21 38.28N 43.21E
Vancouver 38 49.13N123.06W
Vancouver I. 38 50.00N126.00W
Van Diemen G. 34 11.50S132.00E
Vänern *l.* 19 59.00N 13.15E
Vänersborg 19 58.22N 12.19E
Vanga 53 4.37S 39.13E
Vännäs 18 63.58N 19.48E

Vannes 12 47.40N 2.44W
Van Rees, Pegunungan *mts.* 27 2.35S138.15E
Vanrhynsdorp 54 31.37S 18.42E
Vanuatu 30 16.00S167.00E
Var *r.* 16 43.39N 7.11E
Vārānasi 25 25.20N 83.00E
Varaždin 14 46.18N 16.20E
Varberg 19 57.06N 12.15E
Vardak *r.* Yugo. *see* Axiós *r.* 15
Vardar 20 55.18N 46.00E
Varel 16 53.23N 8.10E
Varennes 12 46.19N 3.24E
Varna 17 43.13N 27.57E
Värnamo 19 57.11N 14.02E
Vasa *see* Vaasa 18
Vasilkov 17 50.12N 30.15E
Västerås 19 59.36N 16.33E
Västervik 19 57.45N 16.38E
Vatican City 14 41.54N 12.27E
Vatnajökull *mts.* 18 64.20N 17.00W
Vättern *l.* 19 58.30N 14.30E
Vaughn N.Mex. 40 34.35N105.14W
Växjö 19 56.52N 14.49E
Vaygach 22 70.28N 58.59E
Vega *i.* 18 65.39N 11.50E
Vejle 19 55.42N 9.32E
Velhas *r.* 45 17.20S 44.55W
Velikiye-Luki 20 56.19N 30.31E
Velletri 14 41.41N 12.47E
Vellore 25 12.56N 79.09E
Venado Tuerto 49 33.45S 61.56W
Vendas Novas 13 38.41N 8.27W
Vendôme 12 47.48N 1.04E
Venezia 14 45.26N 12.20E
Venezuela 46 7.00N 65.20W
Veniaminof Mtn. 38 56.05N159.20W
Venice *see* Venezia 14
Vera 13 37.15N 1.51W
Veracruz 42 19.11N 96.10W
Vercelli 14 45.19N 8.26E
Verdon *r.* 12 43.42N 5.39E
Verdun Meuse 12 49.10N 5.24E
Vereeniging 54 26.40S 27.55E
Verín 13 41.55N 7.26W
Verkhoyanskiy Khrebet *mts.* 23 66.00N130.00E
Vermont *d.* 44 43.50N 72.45W
Verona 14 45.27N 10.59E
Versailles 12 48.48N 2.08E
Vert, Cap *c.* 50 14.45N 17.25W
Verviers 7 50.36N 5.52E
Vesoul 12 47.38N 6.09E
Vesuvio *mtn.* 14 40.48N 14.25E
Vetlanda 19 57.26N 15.04E
Vettore, Monte *mtn.* 14 42.50N 13.18E
Vézère *r.* 12 44.53N 0.53E
Viana do Castelo 13 41.41N 8.50W
Viangchan *see* Vientiane 27
Viborg 19 56.26N 9.24E
Vic 13 41.56N 2.16E
Vicenza 16 45.33N 11.32E
Vichuga 20 57.12N 41.50E
Vichy 12 46.07N 3.25E
Victor Harbor 36 35.36S138.35E
Victoria Canada 38 48.26N123.20W
Victoria Hong Kong 26 22.16N114.13E
Victoria *d.* 37 37.20S145.00E
Victoria *r.* 32 15.12S129.43E
Victoria, L. 53 1.00S 33.00E
Victoria, Mt. 34 8.55N147.35E
Victoria de las Tunas 43 20.58N 76.59W
Victoria Falls *f.* 54 17.58S 25.45E
Victoria I. 38 71.00N110.00W
Victoria Nile *r.* 53 2.14N 31.20E
Victoria River *town* 34 15.36S131.06E
Victoria West 54 31.24S 23.07E
Vidin 17 43.58N 22.51E
Viedma 49 40.50S 63.00W
Vienna *see* Wien 16
Vienne 12 45.32N 4.54E
Vienne *r.* 12 47.13N 0.05W
Vientiane 27 17.59N102.38E
Vieques *i.* 43 18.08N 65.30W
Vierwaldstätter See *l.* 16 47.10N 8.50E
Vierzon 12 47.14N 2.04E
Vietnam 27 15.00N108.30E
Vigan 27 17.35N120.23E
Vigo 13 42.15N 8.44W
Vijayawāda 25 16.34N 80.40E
Vikna 18 64.52N 10.57E
Vila 30 17.44S168.18E
Vila da Maganja 53 17.25S 37.32E
Vila Real 13 41.17N 7.45W
Vila Velha 45 20.20S 40.17W
Vila Verissimo Sarmento 52 8.08S 20.38E
Vilhelmina 18 64.37N 16.39E
Vilhena 46 12.40S 60.08W
Villa Angela 48 27.34S 60.45W
Villach 16 46.37N 13.51E
Villagarcía 13 42.35N 8.45W
Villahermosa 42 18.00N 92.53W
Villajoyosa 13 38.31N 0.14W
Villa María 49 32.25S 63.15W
Villa Montes 48 21.15S 63.30W
Villanueva de la Serena 13 38.58N 5.48W
Villarrobledo 13 39.16N 2.36W
Villavicencio 46 4.09N 73.38W
Villena 13 38.39N 0.52W
Villeneuve 12 44.25N 0.43E
Villeurbanne 16 45.46N 4.54E
Vilnius 17 54.40N 25.19E
Vilyuy *r.* 23 64.20N126.55E
Vimmerby 19 57.40N 15.51E
Viña del Mar 49 33.02S 71.34W
Vincennes 44 38.42N 87.30W
Vindel *r.* 18 63.54N 19.52E
Vinnitsa 17 49.11N 28.30E
Vire 12 48.50N 0.53W
Virgin Is. 43 18.00N 64.30W
Virginia 41 47.30N 92.28W
Virginia *d.* 41 37.30N 78.45W
Virovitica 17 45.51N 17.23E
Vis *i.* 14 43.03N 16.10E
Visby 19 57.38N 18.18E
Viscount Melville Sd. 38 74.30N104.00W

Višegrad 15 43.47N 19.20E
Viseu 13 40.40N 7.55W
Vishākhapatnam 25 17.42N 83.24E
Viso, Monte *mtn.* 14 44.38N 7.05E
Vistula *r. see* Wisła *r.* 17
Vitebsk 20 55.10N 30.14E
Viterbo 14 42.26N 12.07E
Viti Levu *i.* 30 18.00N178.00E
Vitim *r.* 23 59.30N112.36E
Vitoria 13 42.51N 2.40W
Vitória 45 20.19N 40.21E
Vittoria 14 36.57N 14.21E
Vjosë *r.* 15 40.39N 19.20E
Vladikavkaz 21 43.02N 44.43E
Vladimir 20 56.08N 40.25E
Vladivostok 23 43.09N131.53E
Vlorë 15 40.28N 19.27E
Vltava *r.* 16 50.22N 14.28E
Voghera 14 44.59N 9.01E
Voi 53 3.23S 38.35E
Voiron 12 45.22N 5.35E
Volga *r.* 21 45.45N 47.50E
Volgograd 21 48.45N 44.30E
Volkhov *r.* 20 60.15N 32.15E
Vologda 20 59.10N 39.55E
Vólos 15 39.22N 22.57E
Volsk 20 52.04N 47.22E
Volta, L. 50 7.00N 0.00
Volta Redonda 45 22.31S 44.05W
Volterra 14 43.24N 10.51E
Volturno *r.* 14 41.02N 13.56E
Volzhskiy 21 48.48N 44.45E
Voorburg 16 52.04N 4.21E
Vopnafjórdhur *town* 18 65.46N 14.50W
Vordingborg 19 55.01N 11.55E
Vóraï Sporádhes *is.* 15 39.00N 24.00E
Vorkuta 20 67.27N 64.00E
Voronezh 21 51.40N 39.13E
Vosges *mts.* 16 48.10N 7.00E
Voss 19 60.39N 6.26E
Votuporanga 48 20.26S 49.53W
Vouga *r.* 13 40.41N 8.38W
Voves 12 48.16N 1.37E
Voznesensk 21 47.34N 31.21E
Vranje 15 42.34N 21.52E
Vratsa 15 43.12N 23.33E
Vrbas *r.* 15 45.06N 17.29E
Vrede 54 27.24S 29.09E
Vredefort 54 27.00S 27.23E
Vryburg 54 26.57S 24.42E
Vryheid 54 27.45S 30.48E
Vyazma 20 55.12N 34.17E
Vyazniki 20 56.14N 42.08E
Vyborg 20 60.45N 28.41E
West Felton 8 52.49N 2.58W
Vyrnwy, L. 8 52.46N 3.30W
Vyshniy-Volochek 20 57.34N 34.23E

W

Wabash *r.* 41 38.25N 87.45W
Waco 41 31.33N 97.10W
Wad 25 27.21N 66.23E
Waddeneilanden *is.* 16 53.20N 5.00E
Waddenzee *b.* 16 53.15N 5.05E
Waddington, Mt. 38 51.30N125.00W
Wadhurst 9 51.03N 0.21E
Wādi Halfa' 51 21.55N 31.20E
Wad Madani 51 14.24N 33.30E
Wager Bay *town* 39 65.26N 88.40W
Wagga Wagga 37 35.07S147.24E
Wahpeton 41 46.16N 96.36W
Waigeo *i.* 27 0.05S130.30E
Waikabubak *r.* 29 43.23S172.40E
Waimate 29 44.45S171.03E
Waingapu 27 9.30S120.10E
Wainwright 38 70.39N160.00W
Waiouru 29 39.39S175.40E
Waipukurau 29 40.00S176.33E
Wairau *r.* 29 41.32S174.08E
Wairoa 29 39.03S177.25E
Waitaki *r.* 29 44.56S171.10E
Waitara 29 38.59S174.13E
Waiuku 29 37.15S174.44E
Wajir 53 1.46N 40.05E
Wakatipu, L. 29 45.10S168.30E
Wakayama 28 34.13N135.11E
Wakefield 8 53.41N 1.31W
Wakkanai 26 45.26N141.43E
Wałbrzych 16 50.48N 16.19E
Walcha 37 31.00S151.36E
Wales *d.* 9 52.30N 3.45W
Walgett 37 30.03S148.10E
Walsall 9 52.36N 1.59W
Walton on the Naze 9 51.52N 1.17E
Walvis B. 54 22.59S 14.30E
Walvis Bay *town see* Walvisbaai 54
Wamba *r.* 52 4.35S 17.15E
Whyalla 36 33.02S137.35E
Wichita 41 37.43N 97.20W
Wichita Falls *town* 40 33.55N 98.30W
Wick 11 58.26N 3.06W
Wicklow 10 52.59N 6.03W
Wicklow *d.* 10 52.59N 6.25W
Wicklow Mts. 10 53.06N 6.20W
Widnes 8 53.22N 2.44W
Wien 16 48.13N 16.22E
Wiener Neustadt 16 47.49N 16.15E
Wiesbaden 16 50.05N 8.15E
Wigan 8 53.33N 2.38W
Wight, Isle of 7 50.40N 1.17W
Wigton 8 54.50N 3.09W
Wigtown 11 54.47N 4.26W
Wigtown B. 11 54.47N 4.15W
Wilcannia 36 31.33S143.24E
Wildhorn *mtn.* 12 46.22N 7.22E
Wildwood 44 38.59N 74.49W
Wilhelmshaven 16 53.32N 8.07E
Wilkes-Barre 44 41.15N 75.50W
Willemstad 46 12.12N 68.56W
Williamsport Penn. 44 41.14N 77.00W
Williston L. 38 56.00N126.00W
Willmar 41 45.06N 95.00W
Willowmore 54 33.18S 23.28E
Wilungga 36 35.18S138.33E
Wilmington N.C. 41 34.14N 77.55W
Wilmslow 8 53.19N 2.14W
Wilson's Promontory *c.* 37 39.06S146.23E
Wilton 9 51.05N 1.52W

Washington D.C. 44 38.55N 77.00W
Wasian 27 1.51S133.21E
Wasior 27 2.38S134.27E
Waswanipi Lac *l.* 44 49.36N 76.39W
Watchet 9 51.10N 3.20W
Waterbury 44 41.33N 73.03W
Waterford 10 52.16N 7.08W
Waterford *d.* 10 52.10N 7.40W
Waterloo Iowa 41 42.30N 92.20W
Waterville 44 41 52.50N 10.11W
Watford 9 51.40N 0.25W
Watson Lake *town* 38 60.07N128.49W
Wauchope 37 31.27S152.43E
Wausau 41 44.58N 89.40W
Waveney *r.* 9 52.29N 1.46E
Wāw 51 7.40N 28.04E
Wear *r.* 8 54.55N 1.21W
Wedmore 9 51.14N 2.48W
Weiden in der Oberpfalz 16 49.40N 12.10E
Weimar 16 50.59N 11.20E
Weissenfels 16 51.12N 11.58E
Welkom 54 27.59S 26.42E
Welland 44 42.59N 79.14W
Welland *r.* 8 52.53N 0.00
Wellingborough 9 52.18N 0.41W
Wellington *d.* 29 40.00S175.30E
Wellington New Zealand 29 41.17S174.47E
Wellington Shrops. 9 52.42N 2.31W
Wells 9 51.12N 2.39W
Wells-next-the-Sea 8 52.57N 0.51E
Welshpool 9 52.40N 3.09W
Welwyn Garden City 9 51.48N 0.13W
Wem 8 52.52N 2.45W
Wembere *r.* 53 4.07S 34.15E
Wenatchee 40 47.26N120.20W
Wensleydale *f.* 8 54.19N 2.04W
Wentworth 36 34.06S141.56E
Wenzhou 26 28.02N120.40E
Wepener 54 29.43S 27.01E
Werris Creek *town* 37 31.20S150.41E
Weser *r.* 16 53.15N 8.30E
Wessel, C. 34 10.59S136.46E
West Bengal *d.* 25 23.00N 88.00E
West Bromwich 9 52.32N 2.01W
Western Australia *d.* 32 24.20S122.30E
Western Isles *d.* 11 57.40N 7.10W
Western Sahara 50 25.00N 13.00W
Western Samoa 30 13.55S172.00W
West Felton 8 52.49N 2.58W
West Frisian Is. *see* Waddeneilanden 16
West Glamorgan *d.* 9 51.42N 3.47W
West Linton 11 55.45N 3.21W
Westmeath *d.* 10 53.30N 7.30W
West Midlands *d.* 9 52.28N 1.50W
West Nicholson 54 21.06S 29.25E
Weston 27 5.14N115.35E
Weston-Super-Mare 9 51.20N 2.59W
West Palm Beach *town* 41 26.42N 80.05W
Westport 10 53.48N 9.32W
Westray *i.* 11 59.18N 2.58W
Wexford 10 52.20N 6.28W
Wexford *d.* 10 52.20N 6.30W
Weymouth 9 50.36N 2.28W
Whakatane 29 37.56S177.00E
Whangarei 29 35.43S174.20E
Wharfe *r.* 8 53.50N 1.07W
Wharfedale *f.* 8 54.00N 1.58W
Wheeling 44 40.05N 80.43W
Whernside *mtn.* 8 54.14N 2.25W
Whitburn 11 55.52N 3.41W
Whitby 8 54.29N 0.37W
Whitchurch Shrops. 8 52.58N 2.42W
White *r.* 41 33.53N 91.10W
White *r.* Ind. 44 38.29N 87.45W
White *r.* S.Dak. 40 43.40N 99.30W
Whitehaven 8 54.33N 3.35W
Whitehorse 38 60.41N135.08W
White Nile *r. see* Abyaḍ, Al Baḥr al *r.* 24
White Sea *see* Beloye More *sea* 20
White Volta *r.* 50 9.13N 1.15W
Whithorn 11 54.44N 4.25W
Whitley Bay *town* 8 55.03N 1.25W
Whitney, Mt. 40 36.35N118.17W
Whitstable 9 51.21N 1.02E
Whitton 8 53.42N 0.39W

Wiltshire *d.* 9 51.20N 0.34W
Winam, *b.* 53 0.15S 34.30E
Winburg 54 28.30S 27.01E
Wincanton 9 51.03N 2.24W
Winchester 9 51.04N 1.19W
Windermere *l.* 8 54.20N 2.56W
Windhoek 54 22.34S 17.06E
Windsor U.K. 9 51.29N 0.38W
Windsor Ont. 44 42.18N 83.01W
Windward Is. 43 13.00N 60.00W
Windward Passage *str.* 43 20.00N 74.00W
Winisk *r.* 39 55.20N 85.20W
Winnebago, L. 44 44.00N 88.25W
Winnipeg 39 49.53N 97.10W
Winnipeg, L. 39 52.00N 98.00W
Winnipegosis, L. 39 52.00N100.00W
Winona Minn. 41 44.02N 91.37W
Winschoten 16 53.07N 7.02E
Winsford 8 53.12N 2.31W
Winslow Ariz. 40 35.01N110.43W
Winston-Salem 41 36.05N 80.05W
Winton 34 22.22S143.00E
Wisbech 9 52.39N 0.10E
Wisconsin *d.* 41 45.00N 90.00W
Wisconsin Rapids *town* 41 44.24N 89.55W
Wisła *r.* 17 54.23N 18.52E
Wismar 16 53.54N 11.28E
Witham *r.* 8 52.56N 0.04E
Withernsea 8 53.43N 0.02E
Wittenberg 16 51.52N 12.39E
Wittenberge 16 52.59N 11.45E
Witu 53 2.22S 40.20E
Wiveliscombe 9 51.02N 3.20W
Wodonga 37 36.08S146.09E
Woking 9 51.20N 0.34W
Wolfenbüttel 16 52.10N 10.33E
Wolfsberg 16 52.27N 10.49E
Wolin 16 53.51N 14.34E
Wollaston L. 38 58.15N103.30W
Wollongong 37 34.25S150.52E
Wolmaransstad 54 27.11S 25.58E
Wolseley 36 36.21S140.55E
Wolverhampton 9 52.35N 2.06W
Wŏnsan 26 39.07N127.26E
Wonthaggi 37 38.38S145.37E
Woodbridge 9 52.06N 1.19E
Woodside 37 38.31S146.52E
Wooler 8 55.33N 2.01W
Woomera 36 31.11S136.54E
Woonsocket 44 42.00N 71.31W
Wooroorooka 37 28.59S145.40E
Worcester U.S.A. 44 42.16N 71.48W
Worcester U.K. 9 52.12N 2.12W
Workington 8 54.39N 3.34W
Worksop 8 53.19N 1.09W
Worland 40 44.01N107.58W
Worms 16 49.38N 8.23E
Worthing 9 50.49N 0.23W
Worthington Minn. 41 43.37N 95.36W
Wragby 8 53.17N 0.18E
Wrangel I. 23 71.00N180.00
Wrangell 38 56.28N132.23W
Wrangle 8 53.03N 0.09E
Wrath, C. 11 58.37N 5.01W
Wrexham 8 53.05N 3.00W
Wrigley 38 63.16N123.39W
Wrocław 17 51.05N 17.00E
Wuhan 26 30.37N114.19E
Wuhu 26 31.23N118.25E
Wulian Shan *mts.* 26 24.27N100.43E
Wuppertal 16 51.15N 7.10E
Würzburg 16 49.48N 9.57E
Wuwei 26 38.00N102.59E
Wuxi 26 31.34N120.20E
Wuzhou 26 23.28N111.21E
Wyandotte 44 42.11N 83.10W
Wyangala Resr. 37 33.58S148.55E
Wye 9 51.11N 0.56E
Wye *r.* 9 51.37N 2.40W
Wymondham 9 52.34N 1.07E
Wyndham 32 15.29S128.05E
Wyoming *d.* 40 43.00N108.00W

X

Xai-Xai 54 25.05S 33.38E
Xangongo 52 16.31S 15.00E
Xánthi 15 41.07N 24.55E
Xau, L. 54 21.15S 24.50E
Xiaguan 26 25.33N100.09E
Xiamen 26 24.30N118.08E
Xi'an 26 34.11N108.55E
Xiangfan 26 32.04N112.04E
Xingu *r.* 47 1.40S 52.15W
Xining 26 36.35N101.55E
Xugou 26 34.40N119.26E
Xuzhou 26 34.14N117.20E

Y

Yablonovyy Khrebet *mts.* 23 53.20N115.00E
Yahuma 52 1.06N 23.10E
Yakima 40 46.37N120.30W
Yakutsk 23 62.10N129.20E
Yalong Jiang *r.* 25 26.35N101.44E
Yaman Tau *mtn.* 20 54.20N 58.10E
Yamuna *r.* 25 25.25N 81.50E
Yana *r.* 23 71.30N135.00E
Yanchuan 26 36.51N110.05E
Yangtze *see* Chang Jiang *r.* 26
Yanqi 25 42.00N 86.30E
Yantabulla 37 29.13S145.01E
Yantai 26 37.27N121.26E
Yao 28 34.37N135.36E
Yaoundé 52 3.51N 11.31E
Yap *i.* 30 9.31N138.06E
Yaqui *r.* 42 27.40N110.30W
Yare *r.* 9 52.34N 1.45E
Yarkant He *r.* 25 40.30N 80.55E
Yarlung Zangbo Jiang *r.* China *see* Brahmaputr *r.* 25
Yarmouth 44 43.50N 66.08W
Yaroslavl 20 57.34N 39.52E
Yarrow *r.* 11 55.32N 2.51W
Yass 37 34.51S148.55E

Yatakate 50 14.52N 0.22E
Ya Xian 27 18.19N109.32E
Yegorlyk *r.* 21 46.30N 41.52E
Yegoryevsk 20 55.21N 39.01E
Yegros 45 26.24S 56.25W
Yell *i.* 11 60.35N 1.05W
Yellow Sea 26 35.00N123.00E
Yellowknife 38 62.30N114.29W
Yellowstone *r.* 40 47.55N103.45W
Yellowstone L. 40 44.30N110.20W
Yell Sd. 11 60.30N 1.11W
Yelwa 50 10.51N 4.46E
Yemen 24 14.20N 45.50E
Yeovil 9 50.57N 2.38W
Yerbent 22 39.23N 58.35E
Yerevan 21 40.10N 44.31E
Yershov 21 51.22N 48.16E
Yerushalayim 24 31.47N 35.13E
Yeu, Île d' *i.* 12 46.43N 2.20W
Yeysk 21 46.43N 38.17E
Yibin 26 28.42N104.34E
Yichang 26 30.21N111.21E
Yinchuan 26 38.27N106.18E
Yingtan 26 28.11N116.55E
Yogyakarta 27 7.48S110.24E
Yokkaichi 28 34.58N136.37E
Yokohama 28 35.27N139.39E
Yokosuka 28 35.18N139.40E
Yola 50 9.14N 12.32E
Yonne *r.* 12 48.22N 2.57E
York U.K. 8 53.58N 1.07W
York Penn. 44 39.58N 76.44W
York, C. 34 10.42S142.31E
Yorkshire Wolds *hills* 8 54.00N 0.39W
Yorkton 38 51.12N102.35W
Yoshkar Ola 20 56.38N 47.52E
Youghal 10 51.58N 7.51W
Young 37 34.19S148.20E
Youngstown 44 41.05N 80.40W
Yoxford 9 52.16N 1.30E
Yozgat 21 39.50N 34.48E
Ystad 19 55.25N 13.49E
Ythan *r.* 11 57.21N 2.01W
Yuan Jiang *r.* Yunnan China *see* Hong Hâ *r.* 26
Yucatan Pen. 42 19.00N 90.00W
Yugoslavia 15 44.00N 20.00E
Yukon *r.* 38 62.35N164.20W
Yukon Territory *d.* 38 65.00N135.00W
Yulara 34 25.14S130.59E
Yuma Ariz. 40 32.40N114.39W
Yumen 26 40.19N 97.12E
Yungera 36 34.48S143.10E
Yvetot 12 49.37N 0.45E

Z

Zaandam 16 52.27N 4.49E
Zacapa 43 15.00N 89.30W
Zacatecas 42 22.48N102.33W
Zadar 14 44.08N 15.14E
Zafra 13 38.25N 6.25W
Zagorsk 20 56.20N 38.10E
Zagreb 14 45.49N 15.58E
Zágros, Kúhhá-ye *mts.* 24 32.00N 51.00E
Zagros Mts. *see* Zágros, Kúhhá-ye *mts.* 24
Záhedān 24 29.32N 60.54E
Zaïre 52 2.00S 22.00E
Zaïre *r.* 52 6.00S 12.30E
Zaječar 15 43.56N 22.15E
Zákinthos *i.* 15 37.45N 20.46E
Zákinthos *i.* 15 37.46N 20.46E
Zakatały 21 41.39N 46.40E
Zalaegerszeg 16 46.51N 16.51E
Zambeze *r.* 53 18.15S 35.55E
Zambezi 52 13.30S 23.12E
Zambia 53 14.00S 28.00E
Zamboanga 27 6.55N122.05E
Zamora 13 41.30N 5.45W
Zamość 17 50.43N 23.15E
Záncara *r.* 13 39.10N 3.00W
Zanzibar 53 6.10S 39.12E
Zanzibar I. 53 6.00S 39.20E
Zapala 49 38.55S 70.05W
Zaporozhye 21 47.50N 35.10E
Zara 21 39.55N 37.44E
Zaragoza 13 41.39N 0.54W
Zárate 49 34.05S 59.02W
Zaraza 46 9.23N 65.20W
Zaria 50 11.01N 7.44E
Zave 53 17.14S 30.02E
Zaysan, Ozero *l.* 22 48.00N 83.30E
Zebediela 54 24.19S 29.17E
Zeebrugge 16 51.20N 3.13E
Zeehan 35 41.55S145.21E
Zeerust 54 25.32S 26.04E
Zémio 51 5.00N 25.09E
Zeya *r.* 23 50.20N127.30E
Zeya 23 53.48N 127.20E
Ž

Žêzere *r.* 13 39.28N 8.20W
Zhangjiakou 26 40.47N114.56E
Zhangzhou 26 24.57N118.32E
Zhanjiang 26 21.08N110.22E
Zhengzhou 26 34.47N113.38E
Zhitomir 17 50.18N 28.40E
Zhlobin 17 52.50N 30.00E
Zibo 26 36.50N118.00E
Zielona Góra 16 51.57N 15.30E
Zile 21 40.18N 35.52E
Zimatlán 42 16.52N 96.45W
Zimbabwe 54 18.55S 30.00E
Zimnicea 17 43.38N 25.22E
Zinder 50 13.46N 8.58E
Znamenka 21 48.42N 32.40E
Znojmo 16 48.52N 16.05E
Zomba 53 15.25S 35.22E
Zonguldak 21 41.26N 31.47E
Zrenjanin 15 45.22N 20.23E
Zug 16 47.10N 8.31E
Zújar *r.* 13 38.58N 5.40W
Zumbo 53 15.36S 30.24E
Zunyi 26 27.39N106.48E
Zürich 14 47.23N 8.33E
Zwickau 16 50.43N 12.30E
Zwolle 16 52.31N 6.06E
Zyryanovsk 22 49.45N 84.16E